EAI/Springer Innovations in Communication and Computing

Series Editor

Imrich Chlamtac, European Alliance for Innovation, Ghent, Belgium

The impact of information technologies is creating a new world yet not fully understood. The extent and speed of economic, life style and social changes already perceived in everyday life is hard to estimate without understanding the technological driving forces behind it. This series presents contributed volumes featuring the latest research and development in the various information engineering technologies that play a key role in this process.

The range of topics, focusing primarily on communications and computing engineering include, but are not limited to, wireless networks; mobile communication; design and learning; gaming; interaction; e-health and pervasive healthcare; energy management; smart grids; internet of things; cognitive radio networks; computation; cloud computing; ubiquitous connectivity, and in mode general smart living, smart cities, Internet of Things and more. The series publishes a combination of expanded papers selected from hosted and sponsored European Alliance for Innovation (EAI) conferences that present cutting edge, global research as well as provide new perspectives on traditional related engineering fields. This content, complemented with open calls for contribution of book titles and individual chapters, together maintain Springer's and EAI's high standards of academic excellence. The audience for the books consists of researchers, industry professionals, advanced level students as well as practitioners in related fields of activity include information and communication specialists, security experts, economists, urban planners, doctors, and in general representatives in all those walks of life affected ad contributing to the information revolution.

Indexing: This series is indexed in Scopus, Ei Compendex, and zbMATH.

About EAI

EAI is a grassroots member organization initiated through cooperation between businesses, public, private and government organizations to address the global challenges of Europe's future competitiveness and link the European Research community with its counterparts around the globe. EAI reaches out to hundreds of thousands of individual subscribers on all continents and collaborates with an institutional member base including Fortune 500 companies, government organizations, and educational institutions, provide a free research and innovation platform.

Through its open free membership model EAI promotes a new research and innovation culture based on collaboration, connectivity and recognition of excellence by community.

More information about this series at http://www.springer.com/series/15427

Liliana Mâță

Editor

Ethical Use of Information Technology in Higher Education

Editor
Liliana Mâţă
"Vasile Alecsandri" University of Bacău
Bacău, Romania

ISSN 2522-8595   ISSN 2522-8609   (electronic)
EAI/Springer Innovations in Communication and Computing
ISBN 978-981-16-1953-3   ISBN 978-981-16-1951-9   (eBook)
https://doi.org/10.1007/978-981-16-1951-9

This Springer imprint is published by the registered company Springer Nature Singapore Pte Ltd.
The registered company address is: 152 Beach Road, #21-01/04 Gateway East, Singapore 189721,
Singapore

Preface

The unethical use of technology in education has become a topic of current interest to researchers in the fields of social sciences, ethics, and computer science. Although the investigation of ethical issues generated by computer use appeared in the 1980s, it grew in importance in the following decades [1]. The ethical questions posed by the massive introduction of technology cover topics such as confidentiality, neutrality, the digital divide, cybercrime, and transparency [2]. If ethics and technology are analyzed in close connection with education, even more questions arise. The use of information technology in educational activities raises more and more difficulties and problems. In the context of the increasingly frequent use of technology in education, the issue of ethical responsibility has become a serious problem.

Students and teachers use information technology daily in the academic environment to achieve different educational activities. The introduction of new information technologies in the academic environment determines a "wave effect" [3], which leads to the emergence of new ethical, social, and political issues, which must be addressed at the individual, social and political levels. The use of information technologies has raised new ethical issues [4]. These technologies provide many benefits but give rise to the danger of their use for dishonest purposes such as piracy, invasion of privacy, unauthorized access to data. In this situation, there are favored unethical behaviors, especially among students [5]. Unethical IT use by students and teachers is a major challenge in educational institutions [6–7]. The impact of unethical use of information technology is obvious for the academic institutions in general, by increasing the knowledge base about areas of cyber-ethics and professorial ethics.

In the current context of the pandemic period, some authors [8] have identified the extent to which the types of digital public health technologies determine ethical and legal considerations that are specific to the field. These considerations are based on the moral considerations of public health ethics and data ethics, in particular the principles of autonomy, justice, non-malice, privacy, and solidarity. It is very important to formulate principles and values in the context of digital technologies in higher education, which help to clarify ethical issues for students, teachers, researchers, and policymakers. The moral dimensions regarding the use of information technology are the following [3]: information rights and obligations, property rights and obligations, quality of a system, quality of life, and responsibility, and control.

This book provides a current perspective on the ethical problems and solutions involved in the use of information technology in higher education. The issues regarding the ethical use of digital resources are analyzed in a holistic vision, by combining the perspectives of education specialists and those in the field of computer science at the level of higher education. Built out of the need to respond to the ethical challenges of using technology in academia, the book is an innovative and current approach.

The Challenges

The main ethical issues that arise from the impact of technology use in educational activities are the following [9, 10]: privacy, security and ownership of personal data, hacking, intellectual property, netiquette, vandalism, access, the accuracy of inferencing, the effect of personalization on individual capability, the commodification of education, improper use of computer resources, academic dishonesty in online assessment, anonymity and pseudonymity, online harassment and hate speech, academic freedom and free speech online. Olcott [2] believes that the ethical challenges of using information technology affect people both individually and collectively. These challenges are multiple and range from digital identity and reputation to critical information use, technology abuse, and online security and privacy.

The data of studies conducted in higher education show that students have misconceptions about ethics in IT use [11], as well as the fact that they lack knowledge in this field [12]. The possibility for various types of academic dishonesty, such as fraudulence, falsification, plagiarism, delinquency, unauthorized help to occur following the use of digital resources in universities is high [13]. Some authors [14] point to the emergence of ethical issues at the level of higher education institutions in the field of engineering and applied sciences. In this context, several specific problems are highlighted at technological universities, which concern the relations of institutions with industrial partners. It also highlights the issue of educating the new generation of engineers and scientists to meet the future challenges facing humanity, while respecting the highest moral standards of academic conduct and research integrity.

In most cases, academic dishonesty has been addressed unilaterally, only from the perspective of students. Teachers have been ignored in research, although education is achieved through partnership. The attitudes of teachers toward cheating are less investigated. Teachers have reacted to academic cheating more like "detectives" and less as "educators" [15]. The main problems of unethical information technology use by teachers from academia cover issues like plagiarism, ignoring copyright, file sharing, posting incorrect information, cyber-bullying, delivering courses and exams in laboratories with IT equipment, distance learning, use of licensed software, communication through Facebook and YouTube, lack of academic integrity [7, 16]. Teachers prepare courses by downloading materials on the Internet, apply assessments online, use email to send and receive feedback, provide students with CDs and web links related to the course content so that all these activities raise ethical issues of which teachers and students should be aware [17]. According to Akdemir et al. [18], prospective teachers are more prone to unethical behavior in the virtual environment than in real life. Kuzu [19] proposes solutions regarding the problems related to computer ethics through the help of practitioners with an information and communication technology background.

The analysis of current studies reveals that some of these are focused on researching ethical or unethical behavior related to computer and information technology use [18, 20–23], while others aim to identify attitudes towards ethical computer and information technology use [6, 11, 13, 17, 24–25]. In terms of studies conducted in the academic environment, there may be observed the fact that there is increased interest in investigating students' attitudes towards ethical information technology use in particular [5, 11–13, 24–27] and less those of teachers [17, 27]. There is an extension of exploring such issues at elementary school teachers also [6]. The analysis of research in the field of ethical issues of the use of information technology indicates the need to design new studies that primarily target the perspective of teachers in higher education. Another finding from the analysis of the research is the fact that there are no studies in the field of information technology ethics in education in recent years, which shows that a signal must be formulated to all interested researchers. Therefore, this book covers these gaps and complements the theoretical approaches with new current models, as well as with research of interest among students and teachers in academia.

Solutions

The novelty aspects of this approach are multiple. Firstly, the concept of unethical information technology use is defined following the latest studies. Secondly, there are presented the results of scientific research on the current problems of unethical use of information technology in academia and the rules of online communication between teachers and students. Thirdly, there are developed models for the ethical use of information technology in higher education. Not least, pertinent solutions for university students and teachers regarding online communication, online teaching, and evaluation are outlined.

Through the new approach, the book supports students, teachers, and researchers to recognize and raise awareness of the ethical issues involved in the transfer of technological resources in educational activities. The development of ethical attitudes and behaviors for the beneficiaries of education represents an important strategy of the current educational policies. Johnson and Simpson [28] highlighted the importance of understanding the legal and illegal use of computers by students and teachers in the academic environment, and the ethical role models that teachers should represent for students. Igwe and Ibegwam [16] highlight the importance of cyberethics education as it facilitates the development of moral and responsible behavior in information technology use by citizens. The priority is for teachers to feel responsible for educating students about "what is right and what is wrong" in the use of information technology [29–30]. The responsibility of academic teachers is to contribute to the training of students to understand and apply the ethical rules underlying the use of technologies both in the institutional setting and outside the educational organizations. Soon, it is expected that study courses dedicated entirely to the ethical issues of information and communication technology in universities will be created [31].

Olcott [2] formulates a set of valuable principles of action that help make decisions about the use of information technology in education and society. The proposed principles are formulated in the form of five premises:

- premise 1—"Training in the responsible, secure and ethical use of technologies must reach all members of society".
- premise 2—"Education is based on values, and education is provided in, with and from values".
- premise 3—"Technologies should be used appropriately (judiciously and respectfully), not just used".
- premise 4—"Individual and collective commitment determines the responsible and exemplary use of technologies".

The knowledge of ethical rules by students and teachers has become increasingly stringent as the educational activities moved beyond the boundaries of schools, in the informal context. The use of technologies by students to study at home and by teachers to teach in the online environment has given rise to wide-ranging ethical dilemmas. The adoption of new technologies in higher education institutions implies greater "corporate responsibility" [32], as technologies require increased attention to ethical issues during design, and design choices are governed by corporations. One of the basic solutions is the introduction of an ethical code of conduct regarding information technology use at the level of higher education. Sensitizing teachers and students to these ethical issues of using information technology can contribute to their awareness [33] to successfully carry out educational activities, but also a responsible practice in research and innovation.

Organization of the Book

The book is organized into thirteen chapters. Three coordinates of this book can be delimited. The first of these is found in chapters one, two, and three, which include recent theoretical approaches in the field of the ethical use of information technology in higher education. The second coordinate extends from chapter four to chapter ten and addresses the ethical issues that students face in terms of the increasing use of technological resources. The last chapters form the third coordinate of the book, which illustrates the perception of university teachers towards the ethical requirements of the use of digital technologies, as well as the ethical competencies that are involved in online teaching and evaluation. A brief description of each of the chapters follows.

The first chapter "Academic Integrity in the Technology-Driven Education Era", systematizes the current challenges of academic integrity from the perspective of the digital age. Also, there are highlighted a series of specific and general measures to reduce the forms of academic dishonesty.

The second chapter "Unethical Information Technology Use in Higher Education: A Review of Literature in Sub-Saharan Africa", provides a current perspective on the examination of the key factors allowing the rise of unethical practices in information technology in sub-Saharan Africa.

In the third chapter "A Model for Ethical Behavior in the Use of IT by Academicians in Mali", there are highlighted the main factors that may affect the ethical behavior in the use of information technology. The results of the study indicate that the attitude, subjective norm, and perceived control were the factors that affect the ethical behavior of academics.

The fourth chapter "Raising Students' Awareness of Unethical Information Technology Use", presents issues related to unethical information technology use in higher education as a theoretical basis for providing practical suggestions on how academic teachers may raise students' awareness of unethical information technology use.

The fifth chapter "Investigating the Relationship Between Internet Ethics and Motivational Orientations in Higher Education", includes innovative research based on the investigation of the correlation between the students' type of motivation (extrinsic/intrinsic) and their attitude towards the ethics of the use of information technologies, as well as the individual differences in students' unethical Internet use concerning intrinsic and extrinsic motivational orientations.

The sixth chapter "Students' Attitude Toward the Unethical Use of Information Technology", integrates the coordinates of research focused on the analysis of students' attitudes towards the unethical use of information technology as educational actors benefit from increasingly sophisticated technology. There was used a quantitative research methodology, based on a questionnaire.

In the seventh chapter "Ethical Rules of Online Communication Between University Teachers and Students", there are presented the theoretical considerations and a qualitative research referring to the students' perceptions of the ethical issues involved in online communication with the university professor.

The eighth chapter "Ethics and Privacy in Learning Analytics: The Rise of Chief Privacy and Chief Ethics Officers", outlines the ethical and privacy issues and challenges of using learning analytics, the frameworks proposed for the trustworthy utilization of learning analytics, as well as the learning analytics policy progresses.

The ninth chapter "Evaluation of Text Entities for Redundancy Detection on Written and Multimedia Contents", focuses on the determination of intrinsic and extrinsic redundancy on text entities for the study of information replication. Redundancy presumes on the one hand that different entities behave in the same way when we talk about software and on the other hand, it contains the same information when we talk about data structures.

The tenth chapter "Critical Media Literacy: A Comprehensive Approach Enabling Students (as Citizens) To Use ICT in the Quest for a Just Society", includes a review of the benefits and perils associated with ICT and discuss the importance of Critical

Media Literacy: a comprehensive approach that teaches critical skills and enables students-as citizens to use ICT as instruments of social communication but also as tools for change.

The eleventh chapter "Current Issues of Ethical Use of Information Technology from the Perspective of University Teachers", is a reference point for research of the teachers' perception regarding the ethical problems of the use of information technology in higher education teaching-learning-evaluation and research-development.

In the twelfth chapter "Ethical Responsibility of the University Teachers in Online Teaching and Evaluation", there are described the ethical competencies of the university teachers regarding the achievement of online teaching and evaluation. In the first part of the chapter, there are presented the current meanings of the concept of ethical competence and in the second part, there are analyzed the main digital and ethical competencies that university teachers must possess.

The thirteenth chapter "Responsible Online Ethical Teaching in Higher Education During the COVID-19 Pandemic", represents a challenge to identify the problems connected to online (un)ethical teaching and to propose a series of guidelines to be included in the teacher training curriculum as soon as possible.

All the chapters of the book are an invitation for all educational actors to know the problems, but also to apply the rules regarding the responsible ethical use of information technology.

Bacău, Romania   Liliana Mâță

References

1. Halawi, L.: Evaluation of ethical issues in the knowledge age: an exploratory study. Issues Inf. Syst. **14**(1), 106–112 (2013)
2. Olcott Jr., D., Carrera Farran, X., Gallardo Echenique, E.E., González Martínez, J.: Ethics and education in the digital age: global perspectives and strategies for local transformation in Catalonia. RUSC. Univ. Knowl. Soc. J. **12**(2), 59–72 (2015). http://dx.doi.org/10.7238/rusc.v12i2.2455
3. Cvejic, R., Kostic, D., Crvenković, B.: Emerging ethical concerns in information systems. Ann. Univ. Oradea Fascicle Manage. Technol. Eng. **1**, 9–14 (2016)
4. Alakurt, T. Bardakçi, S.: ICT Student teachers' judgments and justifications about ethical issues. Turkish Online J. Qual. Inq. **3**(4), 48–63 (2012)
5. Karim, N.S.A., Zamzuri, N.H.A., Nor, Y.M.: Exploring the relationship between Internet ethics in university students and the big five model of personality. Comput. Educ. **53**(1), 86–93 (2009)
6. Özer, N., Uğurlu, C.T., Beycioglu, K.: Computer teachers' attitudes toward ethical use of computers in elementary schools. Int. J. Cyber Ethics Educ. **1**(2), 15–24 (2011)
7. Dika, A., Hamiti, M.: Challenges of implementing the ethics through the use of information technologies in the university. Procedia Soc. Behav. Sci. **15**, 1110–1114 (2011)
8. Gasser, U., Ienca, M., Scheibner, J., Sleigh, J., Vayena, E.: Digital tools against COVID-19: taxonomy, ethical challenges, and navigation aid. Health Policy. **2**(8), E425–E434 (2020). https://doi.org/10.1016/S2589-7500(20)30137-0

9. Ashman, H., Brailsford, T., Cristea, A.I., Sheng, Q.Z., Stewart, C., Toms, E.G., Wade, V.: The ethical and social implications of personalization technologies for e-learning. Inf. Manage. **51**(6) (2014). https://doi.org/10.1016/j.im.2014.04.003

10. Cilliers, L.: Evaluation of information ethical issues among undergraduate students: an exploratory study. S. Afr. J. Inf. Manage. **19**(1), a767 (2017). https://doi.org/10.4102/sajim. v19i1.767

11. Calluzzo, V.J., Cante, Ch.J.: Ethics in information technology and software use. J. Bus. Ethics. **51**, 301–312 (2004)

12. Hamiti, M., Reka, B., Baloghová, A.: Ethical use of information technology in high education. Procedia Soc. Behav. Sci. **116**, 4411–4415 (2013)

13. Hosny, M., Fatima, S.: Attitude of students towards cheating and plagiarism: university case study. J. Appl. Sci. **14**, 748–757 (2014)

14. Taebi, B., van den Hoven, J. Bird, S.J.: The importance of ethics in modern universities of technology. Sci. Eng. Ethics. **25**, 1625–1632 (2019). https://doi.org/10.1007/s11948-019-00164-6

15. Scanlon, P.M.: Student online plagiarism: how do we respond? Coll. Teach. **51**(4), 161–165 (2003)

16. Igwe, K.N., Ibegwam, A.: Imperative of cyber ethics education to cyber crimes prevention and cyber security in Nigeria. Int. J. ICT Manage. **2**(2), 102–113 (2014)

17. Jamil, M., Tariq, R.-u.-H., Shah, J.H.: Ethical attitudes towards the use of computer and information technology. Int. Res. J. Arts Soc. Sci. **2**(4), 72–78 (2013)

18. Akdemir, O., Vural, O.F., Çolakoğlu, O.M.: Prospective teachers' likelihood of performing unethical behaviors in the real and virtual environments. The Turkish Online J. Educ. Technol. **14**(2), 130–137 (2015)

19. Kuzu, A.: Problems related to computer ethics: origins of the problems and suggested solutions. The Turkish Online J. Educ. Technol. **8**(2), 91–110 (2009)

20. Kavuk, M. Keser, H., Teker, N.: Reviewing unethical behaviors of primary education students' internet usage. Procedia Soc. Behav. Sci. **28**, 1043–1052 (2011)

21. Kaya, S., Durmus, A.: Investigation of Relationship between Preservice Teachers' Unethical Computer Using Behavior and Attitudes towards the Using of Internet. Procedia Soc. Behav. Sci. **28**, 667–672 (2011)

22. Abolarinwa, O.L., Tiamiyu, M.A., Eluwa, S.E.: Computer ethics and security awareness behaviour of tertiary institution students in South-Western, Nigeria. Eng. Sci. Technol. Int. J. (ESTIJ). **5**(3), 260–265 (2015)

23. Seif, M.H.: Presenting a casual model for ethical behavioral intention of information technology among students of Shiraz University of Medical Sciences. Med. Ethics J. **10**(35), 177–198 (2016)

24. Liu, X. Chen, Y.: A cross-cultural comparison between Americans and Chinese in their attitudes towards information ethics. Issues Inf. Syst. **13**(1), 59–67 (2012)

25. Almseidein, T.A.: Attitudes of undergraduate management information systems students towards computer ethics at Al-Balqa' Applied University. Asian J. Inf. Technol. **13**, 438–441 (2014)

26. Acilar, A.: Demographic factors affecting freshman students' attitudes towards software piracy: an empirical study. Issues Inf. Sci. Inf. Technol. **7**, 321–328 (2010)

27. Mohamed, N., Karim, N.S.A., Hussein, R.: Computer use ethics among university students and staffs: the influence of gender, religious work value and organizational level. Campus-Wide Inf. Syst. **29**(5), 328–343 (2012)

28. Johnson, D., Simpson, C.: Are you the copy cop? learning and leading with technology. **323**(7), 14–20 (2005)

29. Beycioglu, K.: A cyberphilosophical issue in education: unethical computer using behavior—the case of prospective teachers. Comput. Educ. **53**, 201–208 (2009)

30. Woodward, B., Martin, N., Imboden, T.: Expansion and validation of the PAPA framework. Inf. Syst. Educ. J. **9**(3), 28–34 (2011)

31. Pólkowski Z.: Ethical issues in the use and implementation of ICT. In: Khajuria, R., Banerjee, R., Sinha, K. (eds.) 4th International Conference on "Business Ethic for Good Corporate Governance & Sustainability", Gujarat Technological University, Ahmedabad 2–5 (2015)
32. Martin, K., Shilton, K. Smith, J.: Business and the ethical implications of technology: introduction to the symposium. J. Bus. Ethics. **160**, 307–317 (2019). https://doi.org/10.1007/s10 551-019-04213-9
33. Stahl, B.C., Timmermans, J., Flick, C.: Ethics of emerging information and communication technologies: on the implementation of responsible research and innovation. Sci. Public Policy. **44**(3), 369–381 (2017)

Acknowledgments

The volume is an important result of the research project, PN-III-P1-1.1-TE-2016-0773, with the title "Factors influencing teachers' attitudes towards the unethical information technology use in higher education" (TAUITUHED). The project was funded by The Executive Agency for Higher Education, Research, Development and Innovation Funding (UEFISCDI).

The main goal of the project was to assess the influence of a set of factors on the attitudes of teachers towards unethical information technology use in higher education. From the theoretical perspective, there were analyzed the current approaches and studies on ethical issues of information technology use and there was elaborated an initial theoretical model on the factors that influence attitudes towards unethical information technology use. Regarding the research methodology, there was proposed a mixed exploratory sequential approach based on qualitative and quantitative data collection in two phases. In the first phase of the research, there was used a qualitative approach to explore the ethical issues of information technology use. There were conducted semi-structured interviews with at least 31 teachers from higher education with experience in this field. Data analysis supported the development of the framework matrix with the categories of ethical issues of information technology use in higher education. In the second phase of the research, there was designed a quantitative study to measure the attitude of teachers towards unethical information technology use in higher education.

Bacău, Romania   Liliana Mâță

Contents

Editor and Contributors

About the Editor

 **Liliana Mâţă** is a Ph.D. in Educational Sciences and Associate Professor at the Teacher Training Department of the "Vasile Alecsandri" University of Bacău, Romania. She has published books, book chapters, and articles in international journals on current issues in the domain of Educational Sciences. She also worked as a research expert, member, and director in national and international research projects on current educational themes: pedagogical competences, curricular innovations, ethical use of information technology in higher education. Also, she is the Chief Editor of the *Journal of Innovation in Psychology, Education and Didactics* (JIPED). e-mail: liliana.mata@ub.ro

Contributors

Richard Afedzie, Ph.D. is a Lecturer of Human Resource Development at the Pentecost University, Accra, Ghana. He has published several academic journals and book chapters on Disaster Management, Business Ethics, Organisational Development, Human Resource, and Environmental Sustainability. Richard has also participated in several academic conferences in Europe and North America over the past decade.

Elena Roxana Ardeleanu is a Ph.D. in Mathematics and Associate Professor at the Mathematics—Informatics Department of the "Vasile Alecsandri" University of Bacău, Romania. She has published books and articles in international journals on current issues in the domain of Mathematics and Educational Sciences. Her experience includes Mathematics applied in Biology, Probability and Statistics, and Mathematics for teacher education. She also was involved as a researcher member in national research projects on current educational themes: pedagogical competences, curricular innovations, ethical use of information technology in higher education.

Nuri Balta is a Physics Professor at the Suleyman Demirel University, Almaty, Kazakhstan. He received his BA in Physics Education from Bogazici University, Istanbul, Turkey, and his Doctorate in Physics Education from Middle East Technical University, Ankara, Turkey. He has taught Physics at high schools in Turkey, Kazakhstan, and Uzbekistan for more than 20 years, and prepared students for international Physics Olympiads. His research areas include physics teachers' professional development, counterintuitive physics problems, and technology integration.

Ioana Boghian holds a Ph.D. in Philology; she is a Lecturer at the Teacher Training Department of the "Vasile Alecsandri" University of Bacău, Romania. She has published books, book chapters, and articles in international journals on current issues in the domains of literary and cultural studies, and the sciences of education: the didactics of foreign languages (English and French), intercultural education, teacher training. She also worked as a research expert and member in national and international research projects on current educational themes: pedagogical competences, curricular innovations, ethical use of information technology in higher education. e-mail: ioana.boghian@ub.ro

Otilia Clipa is Head of the Science of Education Department and Associate Professor with a Ph.D. in the Sciences of Education, at the "Stefan cel Mare" University of Suceava. She has a BA in Pedagogy and Psychology and MD in Integrated Pedagogy. She published and/or coordinated over 12 books and many articles in international journals (over 70 articles). Also, she is involved in many research projects (national or European) in the domain of the Sciences of education. Areas of interest: preschool and primary education, assessment in education, teacher education, and didactics for university teachers. email: otilia.clipa@usm.ro

Venera-Mihaela Cojocariu is a Ph.D. in Educational Sciences and Professor at the Pre- and In-Service Teacher Training Department, the "Vasile Alecsandri" University of Bacău, Romania. She has published books, book chapters, and articles in international journals on current issues in the domain of Educational Sciences: the philosophy of education, training theory, and methodology, student-centered educational strategies, teacher education. She also worked as a research expert and member in national and international research projects on current educational themes: the axiologic universe of the teacher; interactive teaching strategies; teaching strategies used in higher education. e-mail: venera@ub.ro

Macire Kante achieved his Ph.D. in Information Systems at the University of Nairobi (Kenya). He worked as a Research Associate at the National Center for Scientific and Technological Research in Mali. Currently, he is pursuing a postdoctoral fellowship at the University of Johannesburg (South Africa). His recent work is largely in the area of Information and Communication Technology for Development in the following thematic areas: ICT for Agriculture and Health Informatics and Knowledge Management for Development.

Gabriel Mares has a Bachelor's Degree in Educational Sciences and in Psychology, a Master's Degree in Communication and a Ph.D. in Educational Sciences. His research is in experiential education, adult and parent education, therapeutic relationships, therapy and education of people with special needs. His research is reflected in articles and chapters of books, textbooks, and course materials, participation at conferences. He has clinical expertise in working with HIV infected people and autistic children, also he has experience as trainer in life skills development programs for children and young people, critical thinking and career counseling.

Lefkios Neophytou has been working, since 2019, as an education officer at the Cyprus Quality Assurance Agency in Higher Education (CYQAA). He attended undergraduate and graduate studies at the University of Cyprus (B.A. in Educational Sciences, 1999; M.A. in Educational Administration and Curriculum Development, 2004; Ph.D. in Curriculum and Instruction, 2009). He also worked as an educational officer at the Cyprus Pedagogical Institute and as Commissioner for Children's Rights. He is a board member in academic/research organizations and has participated in ad hoc scientific committees in Cyprus and abroad. He is actively involved in research projects funded by the EU or the government of Cyprus. His research interests and publications focus on effective differentiated instruction and teacher professional development.

Paul Adjei Onyina holds a Ph.D. in Economics from the Macquarie University. He is a Senior Lecturer at the Pentecost University, Sowotoum-Accra, Ghana. He has authored a book, book chapters, and articles on contemporary issues in international journals to his credit. His writings cover finance, corporate governance, and gender issues. Additionally, he works as an administrator and a dean, ensuring that lecturers are well informed and have current materials in teaching students of the faculty. e-mail: paonyina@pentvars.edu.gh

Alexandra-Georgiana Poenaru is a Ph.D. student at the "Alexandru Ioan Cuza" University of Iași, sociology, with the thesis "Discrimination and social inequities on the labor market. The case of Romanian migrants from Italy". She has participated in national and international conferences and has published many research studies, book chapters, and articles in professional journals on various issues related to international migration: social representations of migrants, discrimination against Romanian migrants in Italy, international labor migration in Europe, migration, and entrepreneurship, the political participation of Romanian migrants from Diaspora, the cultural projects developed by Romanian associations in Tuscany, the exploitation of Romanian migrants on the labor market in Italy. She also involved in a research assistant in a national project on the ethical use of information technology in higher education.

Carmen-Violeta Popescu holds a Ph.D. in Mathematics, she is an Associate Professor and Head of the Teacher Training Department of the "Vasile Alecsandri" University of Bacău, Romania. Her main subjects/occupational skills covered are Numerical Analysis. Mathematics. Mathematical Software. Didactics of Mathematics. She also was involved as a research expert, member, or director in national and international research projects on educational themes such as e-learning, innovative teaching, or training of teachers from the preuniversity education system.

Roxana Timofte is a Lecturer at the Babeş-Bolyai University, the Faculty of Psychology and Education Sciences, Cluj-Napoca, Romania. She achieved a Ph.D. in Organic Chemistry from Southampton University in the UK and a Master's degree in Education Sciences at the Babeş-Bolyai University, Cluj-Napoca, Romania. Her interests span from Chemistry Education to the utilization of new technologies for the improvement of education at the university level.

Cosmin-Ion Tomozei is Lecturer Ph.D. at the "Vasile Alecsandri" University of Bacău, Faculty of Sciences, Department of Mathematics and Computer Science. He holds a Ph.D. in Economic Informatics, from the Bucharest University of Economic Studies, Faculty of Economic Cybernetics, Statistics, and Informatics, achieved in 2012. His research area is centered on the field of software engineering and reengineering, applied to Government, Education, and Health. In the last years, he has been an IT Expert, researcher, or team leader in many European funded research and development projects. He gained international expertise in the definition and implementation of smart specializations strategies for regional development.

Academic Integrity in the Technology-Driven Education Era

Venera-Mihaela Cojocariu and Gabriel Mareş

Abstract This chapter aims to explore academic integrity and how we can relate to it in the technology-driven education era. To this end, we aim to systematize some of the current challenges of academic integrity from the perspective of the digital age; to list the most common forms of academic dishonesty; to highlight a series of specific and general measures to reduce them; to argue how higher education institutions can intervene for adequate training in this regard; to explain what the codes of honor/ethics represent in this context; to systematize the most important fundamental values that guide them.

Keywords Academic integrity · Code of ethic · Digital age · Model

1 Current Challenges of Academic Integrity in the Age of Technology

Academic integrity should be a major concern of the social macrosystem, the effects of its manifestation being reflected at the level of society as a whole, on all types of activities, from profit-oriented to non-profit, from budgetary to the private type, from the educational/cultural to the economic, social, political type, starting from an early age. The results of some studies show that there are two major categories of causes (internal and external) that determine the struggle to maintain academic integrity: changes in people and changes in the learning environment, respectively, "shifting generational attitudes and prevalence of information technology" [1, p. 579].

Various authors suggest that there is a lack of clarity in defining academic integrity, which should not mean more leniency toward a violation of its principles [2]. The

V.-M. Cojocariu (✉) · G. Mareş
Vasile Alecsandri University of Bacău, Bacău, Romania
e-mail: venera@ub.ro

G. Mareş
e-mail: mares.gabriel@ub.ro

© The Author(s), under exclusive license to Springer Nature Singapore Pte Ltd. 2022
L. Mâță (ed.), *Ethical Use of Information Technology in Higher Education*,
EAI/Springer Innovations in Communication and Computing,
https://doi.org/10.1007/978-981-16-1951-9_1

effort to define the term integrity can be considered both by reference to dictionary-type sources, where integrity appears as "the quality of being honest and having strong moral principles" [3], and dishonesty is defined as "lack of honesty or integrity: the disposition to defraud or deceive" [4], the results of specialized studies on the subject, that have increased over the last decade. In a synthetic approach, the answer to the question of *what is academic integrity* could be condensed as follows: "Academic integrity is a set of specific practices revolving around independent work, production of original scholarship, accurately and transparently tracing of sources and others' contributions, and following stated and unstated norms of academic conduct for academic rewards" [5–7]. "It refers to honesty and trust in all aspects of academic work. It involves a commitment to such fundamental values as honesty, trust, fairness, respect, and responsibility within all academic endeavors" [8, p. 227]. Macfarlane's [9] study highlights the relative synonymy between academic integrity and academic honesty. Against this background, two directions of analysis of academic integrity are highlighted, as an umbrella term, which brings together several aspects, as follows: (1) Honest academic practices, which refer specifically to the teaching process, to the research process [10, 11], and services; (2) The ensemble of "values, behavior, and conduct of academics in all aspects of their practice (teaching, research, and service")" [9, p. 341].

Consequently, if we reflect on the academic environment, integrity designates the coherent and consistent observance and promotion of ethical values and principles in the area of university education in all contexts (theoretically—as values, norms, rules, principles; at the level of action—conduct; managerially—codes, regulations, measures, sanctions). For the academic world, the digitization of scientific resources and the transformation of the instructive–educational process into e-learning or blended learning activity represent not only a new type of resources/process that changed the paradigm of approaching education, but also a real problem with ethical implications, both from the perspective of the quality of teaching–learning-evaluation [12] and reaching the pre-established standards [13], as well as of the general-human training of the beneficiaries of the process [14]. Regarding the effects of violating academic integrity, Jones and Sheridan [15] point out that these are not restricted to reducing school effort but reflect on student equity, reduced reading, decreased ability to operate rationally, decreased creativity, and originality. As such, most of the time, the lack of academic integrity will correlate with a moral deficit in real life. It follows that the phrase *academic integrity* does not designate a concept isolated from real life [5], but only one aspect of the formation of human personality for a profession, social life, with deep roots in the entire existence and previous evolution of the student. There are studies [5, pp. 3–14] that highlight and analyze several generative sources of how the student relates to the dimension of academic integrity: social and economic contexts of higher education (unprecedented increase in the number of students of different ages; the existence of students who work full or part-time during their studies; the costs of higher education; the family and financial situation of students), contexts with direct bearing on academic integrity (support for academic integrity norms; authorship; norms of sharing), contexts with an indirect bearing on academic integrity (motivations and incentives contrary to academic integrity;

pressure to achieve; lack of interest; lack of time; temptations; students' roles and identities). Of real utility are the literature review studies, such as Macfarlane's [9], that investigate and systematize three aspects: main literature items demonstrating the ethics of teaching; main literature items demonstrating the ethics of research; main literature items demonstrating the ethics of service. Such analyses highlight, on the one hand, the diversity of students and their axiological backgrounds as well as the difficulty of identifying and implementing successful procedures for ensuring academic integrity, with a desirable impact on all students and all categories of activities.

Rapid access to databases, platforms, applications, etc., as well as the ease (for many people) of procuring, owning, and using mobile devices capable of providing immediate access to them is a challenge for many educators who need to become compliant and resilient in the face of the new situation. This context, called by some specialists "new technological frontier" [2, p. 14], indicates a completely changed educational environment compared to the traditional approach and, thus, much more challenging, both for teachers and students and for university management [5], a context generating genuine moral panic [16]. Although university management and professors start from the assumption that students are motivated, want to learn and, to this end, will show adequate, honest, conducting genuine study activities [17], the reality shows that with the expansion of digitalization and the generation of millennials there is an unprecedented increase in situations of academic dishonesty [9, 18–20]. All the more so as there are, even in the online environment (but not only!) authentic commercial or non-commercial possibilities that ensure access to cheating "services" [21]. In this sense, ensuring academic integrity is becoming one of the new "requirements of the digital age" [22].

Although it may seem strange, the foundations of academic integrity are laid from the first moment a person/child comes into contact with an instructive–educational institution (kindergarten, school, etc.), especially as the age for using new electronic means of learning, documentation, research has greatly decreased.

Among the challenges of academic integrity in the age of technology, we turn to those most often invoked in the literature:

- massification of knowledge [2, 5, 9, 13, 23, 24];
- reduction/elimination of plagiarism [8, 12, 13, 15, 17, 19, 22–31];
- rethinking the forms, methods, and criteria of teaching–learning assessment [10, 12, 13, 19, 22–26, 29, 32, 33];
- increasing the prevalence of academic dishonesty [2] (for the most common forms in academia, see Table 1) ([2, 5, 8, 9, 12, 13, 15, 17–19, 21, 22, 25, 27, 30, 32–34]);
- the decrease in the weight and quality of learning and its results [22];
- overcoming the confusion between training and education, the quantitative perspective on academic training because "education is not only about accessing a collection of facts" [22, p. 158] and replacing it with the formative approach, constructivist–qualitative, in which knowledge is a construct of the subject of learning that marks, expresses, and shapes it.

Table 1 Significant forms of academic dishonesty and some mitigation measures

Forms of violation of academic integrity	Measures
Plagiarism	Anti-plagiarism software Various types of evaluation Annotation of the bibliography Stimulating reflective thinking
Cheating	Academic ethics course Various types of evaluation Stimulating reflective thinking
Collusion	Individual work Individual topics Individual preparation for exams Stimulating reflective thinking Writing reflective essays
Duplicate submission	Submitting a paper to only one publication Multiple checks with anti-plagiarism software Stimulating reflective thinking
Copying	Announcing rules of ethics and sanctions Discussions about temptations and consequences Stimulating reflective thinking
Homework copying	Detecting copying Discern temporal, behavioral, and academic patterns Giving enough time and effort to solve homework independently Presenting and discussing homework solutions in class Stimulating reflective thinking
Deceitfulness	Psychological counseling mechanisms to increase self-confidence Stimulating originality, personal perspectives in solving assessment tasks and tests Stimulating reflective thinking
Misconduct	Consistency in the application of sanctions Increasing your chances of getting caught Stimulating reflective thinking
Improper use of Internet sources	Reflective practices Demonstration through one's academic practices of how the norms of integrity are observed (writing a course, making a ppt, using direct, indirect sources) Stimulating reflective thinking
Back translation	Stimulating an original style of achieving assignments, projects Stimulating reflective thinking

The paradox of the Internet age is that new learning and communication technologies (NTLC) is both a factor in generating dishonesty behaviors ("Technology makes students feel anonymous and free from the situation") and a source of their identification [1, p. 589], and therefore, they can increase the academic integrity or they can determine its lack [30].

As can be seen, all measures to reduce academic dishonesty can be directly linked to two vectors: knowledge/observance of the rules of academic integrity and encouraging freedom of thought and expression. Some authors suggest an algorithm to reduce academic dishonesty that could include the following steps: make academic integrity expectations clear [23]; make the most of the technology, utilize pedagogical strategies [19]; restructuring assessment practices [25] toward "individualized assessments" [24, p. 7]. Other authors integrate into this algorithm interesting formative methods that stimulate critical and reflective thinking [12], about which it is appreciated that although it has always been necessary, it has become imperative for the twenty-first century [35], being considered a "core outcome in higher education" and associated with the increase of academic performances [36, p. 91]. Some of the mentioned authors explain this idea, demonstrating that in the age of Internet seduction it would be useful for students to keep a reflective diary, in which to write down incidents, intentions, thoughts, states manifested during study and homework to allow them to reflect on the content, syllabus or even their conduct, thus encouraging them to become proactive subjects of their learning [12].

If we consider a series of general solutions to the reduction of academic dishonesty, we find that they require an appropriate approach by combining three activities: study, research, and writing with levers and procedures such as education for the concrete implementation of autonomous thinking [20, 29]; stimulating analytical and critical thinking [18]; encouraging the expression of personal points of view, solving problems [20]; cultivating reflective learning and reflective practices [18, 29]; elaborating original works [29]; correct citation of sources; addressing and using electronic sources such as those written on paper; finally giving up any copy–paste procedure used for text, statistics, images, music; the correct capitalization of the paraphrasing [17] but also the knowledge and the assumption of the violation of the norms of academic integrity. Overall, this would mean "embracing a culture of free thought" [15, p. 10].

Just as the university must adapt to current times, it must also re-evaluate the issue of academic integrity in a way appropriate to the age of advanced technology [1]. Some authors [29] even consider that the holistic approach that each institution must take in this direction is called Academic Integrity Education and its beneficiaries are all members of the academic community, from those directly involved in the process, students and teachers, to those indirectly involved, administrators and staff members.

2 Training for Academic Integrity in the Digital Age

Training for ethical academic behavior designed to promote and respect academic integrity must begin at an early age. Even during preschool education, children can be taught elements that have a strong influence in structuring moral norms and shaping objective justice [37] which will then lead to the formation of respect for others, implicitly for their work. The formation of ethical attitudes and later academic integrity is directly related to the ability to structure critical thinking skills [35] which involves good analysis, discrimination, selection, decision making, etc., or, in other words, operations such as "critical evaluation, development of argument and use of evidence" [36, p. 92]. Even from an early age, children can learn how to look for resources (to play) by respecting a few elements such as: requesting the agreement/confirmation/permission of adults responsible for their upbringing and education; compliance with access restrictions according to the age criterion (by recognizing the related symbols); refusal to offer play opportunities on the mobile devices of other children or adults, if the reference adults have not given their consent, etc. In turn, adults themselves must be consistent and follow the rules they set for children; reference adults will not change the rules during the game to their advantage; it is right to acknowledge our mistakes and to show honest attitudes; adults must show respect for their peers; politeness and gentleness in dealing with others must be ingredients with which to operate around children as well. The little ones learn through imitation and contagion, and consequently, the reference adults must be models of ethical behaviors so that the appearance of non-ethical situations determines the appearance of cognitive discrepancies and creates opportunities to clarify those situations. It is important to remember that we learn from mistakes, and the mistake should not be treated catastrophically but as an opportunity to understand, clarify, establish the relationship behavior–consequence. The consequences of the low level of critical thinking training come to light more strongly during university studies when many students take information or even work assignments in a non-selective and non-objective manner [20].

A large proportion of adults, including educators, often feel that ethical norms are somehow implicit and that no effort is required on their part to educate/teach learners about these norms and principles. Educators often forget that from one stage of development to another these moral norms and principles undergo changes and adjustments related to the development of cognitive potential and understanding [38], on the one hand, and on the other, some changes are in step with technological transformations that have facilitated access to huge information and video resources [39]. Beyond the particularizations we referred to earlier, we will list several principles and general elements [20, 40, 41], which education systems must promote from high school:

- the student's understanding (regardless of age) of the individual responsibility assumed through the use of the devices in the institution and personal devices;
- offering the possibility to create individual accounts for access to the relays of the educational units, to different devices or applications;

- training the capacity to verify the scientific correctness of the information identified in the online and offline resources, but also of the information with which the educators or the persons from the social groups to which it belongs operate;
- verifying the timeliness and validity of scientific information, working/intervention methods, etc.;
- verifying the credibility of digital resource providers, including Web sites;
- educating for the acquisition of the ability to analyze the content of advertisements and identify the harmful potential for emotional development or social life;
- ensuring the possibility of respecting the individual learning rhythm and the personal learning style by respecting the principles of the training programmed within the applications/software used in the training;
- achieving the transition to methods used in the education process focused on reading and critical thinking;
- the use of participatory, collaborative methods, teamwork for solving innovatively some tasks with the obligation to highlight the sources of documentation/inspiration;
- the use in the evaluation of problem-solving approaches to the detriment of multiple-choice tests;
- ensuring the possibility to restrict access to online resources that directly or easily provide answers or solutions to items or tasks proposed by educators.

Overall, it is about "providing a range of opportunities for students to acquire academic and study skills relevant to seeking and critically evaluating sources, reading and note-making, and writing and citation" [29, p. 2] in a period in which we witness the increase of temptations to easily and quickly obtain [31], by a simple click, assignments, projects, essays, papers, works for which we can only pay (or not!) and change the author.

Who is responsible for training for academic integrity? Morris [29] argues that the holistic approach that gives us the answer to this question brings together the university, faculties, departments and involves both responsibilities and roles as well as creating opportunities for staff, including professors, academic integrity specialists (academic conduct or integrity officers), learning technologists, educational counselors, and administrators. By relating to the competencies of each category, higher education institutions shall develop their academic integrity policy and establish appropriate responsibilities. Other studies [33] also analyze students' perceptions of this responsibility and identify at least three hypostases: non-involvement, involvement without any result, and fear of such involvement.

The approach to the issue of academic integrity in the university environment must be done, as in the previous stages of schooling, also explicitly and punctually, even in terms of defining the term academic integrity [42]. The specific requirements of the student's life presuppose that the student is familiar with the international norms of academic integrity and with those specific to the university in which he studies. Studies show that millennial students, like many digital natives, are much more result-oriented and much less process-oriented, looking for solutions to achieve rewards as quickly and easily as possible, as copying the answers or some consistent parts of the assignments/projects are considered typical and unsanctionable behavior and called by some authors "the technological detachment phenomenon" [20, p. 1]. That is why teachers need to be directly and explicitly involved in ensuring the transparency of both the codes of values and norms specific to integrity, as well as in the effort to reduce academic dishonesty. Studies show that when teachers decide to do so, the positive effects do not take long to occur [32].

Some of the most frequently suggested directions of action in the literature, ordered from the general to the particular, include

– reviewing institutional policies, existing procedures, resources and associated activities [30];
– the application at the institutional level, on this new basis, of a "holistic approach" [29] or a "systemic approach" [25] which (e.g., in the UK perspective) refers to several activities starting with policy and university procedures; it continues with the correct procedures for recruitment, guidance, and advancement in the academic process of students; teaching–learning assessment practices and effective work with students; it is amplified by the professional development measures of teachers and staff; it is crowned with measures for the proper use of technology and its levers;
– giving sufficient time and effort to explain, analyze, understand, and apply the values and norms that underpin academic integrity in their full complexity [24];
– a clear explanation of university expectations toward students in terms of academic integrity [23, 24];
– including the expectations regarding the academic integrity in the syllabus of each teacher, in all educational disciplines and their presentation/clarification during the first meeting with the students [1, 23, 28];
– analysis of teachers' written courses or their presentations from the perspective of academic integrity [28];
– increasing the intrinsic motivation for counterbalanced learning to the application of punitive measures (that only stimulate academic dishonesty, that can become destructive rather than constructive) [24, 29];
– the elimination of unethical ways of using software (e.g., back translation by using machine translation software) [15];
– the introduction of a course dedicated to university ethics (with compulsory or optional status) in which to study the most important aspects of academic integrity with applicability in the teaching and research process as well as the social life inside the university [10];
– addressing the specific aspects of academic integrity in several courses within the study program (not only in the dedicated course), in a transversal, transdisciplinary manner, involving both the explicit teaching of the values and norms of academic integrity and the implicit training of students in this respect [10];
– re-evaluation and restructuring of evaluation practices [25];
– extending training for academic integrity in the field of research through the participation of students and teachers in ethics training and mentoring, observing

the members of the academic community, effective participation in research teams [10, pp. 25–26];
- awareness, knowledge, and observance by teachers, researchers, and students of ethical standards for writing articles, books, course materials, topics, projects [9, 41, 43];
- education for copyright and intellectual property, including the avoidance of plagiarism [17, 31];
- use of anti-plagiarism software [23, 31].

Beyond these lines of intervention at the academic level, there is the perception of teachers regarding the approach to ensuring academic integrity. The results of some studies [10] show that university professors have different opinions about how academic integrity, in general, and that associated with research should be learned (explicitly or implicitly, reactively or proactively). The same diversity is maintained when it comes to how it should relate to cases of academic dishonesty. In this study, the teachers who were part of the research group highlighted the need for pedagogical training to support the promotion of academic integrity in the field of research in the Internet age [10, 25]. Hyytinen [10] considers that this approach is not at all surprising, given that teacher training in this direction is quite low. Other studies [28] reconfirm this need, only that the data indicate that teachers do not recognize that they must attend such courses, but of academic management that must find levers to promote good practices for implementing academic integrity.

Löfström [28, pp. 441–443] highlights interesting aspects of who teaches academic integrity and how, demonstrating that not all teachers approach the relevant aspects of the topic in the same way, such as: core values can be learned or not; how academic integrity can be learned and whether it can be taught; whether it can be explicit teaching or just modeling; what is integrity-based research; what is the importance of moral codes for research; which is the origin of a personal moral compass. It is certain that this whole issue is preserved, nuanced, and diversified in the digital age we are going through. The obtained results allowed the identification and analysis of five patterns: (1) Teachers teach rules and values; (2) Teachers are the guardians of the academy; (3) Teachers are teaching-oriented social reformers; (4) Teachers are models of academic integrity that emphasize the responsibility of students; (5) Teachers are builders of academic integrity skills.

It is becoming increasingly clear that there can be no question of successful recipes applicable to any university and all professors or university management in general, but that each professor and each university will come to express their approach, according to the context in which they carry out their activity. In this context, there remain in the digital age some open issues of training for academic integrity:

- What does it still mean/how can the collaboration between students yet be realized in achieving projects and what ethical implications does this have?;
- Should or should not students report when their classmates cheat on homework or assessment? [28];
- To what extent is the foundation of the teacher–student relationship based on trust, in the context in which it is necessary to scan the topics with an anti-plagiarism

software? Would increased confidence in the correctness of the anti-plagiarism software thus lead to decreased interpersonal trust? [31];

– What other relationships exist between academic integrity, the nature and role of education and success, respectively, efficiency, in a society and a time massively marked by rapid efficiency rather than the ethics of achievement? [24];
– Is the manifestation of academic dishonesty a warning about the challenges of universities in the age of technology in which "information is easy to access but challenging to sort, distill, evaluate, test, and apply and where approaches to promoting integrity and methodologies for teaching and learning have not been sufficiently adapted"? [24, p. 10].

3 Toward a Model of Academic Integrity in the Digital Age

All types of educational institutions should constitute, in case they have not done that already, a code of honor, in which it is worth making very clear and specific clarifications on the aspects of academic integrity, on the three areas, as shown previously (teaching process, research process, and services). These codes should contain explicit references to the components involved in the use of e-learning, the use of the Internet, online education as well as its means and resources: the use of Web sites, software, applications or educational platforms, etc. Of all educational institutions, universities have been most aware of the need to establish such codes of honor, noting that their appearance leads to a decrease in the level of academic dishonesty [44]. The acceleration of the process of establishing or revising academic integrity codes or policies has also been driven by technological changes, especially in the field of information and communication technologies [45]. Thus, in the last two decades, it has even been necessary to move to concrete measures in the introduction of anti-plagiarism software but also by orienting research toward an evidence-based approach [46]. Universities, in particular, have begun to attach greater importance to the training of students in the sense of paying attention and specifying sources of documentation or citations, critical evaluation of online content or analysis of the credibility of the source of such content, steps achievable through a double effort: knowledge of the norms of academic integrity and continuous training/practice of critical and reflective thinking.

Honor codes are a moral tool for building trust in the university space. Through the values, norms, and procedures they propose, they become a significant part of the solution to enhance academic integrity. They try to change the classical approach of the relationship between us and them, between faculties, professors, and students in a relationship that is traded from the perspective of common expectations related to academic conduct [1].

An essential aspect of initiating the process of changing the approach to academic integrity [25], developing or updating codes of honor is the analysis of the influences that the new computerized society has on the moral life of individuals and society. As the impact of ICT on academia has increased, so has the need to clarify and guide the ethical disorder of which some members of society have become aware [14]. In answer to the question: What kind of virtues should I develop? universities must offer sets of values and codes of honor of academic integrity that allow the meeting of the individual perspective with the social one, the present one with the future one. And this is not easy to undertake!

From the same perspective, to maintain or reconfirm their accreditation, universities must demonstrate that they carry out quality processes, able to diminish the opportunities for students to cheat [19, 24]. Moreover, in some countries, such as the UK, quality assurance standards (in the field of psychology) refer to some aspects of critical thinking [36], the development of which is linked by us to the increasing possibility to decline the forms of manifestation of academic dishonesty.

A series of benchmarks on the core values that guide academic conduct were identified in the detailed analysis conducted by Keohane [47] 21 years ago, highly current and applicable to the challenges of the digital age, which nuances a set of five values that must exist in building academic integrity: honesty, trust, fairness, respect, and responsibility, later "revise and re-vitalize" [48], where the value of courage is added. In their absence, all our actions as teachers, students, researchers lose their verticality and "become suspicious" [47, p. 16].

In the same category, there are studies such as those of Manly [1] (correlating and illustrating two of the values analyzed above, namely the values of respect and responsibility with six online scenarios (three for each of the two values, offered for analysis and evaluation to students to identify their perception of violating the rules of academic integrity) that reveals the universities' concern with how students relate to them and thus identify strategies to improve the behavior of millennials.

If in a condensed vision we restrict the sphere of the fundamental values of academic integrity to the six already mentioned (honesty, trust, fairness, respect, responsibility, courage) and correlate them with the three spheres of academic life specified in the previous subchapter (teaching–learning assessment; research; services), we generate a matrix model of the academic integrity culture, called HTFRRC based on the initial of the six values in its structure (Honesty, Trust, Fairness, Respect, Responsibility, Courage). According to this model, on the one hand, each value is found and manifested in each of the three spheres of academic life (1. Teaching–learning assessment; 2. Research; 3. Services). On the other hand, in each sphere, all six values are manifested and intertwined (more or less) (according to Table 2). Following this, each category of actors (students, professors, representatives of university management, computer scientists, technicians, advisers, and administrative staff) must work together and provide dedicated training sessions as well as the development/application of appropriate conduct guidelines [20].

From a similar perspective, but presented in the form of the necessary measures, [48, pp. 30–31] we will list practical steps, the most significant of which would be the development and clear, honest communication of policies and procedures of academic integrity; promoting the positive aspects of academic integrity on university campuses; training all members of the academic community in the field of integrity standards; systematic and correct practice of the actions described in the policies; the realization, explanation, and fair and transparent administration of the system

Table 2 HTFRRC matrix model of academic integrity

Values	Spheres					
	Honesty 1	Trust 2	Fairness 3	Respect 4	Responsibility 5	Courage 6
Teaching-learning-evaluation (1)						
Research (2)						
Services (3)						

of sanctioning the violation of the norms of academic integrity; ensuring knowledge of the ongoing evolution of educational technologies and practices to anticipate possible risks and problems of academic integrity; ensuring a regular evaluation of the effectiveness of policies, procedures, and practices with a view to their continuous improvement. Such measures demonstrate the efforts of universities to ensure that academic integrity standards are transparent, adequately communicated, and targeted directly for implementation to reduce misconduct [21], as a response to deception on an industrial scale, at the national and international level [25]. A more compact version of these measures belongs to Morris [25, p. 2] which indicates three categories of activities: (1) The use of policies and procedures not necessarily punitive, but aimed at the use of educational penalties; (2) Ensuring numerous training opportunities for students of relevant study skills: search for sources, their critical analysis, reading and selection of information, elaboration of written materials, adequate citation of sources; (3) Improving teaching–learning assessment strategies so that they become predominantly formative, with an emphasis on student involvement in learning, student-centered, creative, engaging tasks.

4 Instead of Conclusions ...

The issue of academic integrity in the digital age is a hot one, demonstrated by the permanent increase in the number of studies on the subject since 2000, the appearance of journals dedicated to the subject (e.g., the Journal of Academic Ethics in 2003) but also the insufficiency, at the same time, of empirical research [9].

In addition to the few dimensions of academic integrity inherent in the digital age previously undertaken, multiple aspects remain to be analyzed. One of the challenges arises from the fact that the authors who wrote literature reviews [9] point out that there is no unitary understanding of the concept, nor of the notions of ethics and academic ethics with which it correlates. The distinct perspectives belong either to the multicriteria approach of the analysis of the causes that determine it (work, health, family, relationships, economy, leisure) and the relation between them [5] or to the scientific fields from which the analysis is performed (mathematics, history, literature, communication, and new communication technologies). Thus, significant differences in understanding the terms are found, resulting in very different ways of constructing and implementing academic integrity strategies [34]. Beyond these different theoretical approaches, it is extremely important that within the same university the faculties, professors, management, and students have the same perspective on academic integrity and its components (values, norms, and rules) [1].

In this sense, the literature on academic integrity expresses the consensus on the need to create "meaningful connections between students and faculty in creating communities of academic honesty" [2, p. 20] and to intervene with authentic academic integrity strategies [25]. Concerns yet remain about how the Internet has morally changed academia (either by modeling and intensifying, traditional aspects, such as plagiarism or copying) or by generating new aspects of what is original and what is copied, especially to the uncertain relationship between them [31]. The same sources underline expectations about what will happen in the future, anticipating an increase in tension between the values and practices inherent in Web technology and external values and practices (such as copyright) that are regarded as quite difficult to match.

That is why "efforts to create and maintain cultures of integrity require continuous ongoing attention" [48, p. 9]. Other *aspects* worthy of interest in the continuation of the analysis of the approached topic would be

- involvement of students in building/ taking responsibility [33] for their entire academic life, especially for their learning (see Chankova's analyses) [22, pp. 169–170);
- maximizing the power of example and peer influences, the influence of student groups when creating policies and codes of honor designed to reduce academic dishonesty [33];
- the effective involvement of students in the development of codes of honor [33] which will ensure an important contribution to the formation of a moral culture of students [15];
- systematic collection of feedback from students on the quality [13] of course content and actual teaching activity (interactive, collaborative teaching strategies, and formative assessment strategies, which value the effort, the process, not necessarily the product [15, 33];
- identification/development of good academic integrity practices for high-risk areas [9];
- identification and optimal use of resources [25] (financial, human, temporal) with which these steps can be taken.

If contemporary society is experiencing a deep moral crisis, it is obvious that the convergent and committed effort to research and ensure academic integrity (faculties, professors, students, management, technicians, counselors, parents, even) is part of the solution for a better world. As Youngsup Kim argues, "Academic integrity is a way to change the world. Change the university first; then change the world" [48, p. 17].

References

1. Manly, T.S., Leonard, L.N.K., Riemenschneider, C.K.: Academic integrity in the information age: Virtues of respect and responsibility. J. Bus. Ethics **127**, 579–590 (2015). https://doi.org/10.1007/s10551-014-2060-8
2. Deranek, J., Parnther, C.: Academic honesty and the new technological frontier. The Hilltop Rev. **8**(1), 14–22 (2015)
3. XXX.: Oxford Learners Dictionaries, Oxford University Press (2020). https://www.oxfordlearnersdictionaries.com/definition/english/integrity?q=integrity. Accessed 20 July 2020
4. XXX.: Merriam-Webster Dictionary. https://www.merriam-webster.com/dictionary/dishonesty. Accessed 20 July 2020
5. Blum, S.D.: What it means to be a student today. In: Bretag, T. (ed.) Handbook of academic integrity, pp. 1–20. Springer, Singapore (2015)
6. Davis, S.F., Drinan, P.F., Bertram Gallant, T.: Cheating in school: What we know and what we can do. Wiley, Chichester (2009)
7. Whitley Jr., B.E., Keith-Spiegel, P.: Academic dishonesty: An educator's guide. Lawrence Erlbaum Associates, Mahwah (2002)
8. Bush, P., Bilgin, A.: Student and staff understanding and reaction: Academic integrity in an Australian University. J. Acad. Ethics. **12**(3), 227–243 (2014). https://doi.org/10.1007/s10805-014-9214-2
9. Macfarlane, B., Zhang, J., Pun, A.: Academic integrity: a review of the literature. Stud. High. Educ. **39**(2), 339–358 (2014). https://doi.org/10.1080/03075079.2012.709495
10. Hyytinen, H., Löfström, E.: Reactively, proactively, implicitly, explicitly? Academics' pedagogical conceptions of how to promote research ethics and integrity. J. Acad. Ethics **15**, 23–41 (2017). https://doi.org/10.1007/s10805-016-9271-9
11. Khaled, K.F.: Scientific integrity in the digital age: data fabrication. Res. Chem. Intermed. **40**, 1815–1849 (2014). https://doi.org/10.1007/s11164-013-1084-5
12. O'Connell, J.: Networked participatory online learning design and challenges for academic integrity in higher education. IJEI **12**(4), 1–15 (2016). https://doi.org/10.1007/s40979-016-0009-7
13. Mahabeer, P., Pirtheepal T.: Assessment, plagiarism and its effect on academic integrity: Experiences of academics at a university in South Africa. S. Afr. J. Sci. **115**(11–12), 1–8 (2019).. https://www.sajs.co.za/article/view/6323
14. Floridi, L. (ed.): The Cambridge handbook of information and computer ethics. Cambridge University Press, New York (2010)
15. Jones, M., Sheridan, L.: Back translation: an emerging sophisticated cyber strategy to subvert advances in 'digital age' plagiarism detection and prevention. Assess. Eval. High. Educ. **40**(5), 1–13 (2014). https://doi.org/10.1080/02602938.2014.950553
16. Clegg, S., Flint, A.: More heat than light: Plagiarism in its appearing. Br. J. Sociol. Educ. **27**(3), 373–387 (2006)
17. XXX: Academic integrity at the Massachusetts Institute of Technology: A handbook for students (2012). http://web.mit.edu/academicintegrity/handbook/handbook.pdf. Accessed 23 July 2020
18. Dalal, N.: Responding to plagiarism using reflective means. IJEI **11**(4), 1–12 (2015). https://doi.org/10.1007/s40979-015-0002-6
19. Mcgee, P.: Supporting Academic Honesty in Online Courses. JEO **10**(1), 1–31 (2013). https://doi.org/10.9743/JEO.2013.1.6
20. Piascik, P., Brazeau, G.A.: Promoting a culture of academic integrity. Am. J. pharma. educ. **74**(6), 113 (2010). https://doi.org/10.5688/aj7406113
21. Harris, L., Harrison, D., McNally, D., Ford, C.: Academic integrity in an online culture: Do McCabe's findings hold true for online, adult learners? J. Acad. Ethics (2019). https://doi.org/10.1007/s10805-019-09335-3
22. Chankova, M.: Teaching Academic Integrity: the Missing Link. J. Acad. Ethics **18**, 155–173 (2020). https://doi.org/10.1007/s10805-019-09356-y

23. Denisova-Schmidt, E.: The challenges of academic integrity in higher education: Current trends and prospects. CIHE Perspectives No. 5. Boston College Center for International Higher Education (2017). https://www.bc.edu/content/dam/files/research_sites/cihe/pubs/CIHE%20Perspective/Perspectives%20No%205%20June%2013%2C%202017%20No%20cropsFINAL.pdf. Retrieved 6 August 2020

24. Fishman, T.: Academic integrity as an educational concept, concern and movement in US institutions of higher learning. In Bretag, T. (ed.), Handbook of academic integrity, pp. 1–12. Springer, Singapore (2015). https://doi.org/10.1007/978-981-287-079-7_1-2

25. Morris, J.E.: Academic integrity matters: five considerations for addressing contract cheating. IJEI **14**(15), 1–12 (2018). https://doi.org/10.1007/s40979-018-0038-5

26. Ramdani, Z.: Construction of academic integrity scale. IJRSP **7**(1), 87–97 (2018). https://doi.org/10.5861/ijrsp.2018.3003

27. Griffin, D., Bolkan, S., Goodboy, A.: Academic dishonesty beyond cheating and plagiarism: Students' interpersonal deception in the college classroom. Quali. Res. Reports in Comm. **16**(1), 9–19 (2015). https://doi.org/10.1080/17459435.2015.1086416

28. Löfström, E., Trotman, T., Furnari, M., Shephard, K.: Who teaches academic integrity and how do they do it? High. Educ. **69**(3), 435–448 (2015). https://doi.org/10.1007/s10734-014-9784-3

29. Morris, J.E.: Academic integrity: A teaching and learning approach. Handbook of Academic Integrity. Springer Science + Business Media, Singapore (2015). https://link.springer.com/content/pdf/10.1007%2F978-981-287-079-7_11-1.pdf. Retrieved 31 July 2020

30. Sutherland-Smith, W.: Academic integrity in the digital age: Introduction. Handbook of Academic Integrity. Springer Science + Business Media, Singapore (2015) https://link.springer.com/content/pdf/10.1007%2F978-981-287-079-7_82-1.pdf. Retrieved 6 August 2020

31. Hinman, M.L.: The impact of the internet on our moral lives in academia. Ethics Inf. Technol. **4**, 31–35 (2002). https://doi.org/10.1023/A:1015231824812

32. Palazzo, J.D., Lee, Y.-J., Warnakulasooriya, R., Pritchard, E.D.: Patterns, correlates, and reduction of homework copying. Physical Review Special Topics—Physics Education Research 6 (2010). https://doi.org/10.1103/PhysRevSTPER.6.029901

33. Teodorescu, D., Andrei, T.: Faculty and peer influences on academic integrity: college cheating in Romania. High. Educ. **57**(3), 267–282 (2009). https://doi.org/10.1007/s10734-008-9143-3

34. Tauginienė, L., Gaižauskaitė, I., Razi, S.: Enhancing the Taxonomies Relating to Academic Integrity and Misconduct. J. Acad. Ethics. **17**, 345–361 (2019). https://doi.org/10.1007/s10805-019-09342-4

35. Halpern, D.F.: Critical thinking across the curriculum: A brief edition of thought & knowledge. Routledge, Hoboken, New York (2014) https://books.google.ro/books?hl=en&lr=&id=yrrKAgAAQBAJ&oi=fnd&pg=PP1&ots=V1tKdY1O-E&sig=gQFBQeETypSDy-w3-UD7qjG1Ro&redir_esc=y#v=onepage&q&f=false. Accessed 15 July 2020

36. Stupple, J.N., Maratos, A.F., Elander, J., Hunt, E.T., Cheung, Y.F., Aubeeluck, V.A.: Development of the critical thinking toolkit (CriTT): A measure of student attitudes and beliefs about critical thinking. Thinking Skills and Creativity **23**, 91–100 (2017) http://dx.doi.org/10.1016/j.tsc.2016.11.007

37. Johansson, E.: Morality in children's worlds: Rationality of thought or values emanating from relations? Studies in Philosophy and Education. Int. Quart. **20**(4), 345–358 (2001). https://doi.org/10.1023/A:1011803327963

38. Johansson, E., Emilson, A.: Toddlers' Life in Swedish Preschool. International journal of early childhood. Int. J. Early Childhood **42**, 165–179 (2010) https://doi.org/10.1007/s13158-010-0017-3

39. Carmichael, C.L., Schwartz, A.M., Coyle, M.A., Goldberg, M.H.: A Classroom Activity for Teaching Kohlberg's Theory of Moral Development. Teach. Psycho. **46**(1), 80–86 (2019). https://doi.org/10.1177/0098628318816180

40. Jimenez, D.F., Garza, D.N.: Predatory publishing and academic integrity: A perspective statement on retraction of neurosurgical publications: A systematic review. World Neurosurgery. **105**, 990–992 (2017). https://doi.org/10.1016/j.wneu.2017.05.157

41. Wager, E., Barbour, V., Yentis, S., Kleinert, S.: Retractions: guidance from the Committee on Publication Ethics (COPE). Obes. Rev. **11**(1), 64–66 (2010). https://doi.org/10.1111/j.1467-789X.2009.00702.x
42. Dyer, K.: Challenges of Maintaining Academic Integrity in an Age of Collaboration, Sharing and Social Networking. In Proceedings of TCC 2010. TCC Hawaii, 168–195 (2010). https://www.learntechlib.org/p/43770/. Retrieved 21 July 2020
43. Nath, S.B., Marcus, S.C., Druss, B.G.: Retractions in the research literature: misconduct or mistakes? Med. J. Australia **185**(3), 152–154 (2006).https://doi.org/10.5694/j.1326-5377.2006. tb00504.x
44. McCabe, D.L., Treviño, L.K., Butterfield, K.D.: Honor codes and other contextual influences on academic integrity: A replication and extension to modified honor code settings. Res. High. Educ. **43**, 357–378 (2002). https://doi.org/10.1023/A:1014893102151
45. Benson, L., Rodier, K., Enström, R., et al.: Developing a university-wide academic integrity E-learning tutorial: a Canadian case. Int. J. Edu. Integrity **15**(5), 1–23 (2019). https://doi.org/10.1007/s40979-019-0045-1
46. Gynnild, V., Gotschalk P.: Promoting academic integrity at a Midwestern University: critical review and current challenges. Int. J. Edu. Integrity **4**(2), 41–59 (2008). https://doi.org/10.21913/IJEI.v4i2.413
47. Keohane, N.: The fundamental values of academic integrity. The Center for Academic Integrity, Duke University. (1999), 1–12. https://www.chapman.edu/academics/academic-integrity/_files/the-fundamental-values-of-academic-integrity.pdf. Accessed 30 July 2020
48. Fishman, T. (ed.): The fundamental values of academic integrity, second edition. International Center for Academic Integrity, Clemson University (2012). https://www.chapman.edu/academics/academic-integrity/_files/the-fundamental-values-of-academic-integrity.pdf. Accessed 21 July 2020

Unethical Information Technology Use in Higher Education: A Review of Literature in Sub-Saharan Africa

Richard Afedzie and Paul Adjei Onyina

Abstract Ethical behavior in academic work is an important standard to ensure effective and quality outcomes. As a result, special focus should be dedicated to dealing with unethical behavior associated with information technology use in higher educational institutions in sub-Saharan Africa. This book chapter examines the world of unethical information technology use in sub-Saharan Africa to find out how and why it has become so rife among young adults in the universities. Based on extensive literature reviews, this chapter reveals that the lack of stringent measures to deter students' plagiarism and cheating leads considerably to unethical use of information technology. This chapter offers recommendations on how unethical behavior among students in higher educational institutions in sub-Saharan African countries can be curtailed.

Keywords Higher education · Literature review · Information technology · Unethical behavior

1 Introduction

Higher educational institutions by their mandates play a critical role in educating young adults to attain scientific, social, and technological knowledge that would ultimately benefit society following graduation. Thus, the importance of information technology cannot be overemphasized. It serves as one of the primary channels to interact, communicate, and deliver educational content to students in many higher educational institutions. In our twenty-first century globalized world, almost all higher institutions utilize the blended format of online and face-to-face learning [1, 2].

R. Afedzie (✉) · P. A. Onyina
Pentecost University, Post Office Box KN1739, Kaneshie, Accra, Ghana
e-mail: rafedzie@pentvars.edu.gh

P. A. Onyina
e-mail: paonyina@pentvars.edu.gh

© The Author(s), under exclusive license to Springer Nature Singapore Pte Ltd. 2022   17
L. Mâță (ed.), *Ethical Use of Information Technology in Higher Education*,
EAI/Springer Innovations in Communication and Computing,
https://doi.org/10.1007/978-981-16-1951-9_2

The use of information technology in higher educational institutions of learning has grown significantly over the past three decades [3]. It has expanded exponentially into every corner of society because of globalization and technological advancement [4]. The growth of information technology in higher institutions of learning has become synonymous with the rate of development attained by such institutions especially in sub-Saharan Africa [5]. Information technology is the use of computers and other electronic devices that ensures the regular flow of work and productivity in every aspect of man's life [6].

Although information technology has created a productive and sustained higher productivity in many higher institutions of learning, there have been several unethical practices that have become rife because of easier access to all kinds of information online, according to Castro [7]. Ethics can be defined as a review of human conduct in light of moral principles [8]. In essence, ethics can also be referred to as a pattern of human behavior that conforms to the values of determining right from wrong. Information technology ethics are the moral rules that regulate the use of online resources and systems related to the computer [9]. Although information technology facilitates the ease at which universities manage their routine activities, the ease of copying, increasing access to numerous collections of online materials have aided the practices of plagiarism. However, there is an urgent need to ensure quality education, which is absent from pedagogical abuses, especially plagiarism from online resources.

2 Background

For [10], higher educational institutions are set up to promote the growth and development of students to be responsible and productive to society. To deliver most of these educational resources to students, technology has become a valuable avenue to offer digital content and ensure interactive classes among students. However, the lack of critical institutional sanctions against software piracy, plagiarism, and cheating has become endemic and gradually degrading the quality of graduates from these institutions [11]. Plagiarism is defined as the intentional use or attributing another person's words, ideas, and thoughts as one's own without acknowledging the person [12]. Software piracy entails the illegal copying of someone's music, games, or computer software without the person's consent [13]. Likewise, students can use technology to cheat during examinations by copying from their electronic wristwatches and other technological gadgets.

Many questions have been raised regarding the extent to which students plagiarize the academic work of others and outsourcing their assignments to researchers online in exchange for a monetary fee [14]. These unethical practices have increased tremendously as students seek to find easier ways to acquire degrees and achieve their academic goals without the diligence and rigorous focus associated with academic work in higher educational institutions [15].

In most academic institutions of higher learning, unethical use of information technology includes the following: plagiarism, online bullying, and infringement of copyright protection laws primarily to benefit the academic goals of the student. Realizing the extent of the negative consequences of unethical use of information technology by students, it is vital to have a code of ethics that regulates the use of online resources. This can be done by regularly reminding students of the harm and negative implications of abusing the benefits of online accessibility. Further, students should be made to sign a code of conduct to abide by the rules and regulations related to the safe use of information technology in their learning environment. Students should also be made to take a course in the first year of higher education geared strictly to ethical and unethical information technological use. In so doing, students would be drawn to the moral values placed on the ethical use of information technology and the sanctions that go with violating the rules. While information technology has become an important component in the delivery of learning in higher education in sub-Saharan African countries, students are not adequately educated on the ethical issues related to the teaching, learning, and research. This is particularly alarming in sub-Saharan African countries where there is less education on ethical awareness and policy regulations on information technology [16].

In particular, for [17], students' understanding of what is regarded as acceptable and unacceptable by higher educational institutions regarding unethical practices has a direct reflection on their behavior at the workplace. Specifically, students' scant understanding of what comprises unethical information technology practices has been shown to directly relate to the incidence of unethical behaviors [18]. Thus, this study seeks to identify the gaps in the literature concerning student's awareness and comprehension of unethical information technology use and higher educational institutions' regulations on information technology. The case of sub-Saharan Africa is unique because these higher educational institutions are still battling with irregular internet accessibility.

This chapter aims to review the literature on information technology use in higher institutions and the unethical practices by students in the pursuit of their academic objectives. In so doing, it highlights two key areas. First, it examines the trend and use of information technology use in higher educational institutions in sub-Saharan Africa. Second, it explores some of the deterrent measures established by these higher education institutions to reduce the level of unethical use of information technology in sub-Saharan Africa. In reviewing key factors leading to the rise of unethical use of information technology in higher educational institutions in sub-Saharan countries, this chapter will be categorized into three sections. The first section would explore the field of information technology in higher learning institutions in sub-Saharan African. The second section would examine some of the key factors allowing for the rise of unethical practices in information technology in sub-Saharan Africa. The third section would offer conclusions and recommendations on the way forward for ethical information technology use in higher educational institutions in sub-Saharan Africa.

3 Method—Literature Review

This section entails a critical review of the literature on the unethical use of information technology in higher educational institutions in sub-Saharan Africa. In so doing, it will analyze the trend of unethical use of information technology in higher educational institutions and provide common ways to address these behaviors among students. It is divided into two sections. The first section outlines some of the reasons why students engage in these unethical behaviors. The second area assesses the impact of students' unethical use of online academic resources. The literature review utilizes database search resources from Pentecost University online library, e-books, textbooks, and academic journal articles on students' unethical use of online academic resources in higher academic institutions in sub-Saharan African countries.

This review will involve literature on higher education and information technology from the periods 2010 to 2020. Special focus is given to highly referenced academic journal articles and e-books over the last decade. Journals reviewed for this study will include Journal of Educational Research, Journal of Higher Education, Journal of Educational Policy, Review of Educational Research, Internet and Higher Education, Journal of Research on Educational Effectiveness, Computers and Higher Education, Research in Higher Education and Studies in Higher Education. Keywords used in the research for this literature include information technology use in higher educational institutions in sub-Saharan Africa, unethical behavior in IT use, and regulations on plagiarism in sub-Saharan African tertiary institutions.

4 Method

4.1 Definitions of Information Technology and Information Ethics

Information technology (IT) is defined as the set of resources that assist students in retrieving the appropriate information for academic purposes and undertaking tasks concerning information use [19]. Marshall [20, p. 64] also defined information ethics as "a set of rules or principles used for moral decision-making regarding computer technology and computer use". Key tasks that can be undertaken using information technology include the following: seeking information, dealing with an assessment on project work, preparing for reports, and communicating with colleagues and lecturers. While carrying out these tasks, ethical issues are sometimes overlooked in acknowledging the sources of information. Scholars in the field of information technology assert that the appropriate authorship of scholarly work is highly essential to guide students and scholars in universities during their academic tasks. The recognition of information sources should be duly cited to encourage ethical practices in higher educational institutions.

Another unethical behavior is plagiarism, and according to Stückelberger [21], this dishonest culture is on the surge in academic circles in sub-Saharan Africa. The Cambridge Learners' Dictionary [22] defines plagiarism as copying somebody's work or ideas. In the field of information technology, it is very easy for students to copy a work "freely" from the Internet. This unethical behavior is becoming more recurrent than it used to be over the past two decades. This unprincipled behavior emanates from the ease of accessing online sources without any restrictions. Thus, academic dishonesty in higher educational institutions in sub-Saharan Africa has become so prevalent to the extent that several reputable institutions in the western world do not trust the authenticity of degrees from job seekers from Africa [23].

Another unethical behavior in the use of information technology in higher education institutions is the problem of software piracy. Software piracy is a situation where an individual uses software illegally, and thus, the person does not pay for the usage of the software [13, 24]. The best practice is to purchase an item before use, however, in the information technology field; in some cases, it is extremely difficult to purchase the item (software), and hence, the only available chance is to pirate the product (if possible) for use. The reason may be numerous such as very expensive to purchase and unavailable facilities to host the software by an institution. In such cases, possible users of a particular software may pirate the product. However, as found by [24] in higher educational institutions in sub-Sahara Africa, the proportion of students who condone plagiarism reduces when the volume of work involved decline.

Maner [25] wrote about the issues surrounding information ethics in the 1990s and the need to consider some of the practices by users which contravene the value of authorship and intellectual property. Although much of the author's earlier work was given less credence because of the focus on computer systems, the introduction of the Internet shifted awareness to the illegal use of online resources by end-users of computers and related technology issues such as plagiarism, software piracy, and privacy issues to be considered with the attention it deserves. The author mentioned that such "an aberrant behavior" which means the inappropriate practices by end-users of computers often has no resulting sanctions or punishment to it.

4.2 Unethical Practices Using Information Technology

Morgan [26] in his report on why students knowingly plagiarize in higher educational institutions argued that most of these students do so for lack of knowledge on how to paraphrase, cite, and do appropriate referencing. He asserts that several of these students resort to using information technology in an unethical function solely because of the chance and availability of the requisite information available online. The author also asserts that in many universities in sub-Saharan Africa, many students do not have adequate research facilities, lack proper supervision, and undergo poor curriculum content and the lecture methodology is often not rigorous. Thus, students seek the easier option by plagiarising and cheating to acquire their certificates. Further, the author also opined that in some of these universities, much of the emphasis is often placed on obtaining certificates which often ignores the appropriate means of achieving the degree. Similarly, students' poor time management and planning because of the focus on social life and engagement in sports results in students pursuing the least effort to complete their assignments. According to the author, some students cheat because of their dismissive attitude toward assignments.

Honig and Bedi [27], in their study, "a critical examination of plagiarism among students of tertiary institutions in South Africa", emphasized that there is a growing incidence of plagiarism among scholars in higher institutions in sub-Saharan African countries because of the intense pressure to publish to get promoted. The authors conducted a qualitative study on four public universities in South Africa to examine why students and lecturers often resort to plagiarism in their publications, assignments, and cheating in their examinations. Their findings indicated that lecturers and students were often burdened by the pressure to succeed against all odds. Likewise, accessibility to academic resources online was an encouraging factor to plagiarize and ultimately succeed in their academic work. Above all, the authors confirmed from their study that students realized that regulations and sanctions were not stringent on plagiarism and thus found it as an easier route to achieve their academic goals.

Halawi and McCarthy [28] investigated the ethical use of information technology by young adults at the universities in Eastern Cape Province of South Africa. They argued about the importance of information technology in universities and the ease at which it allows students to learn flexibly. The authors also emphasized that ethical issues in developing countries are given scant attention because of little ethical education, focus, and policy regulation about the unethical use of information technology.

Kim et al. [29] examined the era of information technology in South Africa universities and how it has contributed to the quality of graduates for the job market. They contend that while unethical issues are inappropriate, there is not much difference from societal ethical issues and that an in-depth knowledge of online practices is essential to understand the basic rationale for such ethical issues.

Obanya [30] in his book on universities and information technology use in Kenya also claimed that management of these universities has taken a laid-back approach to students' and lecturers' unethical practices in using online resources. The author stated that most students in higher educational institutions are not taught rigorous literature methodology and are often neglected with inadequate supervision. The author also articulated that students plagiarize to get better grades and save time. Teston [31] indicated in his assessment of students in universities in Namibia believed that software piracy is entirely appropriate and there was nothing wrong with it. The author opined that the information technology curriculum should incorporate information ethics which will promote the awareness of some of these illegal practices and intensify students understanding of the negative impact of such unethical use of online resources. Following this approach will ensure that students are knowledgeable enough to understand what includes ethical dilemmas and how to deal with it in the course of their use of online information. The author suggested that information ethics should be a core aspect of any curricula and should be a cardinal part of the learning outcomes in universities.

Limo [32] contends in his book, computers, and young adults that "when young adults are taught the moral codes of handling and disseminating information, it will propagate knowledge about issues of privacy, censorship, copyright, fair use and access to information" (p. 34). He states that if a change of attitude by young people concerning unethical use of information online change, it would help reform their social attitude and the advancement of the knowledge era. Significantly, a change of attitude by young adults in universities will result in a society that is morally informed. Ultimately, if information ethics is given the right amount of attention it deserves, it will direct and guide young adults in their moral decision-making in their use of information technology.

Pierce and Henry [12] in their studies on computers and students in higher institutions in South Africa argued that three key factors are always considered by students in committing an unethical act. First, students tend to resort to an unethical way of using resources online because of their code of ethics which he/she nurtured over the years usually through experience and observation. Second, the informal code of ethics is a way of life normally accepted in the workplace or validated by peers, and the final one is the formal code of computer ethics which involves the institutional code or policy. These authors emphasized that an individual's decision-making on how to use information technology is often based on these three conditions.

Ongwen [33] asserts that plagiarism in higher educational institutions has risen primarily because of high occurrences and focus on group work which often results in students copying each other's work online. He maintains further that the growth in class sizes in most universities in sub-Saharan Africa implies that students' ratio to the lecturer is high. This phenomenon leads to students seeking help from the Internet for experts to write their assignments for them. He also holds the view that students in universities plagiarize online resources intentionally because they are not hardworking and wants an easier way to achieve their degree program.

This research study explored the reasons why students in higher educational institutions in sub-Saharan Africa engage in unethical use of information technology and its impact on the quality of graduates on the job market. Much of the information reviewed from the available literature contends that there is a lack of awareness and the easy availability of online resources has given cause to the rampant rise of unethical issues in sub-Saharan African countries. The chapter identified that while certain higher institutions in certain countries in sub-Saharan African are changing higher education policies to rectify these issues, others are not creating any regulatory measures to minimize it. This review asserts that effective regulatory measures in universities in sub-Saharan should put in place punitive structures to combat the trend of unethical practices by students. Next, a presentation of the challenges of using IT in sub-Saharan African Universities is given.

4.3 Challenges of Information Technology Use in Sub-Saharan African Universities

Like any other academic idea that emerges within the environment of higher educational institutions, some issues may need attention, and information technology use is not an exception. We must be quick to add however that some of the challenges are country-specific or region-specific. The challenges facing information and technology education in the sub-Saharan African region was well captured by McMahon [34]. He stated that a major challenge with information technology-based modules is how to maintain the standards in teaching information technology models which keep on changing with time. Furthermore, it has been observed that in less than five years, new areas in information technology continue to emerge, and the changes that come up are usually important in the field.

> It is challenging to stay current and to keep one's skills up to date. How does one stay up with the technology, what technology should be learned, what technology should be taught, and when should the switch-over to the new technology be made are questions that plague IT professors in most universities around the world. If this is a challenge for us in the developed world, one can only imagine the difficulties that exist in the developing countries especially those that want to make information technology a cornerstone of their economy. [34, p. 1]

As captured by [34], the information education requires constant knowledge of the issues emerging; however, in the developing world, this is not the case. It is very difficult to keep up with time in general, let alone with information technology that has a rapidly changing record. These have compounded the problems. For example, in Nigeria, Ogbomo [35] grouped challenges in information technology education as infrastructure-related challenges, capacity building challenges, challenges related to financing the cost of information technology use, the paucity of information technology infrastructure, and lack of access among others. However, conspicuously missing was challenges associated with ethical behavior related to students as outlined by [24] in South Africa. Thus, in less than a decade, unethical behavior in the use of information technology has become a major challenge across the globe [24] identified unethical behavior from students as software piracy, plagiarism, and cheating in the use of information technology.

The following are some categories of challenges confronting the use of information technology on the continent as outlined by Obgomo [35]. As stated earlier, there may be country-based challenges, and these do not exhaust the list. The first that was listed is infrastructure-related challenges. This includes the availability of the desired building. The question we may ask ourselves is "can the old educational structures be renovated to meet the teaching of information technology"? The problem may be compounded when electricity needs and telephone availability are considered. Is Internet service accessible and cheaper for students? A related issue is capacity building such as the development of teachers, educational administrators whose role is crucial, and they must understand the need to examine information technology. There must be technical support professionals available to lead the way. Can we say the technical support professionals are readily available? What about content developers? Even when all these are available, will they be affordable for the educational institutions and students to access them? Farrell and Shafika [36] contend that African universities pay twenty times the cost of information technology services than their counterparts in the western world. Financing the cost of information technology-related issues also come up as a major problem. Though this will help balance education aims with economic conditions, are there funding available in each country for this? Who is willing to provide grants or is it public subsidies, private donations, or fundraising activities? To show how African universities struggle with information technology services, Farrell and Shafika [36] stated categorically that "the average African university has bandwidth capacity equivalent to a broadband residential connection available in Europe, [and] pays 50 times more for their bandwidth than their educational counterparts in the rest of the world" (p. 10).

This captures the exact situations that confront universities in African in their quest for the information technology services for students. As indicated earlier, the accessibility differs from country to country. Table 1 below depicts information technology distribution of major Africa population and Internet users from December 31, 2000, to June 30, 2019, and then Facebook subscribers for December 31, 2018. There is great disparity across African countries as shown in the table. The table highlights twenty-five African countries with stable economies devoid of any major internal conflicts.

From Table 1, the distribution of internet users varies greatly. The highest number of Internet users was 89.9 percent in Kenya, and the smallest number of users was found in Congo with only 11.7% of the population. The rest of the world has a penetration rate of 62.7 percent, and the total for the world is 58.8 percent. A closer look shows that only 15 out of the listed 24 countries (29.3%) have an Internet penetration rate for the population above 50 percent. Again, Africa is made up of 17.1 percent of the world population, but only 11.5 percent of Internet users are in Africa.

The above table gives a clearer picture of information technology users of the Internet in Africa, and the situation is not different from higher learning institutions. Aside from the differences in the availability of information technology in institutions in various countries, there are other challenges. For example, whereas McMahon [34] found that the information technology centers in Rwanda were severely virus infected. In addition to problems of educational infrastructure, South Africa has serious bureaucracy in the national processes in acquiring information technology degrees, and the concentration of information technology centers in two provinces— Cape Town area and Johannesburg-Pretoria area.

There is also the problem of paucity of information technology infrastructure and inadequate access to the facilities. As stated by Butcher [37], available infrastructure is an important ingredient for the development of information technology education in Africa. However, the internet infrastructure availability is not the best on the continent. Thus, the overall statistics may be a huge misrepresentation since there is a great disparity between countries (as seen from the Internet World Stats 2019

Table 1 Africa 2019 population and Internet users statistics

Africa 2019 population and Internet users statistics

AFRICA	Population (2019 Est.)	Internet users December 31, 2000	Internet users June 30, 2019	Penetration (% Population)	Internet growth % 2000–2019	Facebook subscribers December 31, 2018
Algeria	42,679,018	50,000	25,428,159	59.6	50,756	19,000,000
Angola	31,787,566	30,000	7,078,067	22.3	23,493	27,400,000
Botswana	2,374,636	15,000	1,116,079	47.0	6455	840,000
Cameroon	25,312,993	20,000	6,128,422	24.2	30,542	2,700,000
Congo	5,542,197	500	650,000	11.7	129,900	600,000
Cote d'Ivoire	25,531,083	40,000	11,953,653	46.8	29,784	3,800,000
Egypt	101,168,745	450,000	49,231,493	48.7	10,840	35,000,000
Ethiopia	110,135,635	10,000	20,507,255	18.6	204,972	4,500,000
Gabon	2,109,099	15,000	1,307,641	62.0	8617	620,000
Ghana	30,096,970	30,000	11,737,818	39.0	39,026	4,900,000
Guinea	13,398,180	8,000	2,411,672	18.0	30,046	1,500,000
Kenya	52,214,791	200,000	46,870,422	89.8	23,335	7,000,000
Mali	19,689,140	18,800	12,480,176	63.4	66,284	1,500,000
Mauritius	1,271,368	87,000	803,896	63.2	824	700,000
Morocco	36,635,156	100,000	23,739,581	64.8	23,640	15,000,000
Namibia	2,641,996	30,000	1,347,418	51.0	4391	570,000
Nigeria	200,962,417	200,000	123,486,615	61.4	61,643	17,000,000
Rwanda	12,794,412	5,000	5,981,638	46.8	119,532	490,000
Senegal	16,743,859	40,000	9,749,527	58.2	24,274	2,900,000
South Africa	58,065,097	2,400,000	32,615,165	56.2	1259	16,000,000
Tanzania	60,913,557	115,000	23,142,960	38.0	20,024	6,100,000
Tunisia	11,783,168	100,000	7,898,534	67.0	7798	6,400,000
Uganda	45,711,874	40,000	18,502,166	40.5	46,155	2,600,000
Zambia	18,137,369	20,000	7,248,773	40.0	36,144	1,600,000
Total Africa	1,320,038,716	4,514,400	522,809,480	39.6	11,481	204,304,118
Rest of World	6,396,184,493	82.9%	4,013,439,328	62.7	88.5	1,995,104,452
World total	7,716,223,209	100.0%	4,536,248,808	58.8	100.0	2,199,428,570

above) and even inside the same country as found in South Africa [24, 37]. The infrastructure challenges cut across countries.

Another area that comes into mind is the expansion cost for clients in many sub-Saharan African countries. Whereas some institutions in South Africa can meet the cost in the expansion of information technology facilities, the same cannot be said about universities in Niger and the Central Africa Republic for example. The lack of Internet infrastructure coupled with erratic power supply in most countries, as noted by [37], on the continent is a major challenge in using information technology in educational institutions.

5 Conclusions and Recommendations

It can be concluded that the unethical use of information technology in sub-Saharan African countries is rife and is often done without any punitive measures [37]. Students in higher institutions in sub-Saharan African countries tend to plagiarize and cheat using online resources because regulations to monitor them are not stringently enforced. Additionally, the policy of publishing for promotion has also urged many lecturers to also find ways to plagiarize and cheat the system using information technology accessibility. In essence, the policy in many higher institutions placing much emphasis on publication and glorifying certain degree grades is contributing to the widespread unethical practices by both students and lecturers to cheat using information technology [36].

Significantly, implementing a well-designed electronic system to prevent copying and pasting can be one approach to reduce the level of unethical use of information technology among students. Higher educational institutions of learning should integrate ethics in all their curriculum and particularly in the use of information technology in all students' activities. Initiating ethics in higher educational institutions' routine activities requires that ethics plays a critical role in academic management and decision-making. This chapter asserts that while students understand what is meant by software piracy, they do not comprehend the unethical side of plagiarism online primarily because of the ease of doing it [38]. Finally, higher institutions must educate students on the value of authorship so that students do not become susceptible to plagiarism and cheating under the accessibility to information technology. Above all, it undermines the confidence and mutual collegiality fostered within the scientific community if plagiarism and software piracy are not addressed within the higher education environment in sub-Saharan Africa.

There must be creative ways to draw awareness of the detriments to unethical use of information technology and how it devalues the quality of higher education for young adults. This can be seriously pursued with a series of orientation with the freshmen class. Students should also be mentored and coached to value the importance of originality of their assignments and other schoolwork. In so doing, deterrence measures should be built into the design and delivery of instructions primarily to punish and discourage students who engage in such unethical behavior.

Further, student's participation should be given a considerable focus primarily to enhance student learning and generating new knowledge among themselves. Above all, all student's schoolwork should be run through plagiarism software to generate originality and eradicate students' unethical practices often associated with information technology use.

6 Limitations and Future Work

The key limitation is the inability to conduct an extensive qualitative study by interviewing students on their perspectives on the topic. This limitation was due to the outbreak of the coronavirus pandemic which prevented any close contact with the participants. The closure of many academic institutions to stem the outbreak of the virus impeded any effective data collection by the authors. Above all, the lack of time and resources to collect data from participants (students and lecturers) hindered key insight into some of the reasons for the unethical use of information technology in Ghana.

Several factors contributing to the rife of unethical practices by students in their use of information technology in higher educational institutions in sub-Saharan African countries should be empirically tested by utilizing a qualitative approach. By interviewing students to gain insight into their rationale for software piracy, cheating, and plagiarism, higher educational institutions would be able to formulate regulations to minimize these incidents. Further, a qualitative, semi-structured interview approach can also be used to compare the higher educational institutions' regulations on information technology in sub-Saharan countries to the developed world. Furthermore, future research should also be undertaken on ways to encourage students in a higher institution within sub-Saharan African countries on how to effectively use information technology to their benefit.

References

1. Till, G.: Harnessing distance learning and ICT for higher education in Sub-Saharan Africa: An examination of experiences useful for the design of wide-spread and effective tertiary education in Sub-Saharan Africa. Report to the Rockefeller Foundation (2003)
2. Uys. P.: Innovation and management strategies for higher education in Africa: Harmonizing reality and idealism (2003). Retrieved from: http://www.globeonline.com/philip.uys/transform ationofhighereducation.htm
3. Sayed, Y.: Missing the connection? Using ICTs in education. Insights Education #1 (2003). Retrieved from: http://www.id21.org/zinter/id21zinter.exe?a=1&u=3f388ca5
4. Mitcham, C., Englehardt, E.E.: Ethics across the curriculum: Prospects for broader (and deeper) teaching and learning in research and engineering ethics. Sci. Eng. Ethics 25, 6 (2016)
5. World Bank.; Constructing knowledge societies: New challenges for tertiary education. Quoted in William Saint et. al (2004). Higher education in Nigeria: A status report (2002) http://www.wes.org/ewenr/PF/04/PFFeature.htm

6. Internet World Stats. Africa Internet Usage.: Population Stats and Facebook Subscribers (2019). Available at www.internetworldstats.com. Accessed on 22 January 2020
7. Castro, C.: Technology and institutional change: Why some educational institutions use technology and others don't. Tech. Knowlogia. **2**(1), 14–15 (2000)
8. Newton, L.: Ethics in America: Study guide. Pearson, Kittery, ME (2004)
9. Miller, S.: Whither the university? Universities of technology and the problem of institutional purpose. Sci. Eng. Ethics **25**, 6 (2019)
10. Dutton, W.H., Cheong, P., Park, N.: An ecology of constraints on e-learning in higher education: The case of a virtual learning environment. Prometheus **22**(2), 131–149 (2004)
11. Mdlongwa, T.: Information and communication technology (Information Technology) as a means of enhancing education in schools in South Africa: Challenges, benefits and recommendations. Africa Institute of South Africa, Johannesburg (2012)
12. Pierce, M., Henry, J.: Computer ethics: The role of personal, informal and formal codes. J. Bus. Ethics **15**(4), 425–437 (2015)
13. Asongu, S.: Software piracy, inequality and the poor: Evidence from Africa. SSRN Electronic J. **41**(4), 526–553 (2014)
14. Naidoo, V.: IT in education policy—Reflecting on key issues. Paper presented at the Its in African Schools Workshop, Gaborone, Botswana (2003)
15. Escher, G., Noukakis, D., Aebischer, P.: Boosting higher education in Africa through shared massive online courses (MOOCs). Int. Develop. Policy **5**, 1 (2014)
16. Leonard, L., Cronan, T.: Attitude toward ethical behavior in computer use: A shifting model. Indus. Manag. & Data Syst. **105**(9), 1150–1171 (2005)
17. Mutula, S., Mmakola, L.: Information ethics integration in the curriculum at the University of Kwazulu Natal'. Innovations **46**, 1–18 (2013)
18. Underwood, J.: Rethinking the digital divide: Impacts on student-tutor relationships. European J. Educ. **42**(2), 213–222 (2007)
19. Haag, R., Keen, F.: Information technology: Tomorrow's advantage today. McGraw-Hill Companies, New Your City, NY (1996)
20. Marshall, K.P.: Has technology introduced new ethical problems? J. Bus. Ethics **19**(1), 81–90 (1999)
21. Stuckelberger, C.: Ethics in higher education. Globethics.net, Geneva (2017)
22. Cambridge Learners' Dictionary. Cambridge (2016)
23. UNDP.: E-governance and citizens participation in West Africa: challenges and opportunities. Dakar: UNDP (2010)
24. Cilliers, L.: Evaluation of information ethical issues among undergraduate students: An exploratory study. SA J. Info. Manag. **19**(1), 45–60 (2017)
25. Maner, W.: Starter kit in computer ethics. Helvetia Press and the National Information and Resource Center for Teaching Philosophy, Hyde Park, New York (1990)
26. Morgan, C.: Why Students Plagiarise (2005). Retrieved on 23 June 2008. http://www.in.edu. hk/tlc/Learning Matters/10-652005.pdf
27. Honig, B., Bedi, A.: The Fox in the Hen House: A Critical Examination of Plagiarism among members of the Academy of Management. Academy of Manag. Lear. Educ. **11**(1), 101–123 (2012)
28. Halawi, L., McCarthy, R.: Evaluation of ethical issues in the knowledge age: An exploratory study. Issues in Info. Syst. **14**(1), 106–112 (2013)
29. Kim, H., Kim, J., Lee, W.: IE behaviour intent: A study on ICT ethics of college students in Korea. Asia-Pacific Educ. Res. **23**(2), 1–10 (2013)
30. Obanya, P.: The dilemma of education in Africa. Heinemann, Ibadan (2019)
31. Teston, G.: Software piracy among technology education students: Investigating property rights in a culture of innovation. J. Techn. Educ. **20**(1), 66–78 (2008)
32. Limo, A.: Information ethics and the new media: Challenges and opportunities for Kenya's education sector (2010)
33. Ongwen, P., Otike, J.: The extent to which plagiarism is manifested in Africa. School of Information Sciences, Moi University, Eldoret, Kenya (2012)

34. McMahon R.: The challenges of information and communications technology education in Sub-Saharan Africa. Chicago, IL, USA (2015)
35. Obgomo, E.F.: Issues and challenges in the use of information communication technology (information technology) in education. J. Inf. Knowl. Manag. 2(1), 101–134 (2011)
36. Farrell, G., Shafika I.: Survey of information technology and education in Africa: A Summary Report, Based on 53 Country Surveys. Washington, DC: info Dev/World Bank (2007)
37. Butcher, N.: Technological infrastructure and use of information technology in e- education in Africa: An Overview. Association for the Development of Education in Africa, Paris (2003)
38. Bird, S.J.: The survival imperative: Commentary on whither the university? Universities of technology and the problem of institutional purpose. Sci. Eng. Ethics 25, 6 (2019)

A Model for Ethical Behavior in the Use of IT by Academicians in Mali

Macire Kante

Abstract Understanding the ethical behavior in the use of IT by academics remains a critical issue that needs to be addressed. Using the Theory of Planned Behaviour this study gathered data from 20 respondents to contribute to the understanding of the ethical behavior in the use of IT by academics in Mali. The results characterized the academics and revealed that the factors Attitude, Subjective Norm, and Perceived Control explained 87.7% of the variance of ethical behavior in the use of IT by academics. These findings suggest that specific attention should be paid to these identified factors by stakeholders in Mali and elsewhere. Additionally, the results suggest further study with higher sample size and other theories to understand the ethical behavior in the use of IT.

Keywords Ethical behavior · Information technology · Model · University

1 Introduction

Research on the ethical use of Information Technology (IT) has recently received attention from researchers. For instance, Hassan et al. [1] reported ethical use of IT has recently attracted much attention from researchers as well as from the media. The same observation was reported by [2, 3]. The ethical use of IT continues to attract researchers in many fields and many countries. The next question one should ask is what is the definition of IT ethical use.

Ethical use of IT is related to behavior. Ethics can, therefore, be related to some (moral) principles of conducting an activity. Ethical use of IT can be defined in other words as acceptable and good behavior in conducting activity by means of IT. The opposite of such behavior would be considered unethical use of IT. Unethical IT behavior may have severe consequences in the workplace. One such work that has attracted researchers' attention is Accademia. This point was noted by Schilhavy [3]

M. Kante (✉)
University of Johannesburg, Johannesburg, South Africa
e-mail: mkante@uj.ac.za

© The Author(s), under exclusive license to Springer Nature Singapore Pte Ltd. 2022   31
L. Mâță (ed.), *Ethical Use of Information Technology in Higher Education*,
EAI/Springer Innovations in Communication and Computing,
https://doi.org/10.1007/978-981-16-1951-9_3

who argues that concerns about unethical IT behavior have drawn the attention of Information Systems (IS) researchers investigating the phenomenon.

Investigations on the phenomenon of unethical IT use have been conducted by scholars in many countries and fields [2–4]. They investigated the ethical behavior of users (students, users) regarding social media, plagiarism, and cheating. Nevertheless, few studies have been done on the ethical behavior in the use of IT by academics in general and in Mali in particular. Hence, there is a need to study ethical behavior in the use of IT by Malian academics.

The main objective of this chapter is to propose an ethical behavior model for the use of IT by academics in Mali. The specifics objectives are:

1. To identify the factors that may affect ethical behavior in the use of IT;
2. To determine the effect of these factors on ethical behavior in the use of IT;
3. To propose a model for ethical behavior in the use of IT.

2 Literature Review

2.1 Relevant Theories

Information Systems research was built upon the use of theories and models [4]. Some of these relevant theories and models are discussed here. The theory is an important vessel to document our interpretation of the world [5]. Two things define a theory: (1) factors and (2) hypotheses [6]. Therefore, a tested conceptual framework with constructs and the relationship between these constructs constitutes a model.

A survey of the literature done by Lim et al. [4] identified 154 theories in the field of IS research. Amongst these theories, they reported the five most used: Technology Acceptance Model (TAM), Theory of Reasoned Action (TRA), Diffusion of Innovation Theory (DOI/IDT), Theory of Planned Behavior (TPB), and the Social Cognitive Theory (SCT). Each one of these theories is discussed below to see its relevance to thisstudy.

2.1.1 Technology Acceptance Model (TAM)

TAM is an information system theory that models how users come to accept technology and how they use that technology. It was adapted from the Theory of Reasoned Action (TRA). TAM received extensive empirical documentation on the validations, applications, and replications of its power to forecast the behavior of adoption [7].

Perceived Usefulness and Perceived Ease of Use determine an individual's intention to use a system serving as a mediator for the actual system use according to the TAM [8]. It includes beliefs about usefulness and ease of use as the primary determinants of Information and Communication Technology adoption in organizations. The

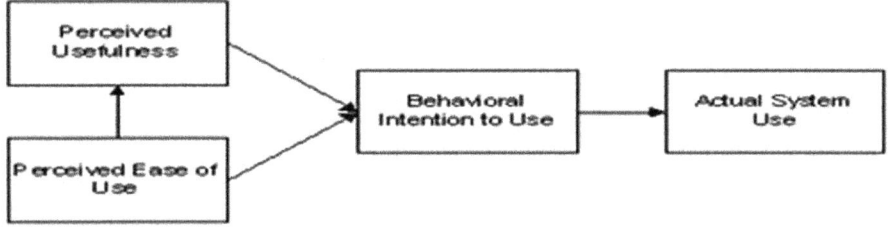

Fig. 1 Technology Acceptance Model (TAM) [9]

two most important individual beliefs of TAM in using IT is the Perceived usefulness and the Perceived ease of use [9]. The literature defines Perceived usefulness as the degree to which a person believes that using a particular system would enhance his or her job performance [7–9]. Besides, perceived ease of use is defined as the degree to which a person believes that using a system would be free of effort. The two behavioral beliefs, perceived usefulness, and perceived ease of use, then lead to individual behavior intention and actual behavior (Fig. 1). Ventkatesh et al. [10] argued that perceived usefulness is also seen as being directly impacted by perceived ease of use.

Researchers have also extended the model. For instance, many other factors such as subjective norm perceived behavioral control, and self-efficacy have added to the model [11, 12]. Other researchers introduce additional belief factors from the diffusion of innovation literature, such as trialability, visibility, or result demonstrability [13, 14]. One of the main extended versions of TAM, which has been widely used is the Unified Theory of Acceptance and Use of Technology (UTAUT).

Despite being the widely used theory, researchers have pointed out some gaps in the theory. Scholars [5–9] argue that though TAM is a useful model, it needs to be expanded to include social and human factors. Moreover, TAM has been barely used in studies related to ethical behavior in the use of IT. Therefore, we will not consider TAM in our study as the theoretical lens as its fitness has been debated amongst scholars.

2.1.2 Unified Theory of Acceptance and Use of Technology (UTAUT)

Venkatesh et al. [10] investigated eight technology acceptance models and formulated a model that integrates and unifies the characteristics and elements of these eight models. The model was labeled the UTAUT Model. The incorporated theories were the Theory of reasoned action (TRA), Theory of Planned Behaviour (TPB), Technology Acceptance Model (TAM), Combination of TPB and TAM, Motivational Model, Personal Computer (PC) Utilization, Diffusion of Innovation (DOI), and the Social Cognitive Theory [5]. The UTAUT integrates the common elements of these eight theories [10]. The validation of the UTAUT was conducted to conclude a 70% variance in usage intention [15]. UTAUT suggests that three constructs are the main

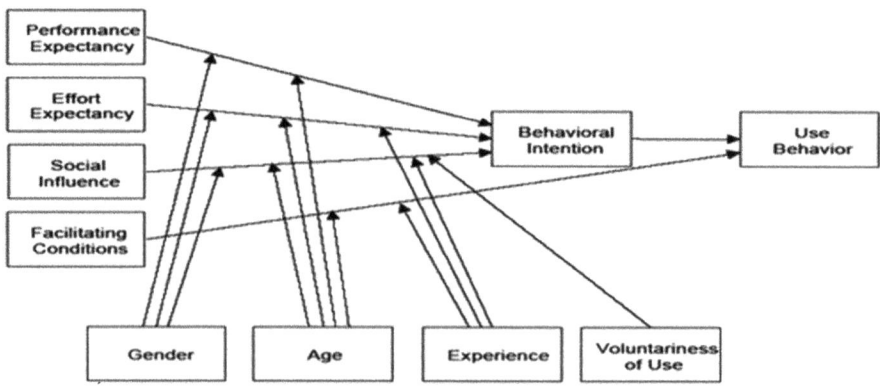

Fig. 2 Unified Theory of Technology Acceptance Model (UTAUT) [15]

determinants of the intention to use information technology (see Fig. 2). The three constructs are performance expectancy, effort expectancy, and social influence [9]. The fourth construct (Facilitating conditions) affects user behavior. Venkatesh et al. [10] define Performance expectancy as the degree to which an individual believes that using the system will help him or her to attain gains in job performance. They argue that Effort expectancy is the level of ease associated with the utilization of the scheme. Social influence is defined as the extent to which an individual perceives that important others believe he or she should use the new system. Finally, they argue that Facilitating conditions are defined as the degree to which an individual believes that an organizational and technical infrastructure exists to support the use of the system. The theory has been extended to UTAUT 2, which has the construct price as affecting the behavioral intention [5]. Figure 2 displays the UTAUT model.

The model and its extensions were criticized. Bagozzi [16] criticized the model and its subsequent extensions. The researcher argues that UTAUT is a well-meaning and thoughtful presentation, but that it presents a model with 41 independent variables for predicting intentions and at least eight independent variables for predicting behavior, and that it contributed to the study of technology adoption "reaching a stage of chaos." [5]. Also, van Raaij and Schepers [17] argue that the grouping and labeling of items and constructs are problematic because a variety of different items were combined to reflect a single psychometric construct. As of the TAM, UTAUT has been barely applied to study ethical behavior and hence it will not be considered in this study.

2.1.3 Theory of Reasoned Action (TRA), Theory of Planned Behaviour (TPB)

Hoffman et al. [18] argued that TRA was developed to better understand relationships between attitudes, intentions, and behaviors. The theory asserts that the most important determinant of behavior is a behavioural intention [19]. Direct determinants of individuals' behavioral intention are their attitude toward performing the behavior and their subjective norm associated with the behavior.

The Theory of Planned Behaviour is an extension of the TRA. The Theory of Planned Behaviour (TPB) is essentially an extension of the Theory of Reasoned Action (TRA) that includes measures of control belief and perceived behavioral control [20]. TPB is like other cognitive decision-making models in that its underlying premises states that individuals make decisions rationally and systematically through the information available to them.

The TRA and TPB, which focus on the constructs of attitude, subjective norm, and perceived control, explain a large proportion of the variance in behavioral intention and predict several different behaviors, including health behaviors [19]. Evidence comes from hundreds of studies that have been summarized in several meta-analyses and reviews [9, 19, 20].

TRA asserts that the most important determinant of behavior is behavioral intention. The factors that affect behavioral intention are their attitude toward performing the behavior and their subjective norm associated with the behavior as depicted in Fig. 3. On the other hand, TPB adds perceived control over the behavior, taking into account situations where one may not have complete volitional control over behavior [19].

According to the literature [19], Attitude is determined by the individual's beliefs about outcomes or attributes of performing the behavior (behavioral beliefs). Similarly, a person's subjective norm is determined by his or her normative beliefs. In other words, whether important referent individuals approve or disapprove of performing the behavior. However, TRA was criticized by the literature. One such critic [19] reported that the TRA components are not sufficient to predict behaviors in which volitional control is reduced. Thus, Ajzen and colleagues [21] added perceived behavioral control to TRA that may affect intentions and behaviors. This addition created the Theory of Planned Behavior (TPB; see shaded boxes in Fig. 3). Perceived control is determined by control beliefs concerning the presence or absence of facilitators and barriers to behavioral performance, weighted by their perceived power or the impact of each control factor to facilitate or inhibit the behavior [19–22].

Regarding studies of ethical behavior in the use of IT, TPB and TRA have been widely used by studies. These studies include [2, 3]. Consequently, we argue that TPB fits our current study better than any other theory. The theory was chosen as the theoretical lens for this study.

2.1.4 Diffusion of Innovation Theory (DOI/IDT)

The Diffusion of Innovation (or Innovation Diffusion Theory –IDT-) of Rogers [24] is one of the theories used in Information System to study the adoption or use of ICT service by users. In such settings, it is used as a technology acceptance model. Many studies [9–28] have emphasized that in the field of information systems, DOI is used as a technology acceptance model. The theory attempts to predict the behavior of

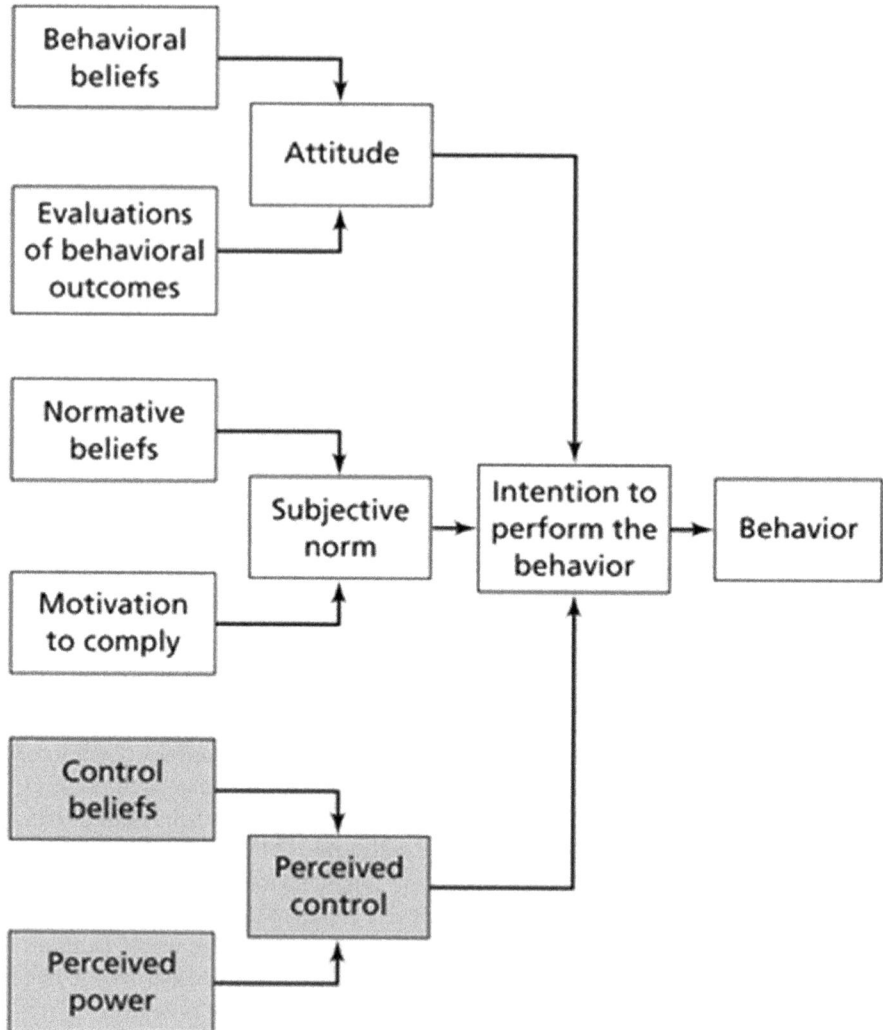

Fig. 3 Theory of planned behavior [19]

individuals and social groups in the process of adoption of innovation, considering their characteristics, their social relations, the time factor, and the features of the innovation. They further argue that in the study of Innovation, which, individuals, most often use the term diffusion to describe the process of adoption of innovation or replace the old one with the new [5].

Explaining the theory, Rogers [24] argues that the characteristics which determine the rate of adoption are: Relative Advantage, Compatibility, Complexity, Trialability, and Observability (Fig. 4). The DOI has been criticized. For instance, a study [29]

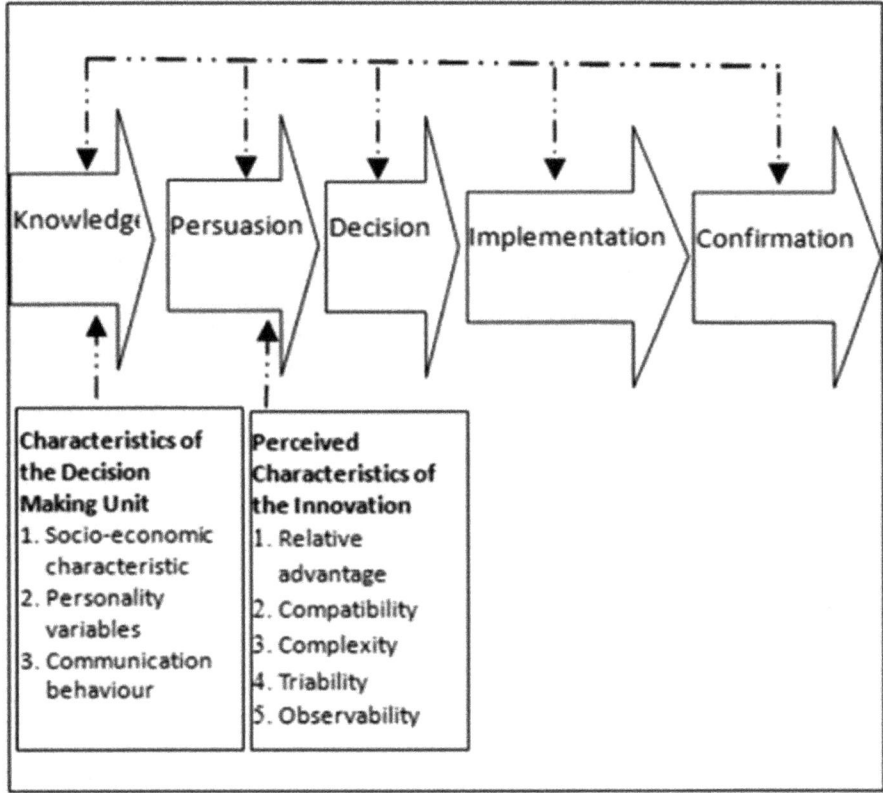

Fig. 4 Diffusion of Innovation Theory (DOI/IDT) [30]

argues that the theory put forward various vague statements and, therefore, requires an address.

Woosley and Ashia [26] criticized the DOI by arguing that it still presents some deficiencies. Additionally, the DOI has been barely applied to studies related to ethical behavior. Hence, we will not use this theory.

2.2 Conceptual Framework and Hypotheses

The conceptual model (see Fig. 5) is drawn below from the TPB. This conceptual framework did not include behavior as ethical behavior in IT use in Mali is a new concept. Furthermore, we did not split the core concepts of the determinants of the TPB as much of them were captured by the items. The hypotheses resulting from the conceptual model were formulated as follows:

$H_1 1$. Attitude has a significant positive effect on Ethical behavior in using IT.

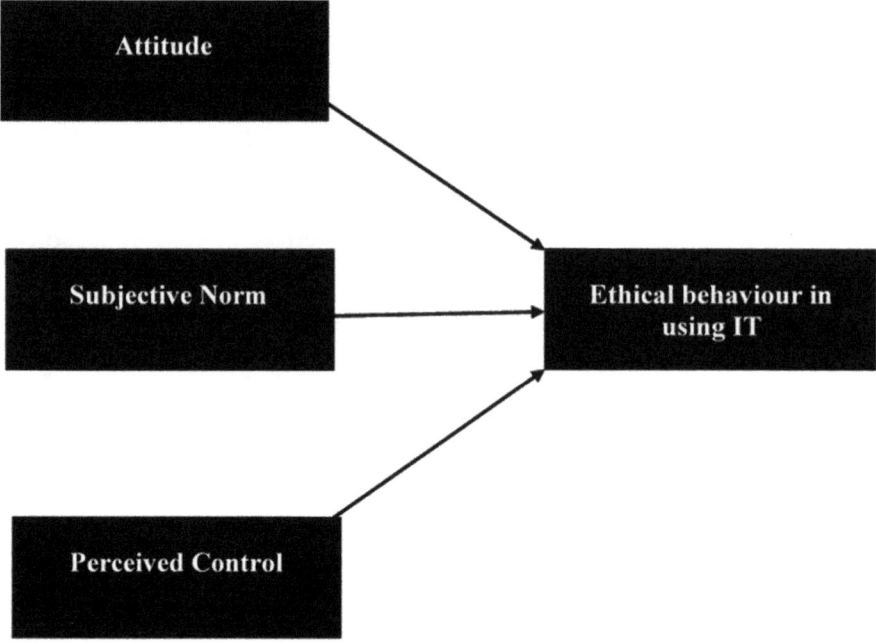

Fig. 5 Conceptual framework

$H_1 2$. Subjective Norm has a significant positive effect on Ethical behavior in using IT.

$H_1 3$. Perceived Control has a significant positive effect on Ethical behavior in using IT.

3   Research Methodology

We collected data from higher education and research institutions in Mali from a convenient sample size of 20 respondents. The survey questionnaire, consisting of 15 items were adapted from [2–23]. The survey instrument is provided in Appendix 1. The instrument was translated from English to French following the guidelines of the literature [31, 32]. Respondents were requested to fill the questionnaires using google forms as appropriate, i.e., to indicate their level of disagreement or agreement on a 5-point Likert scale: 1 = strongly disagree, 2 = disagree, 3 = neutral, 4 = agree, and 5 = strongly agree. We used the Partial Least Square Structural Equation Modelling (PLS-SEM) to analyze our data. PLS-SEM can be used to analyze a small sample size (e.g. 20 respondents) [33–35]. PLS-SEM creates path models that depict causal sequence [34] and it is comprised of two subsequent models, namely the inner model, or structural model, and the measurement model. The inner model displays the relationships between the constructs, while the outer model, also known as the measurement model, is used to evaluate the relationships between the indicator variables and their corresponding constructs [33]. Table 1 provides the criteria used for the PLS-SEM model assessment.

Regarding data management, missing data analysis was performed using SPSS. There were 5 questionnaires with a low rate of responses (missing values higher than 5%), thus excluding them for analysis following the rule of [39]. For the missing values, we applied the Mean Replacement technique [39].

4   Results and Discussion

4.1   Descriptive Statistics

About 93% of our respondents were female. In terms of age, our data set comprised two groups: 80% of our respondents were from 30 years old to 59 years old and 20% were above 60 years old. In terms of degree, 40% of the respondents have a Ph.D., 47% of the respondents posses a master's degree while 13% have a bachelor's degree.

4.2   Factors Affecting Ethical Behavior in the Use of IT (Research Objective 1—Measurement Model Assessment)

The evaluation of the construct validity is done through the evaluation of the Convergent validity and Discriminant validity. Establishing the convergent and discriminant validity of a latent variable implies that the construct can be a determinant in the model under evaluation [33–40].

4.2.1   Convergent Validity

A set of variables presumed to measure the same construct shows convergent validity if their inter-correlations are at least moderate in magnitude [41]. The following measures were used to assess the convergent validity: Composite reliability (greater than 0.6), Cronbach's Alpha (greater than 0.6), Average Variance Extracted (greater than 0.6), Indicator reliability (greater than 0.6). A closer inspection of Table 2 revealed that our constructs passed these criteria, thus establishing their convergent validity.

Table 1 Guidelines when using PLS-SEM [33, 34, 38]

Validity type	Criterion	Description
Indicator reliability	Indicator loading > 0.600	Loadings represent the absolute contribution of the indicator to the definition of its latent variable
Internal consistency reliability	Cronbach's α > 0.6	Measures the degree to which the MVs load simultaneously when the LV increases
	Composite reliability > 0.6	Attempts to measure the sum of an LV's factor loadings relative to the sum of the factor loadings plus error variance. Leads to values between 0 (completely unreliable) and 1 (perfectly reliable)
Content validity	Average Variance Extracted (AVE) > 0.5	The degree to which individual items reflecting a construct converge in comparison to items measuring different constructs
Discriminant validity	Heterotrait-Menotrait Ratio (HTMT) < 1	In Information System research, it was argued that Discriminant validity should be assessed by the Heterotrait-Menotrait Ratio (HTMT) [36]. Its ratio is the geometric mean of the heterotrait-heteromethod correlations (i.e., the correlations of indicators across constructs measuring different phenomena) divided by the average of the monotrait-heteromethod correlations (i.e., the correlations of indicators within the same construct) [37]
Model predictability	Predictive relevance Q^2 > 0.05	By systematically assuming that a certain number of cases are missing from the sample, the model parameters are estimated and used to predict the omitted values. Q^2 measures the extent to which this prediction is successful
Model validity	R^2 > 0.1	Coefficient of determination

(continued)

Table 1 (continued)

Validity type	Criterion	Description
Model validity	Path coefficients Critical t-values for a two-tailed test are 1.65 (significance level = 10%), 1.96 (significance level = 5%), and 2.58 (significance level = 1%).	Structural path coefficients are the path weights connecting the factors

Table 2 Convergent validity assessment results

Construct	Item	Indicator reliability	Cronbach's Alpha	Composite reliability	Average variance extracted (AVE)
Attitude	Attitude_1	0.934	0.893	0.933	0.823
	Attitude_2	0.874			
	Attitude_3	0.913			
Subjective norm	Subjective_norm_1	0.883	0.906	0.780	0.780
	Subjective_norm_2	0.872			
	Subjective_norm_3	0.567[a]			
	Subjective_norm_4	0.242[a]			
	Subjective_norm_5	0.873			
	Subjective_norm_6	0.902			
Ethical behaviour in the use of IT	EB1	0.814	0.881	0.928	0.812
	EB2	0.941			
	EB3	0.942			
Perceived control	Perceived_control_1	0.799	0.693	0.620	0.620
	Perceived_control_2	0.580			
	Perceived_control_3	0.942			

[a]Removed items as their indicator reliability value was below 0.6

4.2.2 Discriminant Validity

The extent to which the construct is empirically distinct from other constructs is defined as Discriminant validity [34] or, in other words, the extent to which the construct measures what it is intended to measure. It can be assessed using three means: the Fornell-Larcker criterion, Cross-loading criterion, and Heterotrait-Menotrait Ratio (HTMT) [42]. The Fornell-Larcker criterion was used to assess the discriminant validity and the results as shown below in Table 3 indicated that the constructs passed the criterion. Only the attitude construct did not pass the criterion. We could not drop it as its convergent validity was established.

Table 3 Fornell-Larcker criterion results

Construct	Attitude	subjective norm	Ethical behaviour in the use of IT	Perceived control
Attitude	0.907			
Subjective norm	0.923	0.901		
Ethical behaviour in the use of IT	0.904	0.874	0.788	
Perceived control	0.878	0.830	0.745	0.883

After establishing the convergent (Table 2) and discriminant validity (Table 3) of our constructs, we can argue that their construct validity was also established. In other words, the construct Attitude, Subjective Norm, and Perceived Control are appropriate variables that can influence Ethical Behaviour in the use of IT. The remaining question is now to what extent. That answer is provided below.

4.3 Hypotheses Validation and Discussion (Research Objective 2)

The structural model represents the causal model [33]. The criteria for the evaluation of that model are the coefficient of determination (R^2); the path coefficient (β) and the Predictive relevance (Q^2). The results of these criteria are described in the following sections.

4.3.1 The Coefficient of Determination (R^2)

As shown in Fig. 6, the variance of the endogenous variable (Ethical Behaviour in the use of IT) is 0.877. That means that the factors Attitude, Subjective Norm, and Perceived control explain 87.7% of the variance in Ethical Behaviour in the use of IT. This value is higher than previous values in measuring the ethical use of IT. For instance, the study of Moores, Chang, Moores, and Chang [43] who reported an R^2 of 21.8% on Ethical Decision Making in the Software industry.

4.3.2 The Path Coefficient (β)

Structural path coefficients are the path weights connecting the factors (β). Regarding the endogenous variable Ethical Behaviour in the use of IT, we found that Attitude has the strongest effect on Ethical Behaviour in the use of IT (0.451), followed by Perceived Control (0.366) and Subjective norm (0.161). We ran the bootstrapping function as suggested [34] (Fig. 6). The results of the bootstrapping are reported below in Table 4. As shown in Table 4, four hypotheses are supported while two are rejected.

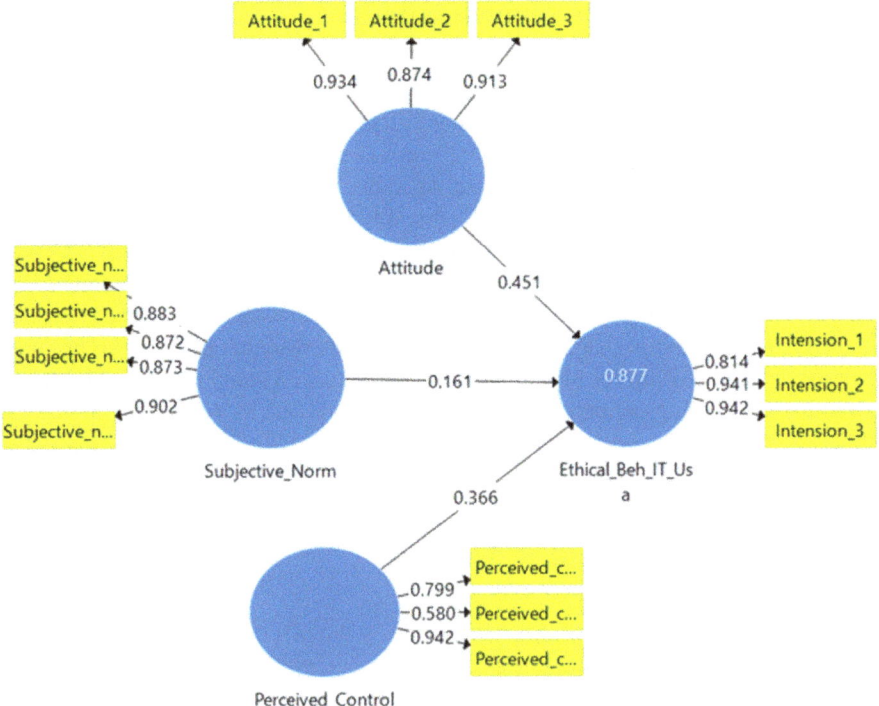

Fig. 6 Model results

Table 4 Path coefficient

Hypothesis	β	T statistics	Comments
Attitude > Ethical behaviour in the use of IT	0.451	0.820	Rejected
Subjective norm > Ethical behaviour in the use of IT	0.161	0.400	Rejected
Perceived control > Ethical Behaviour in the use of IT	0.232	0.766	Rejected

Critical t-values for a two-tailed test are 1.65* (significance level = 10%), 1.96** (significance level = 5%), and 2.58*** (significance level = 1%)

4.3.3 Predictive Relevance (Q^2)

The Blindfolding function of SmartPLS 3.2.9 was run following the recommended guidelines. The factors are highly predictive of the Ethical Behaviour in the use of IT with a high Q^2 (0.402). That assertion was based on the argument provided by [33, 34] who reported that a Q^2 value above 0 indicates that the model is relevant to predicting that (these) factor(s).

5 Conclusions and Recommendations

This study set out to propose an ethical behavior model in the use of IT by academics in Mali. Thereby, it aimed at identifying the factors that may affect ethical behavior and determine the extent of the effects of these factors on that ethical behavior. The first major finding of this study was that Attitude, Subjective Norm, and Perceived Control were the factors that affect the ethical behavior of academics in the use of IT. The second major finding was that these factors were able to explain 87.7% of the variance in the ethical behavior of academics in the use of IT. The evidence from this study suggests that TPB is a suitable model in predicting ethical behavior in the use of IT in Mali and perhaps in other settings. This research has thrown up many questions in need of further investigation. For instance, a study could be conducted in another developing country with more respondents and more cases to assess our model.

6 Limitations and Future Work

The generalisability of these findings is limited by the fact that it was only conducted in Mali with a tiny sample size. Hence, one may need more sample size and contexts to apply these results.

Acknowledgements "We would like to thank all the respondents in this study. Many thanks to Bandiougou Dembele (IER) for helping in the translation of this survey instrument into French."

Appendix 1: Survey Instrument

Construct	Item	Indicator reliability
Attitude	Attitude_1	*Ma décision d'utiliser le système et les outils informatique de mon service en respectant les mesures d'éthique était sage* My decision to use my department's IT system and tools while respecting ethical measures was wise

(continued)

(continued)

	Attitude_2	*Ma décision d'utiliser le système et les outils informatique de mon service en respectant les mesures d'éthique était bonne* My decision to use my department's IT system and tools while respecting ethical measures was good
	Attitude_3	*Ma décision le système et les outils informatique de mon service en respectant les mesures d'éthique a été bénéfique* My decision the system and the IT tools of my service respecting ethical measures was beneficial
Subjective norm	Subjective_norm_1	*Si j'utilise le système et les outils informatique de mon service en respectant les mesures d'éthique ou mise en place, la plupart des gens qui sont importants pour moi ne s'en moqueraient pas ou n'intéresseraient pas* If I use my department's IT system and tools in an ethical or established manner, most of the people who are important to me would not care
	Subjective_norm_2	*Si j'utilise le système et les outils informatique de mon service en respectant les mesures d'éthique en place, la plupart des gens qui sont importants pour moi s'y intéresseraient* If I use my department's IT system and tools following the ethics measures in place, most people who are important to me would be interested
	Subjective_norm_3	*La plupart des gens qui sont importants pour moi pensent que me devrais utiliser le système et les outils informatique de mon service en respectant les mesures d'éthique mise en place* Most of the people who are important to me think that I should use my department's IT system and tools while respecting the ethics measures in place

(continued)

(continued)

	Subjective_norm_4	À mon avis, il est faux d'utiliser le système et les outils informatique de mon service en ne respectant pas les mesures d'éthique mise en place In my opinion, it is wrong to use the system and IT tools of my service by not respecting the ethical measures put in place
	Subjective_norm_5	Je ne me sentirai pas coupable si j'utilise le système et les outils informatique de mon service en ne respectant pas les mesures d'éthique mise en place I will not feel guilty if I use the system and the IT tools of my service while not respecting the ethical measures put in place
	Subjective_norm_6	À mon avis, le système et les outils informatique de mon service en ne respectant pas les mesures d'éthique mise en place est une erreur In my opinion, the system, and the IT tools of my service by not respecting the ethics measures put in place is a mistake
Ethical behaviour in the use of IT	EB1	J'ai l'intention d'utiliser le système et les outils informatique de mon service en respectant les mesures d'éthique dans les prochains mois I intend to use the system and IT tools of my department respecting ethical measures in the coming months
	EB2	Je peux utiliser le système et les outils informatique de mon service en respectant les mesures d'éthique dans les prochains mois I can use my department's IT system and tools while respecting ethical measures in the coming months
	EB3	Je pourrais utiliser le système et les outils informatique de mon service en respectant les mesures d'éthique e dans les prochains mois I could use the IT system and tools of my service while respecting ethical measures e in the coming months

(continued)

(continued)

Perceived control	Perceived_control_1	*Si je le voulais, j'utiliserais le système et les outils informatique de mon service en respectant les mesures d'éthique mise en place* If I wanted, I would use the IT system and tools of my department while respecting the ethical measures put in place
	Perceived_control_2	*Techniquement, il m'est facile d'utiliser le système et les outils informatique de mon service en respectant les mesures d'éthique mise en place* Technically, it is easy for me to use the IT system and tools of my department while respecting the ethical measures put in place
	Perceived_control_3	*Je serais en mesure d'utiliser le système et les outils informatique de mon service en respectant les mesures d'éthique mise en place même s'il n'y avait personne pour me montrer comment* Technically, it is easy for me to use the IT system and tools of my department while respecting the ethical measures put in place

References

1. Hassan, L.M., Shiu, E., Shaw, D.: Assessing the Empirical Evidence of an Intention-Behaviour Gap in Ethical Consumption. J. Bus. Ethics (2014). https://doi.org/10.1007/s10551-014-2440-0Who
2. Jafarkarimi, H., Saadatdoost, R., Sim, A.T.H., Hee, J.M.: Behavioral intention in social networking sites ethical dilemmas: An extended model based on Theory of Planned Behavior. Comput. Hum. Behav. J. **62**, 545–561 (2016). https://doi.org/10.1016/j.chb.2016.04.024
3. Schilhavy, R.: Explaining ethical IT behavior, judgment and awareness using a domain theory context. Association for Information Systems—13th Americas Conference on Information Systems. AMCIS 2007: Reaching New Heights. 7 (2007) 4966–72
4. Lim, S., Saldanha, T., Malladi, S., Melville, N.P.: Theories Used in Information Systems Research : Identifying Theory Networks in Leading IS Journals. ICIS 2009 Proceedings. 91 (2009). https://aisel.aisnet.org/icis2009/91
5. Kante, M., Oboko, R., Chepken, C.: An ICT model for increased adoption of farm input information in developing countries: A case in Sikasso. Mali. Information Processing in Agriculture. **6**(1), 26–46 (2019). https://doi.org/10.1016/j.inpa.2018.09.002
6. Mueller, B., Urbach, N.: Understanding the Why, What, and How of Theories in IS Research. Communications of the Association for Information Systems. 41 (2017) https://doi.org/10.17705/1CAIS.04117

7. Kondo, F. N., Ishida, H., Ghyas, Q. M.: A difference between Japan and the US in the customer satisfaction model for mobile utilitarian information services. 2012 International Conference on Mobile Business. 13 (2013) https://aisel.aisnet.org/icmb2012/13

8. Surendran, P.: Technology Acceptance Model: A Survey of Literature. International Journal of Business and Social Research. **2**(4), 175–178 (2012)

9. Li, L.: A critical review of technology acceptance literature. Southwest Decisino Sciences Institute, Grambling State University (2010) http://swdsi.org/swdsi2010/SW2010_Preceedings/papers/PA104.pdf

10. Venkatesh, V., Morris, M.G., Davis, G.B., Davis, F.D.: User Acceptance of Information Technology: Toward a Unified View. MIS Q. **27**(3), 425–478 (2003)

11. Hartwick, J., Barki, H.: Explaining the role of user participation in information system use. Manage. Sci. **40**(4), 440–465 (1994)

12. Mathieson, K., Peacock, E., Chin, W.W.: Extending the technology acceptance model: the influence of perceived user resources. ACM SIGMIS Database: The DATABASE for Advances in Information Systems. **32**(3), 86–112 (2001)

13. Kochar, D., Kumawat, B.L., Karan, S., Kochar, S.K., Agarwal, R.P.: Severe and complicated malaria in Bikaner (Rajasthan), Western India. The Southeast Asian Journal of Tropical Medicine and Public Health. **28**(2), 259–267 (1997)

14. Karahanna, E., Straub, D.W., Chervany, N.L.: Information technology adoption across time: a cross-sectional comparison of pre-adoption and post-adoption beliefs. MIS Q. **23**(2), 183–213 (1999)

15. Seuwou P., Banissi E., Ubakanma G.: User Acceptance of Information Technology: A Critical Review of Technology Acceptance Models and the Decision to Invest in Information Security. In H. Jahankhani, Eds.: Global Security, Safety and Sustainability—The Security Challenges of the Connected World. ICGS3 2017. Communications in Computer and Information Science, vol. 630. Springer, Cham. (2016). https://doi.org/10.1007/978-3-319-51064-4_19

16. Bagozzi, R.P.: The Legacy of the Technology Acceptance Model and a Proposal for a Paradigm Shift. Journal of the Association for Information Systems. **8**(4), 244–254 (2007)

17. Van Raaij, E.M., Schepers, J.J.L.: The acceptance and use of a virtual learning environment in China. Comput. Educ. **50**(3), 838–852 (2008). https://doi.org/10.1016/j.compedu.2006.09.001

18. Hoffman, W.S., Adler, H., Fishbein, W.I., Bauer, F.C.: Relation of pesticide concentrations in fat to pathological changes in tissues. Archives of Environmental Health: An International Journal. **15**(6), 758–765 (1967)

19. Montaño, D.E., Kasprzyk, D.: Theory of reasoned action, theory of planned behavior, and the integrated behavioral model. Health Behaviour and Health Education. 4th Ed. John Wiley & Sons, San Francisco (2008)

20. Armitage, C.J., Conner, M.: Efficacy of the Theory of Planned Behaviour: A meta-analytic review. Br. J. Soc. Psychol. **40**(4), 471–499 (2001)

21. Beck, L., Ajzen, I.: Predicting dishonest actions using the theory of planned behavior. J. Res. Pers. **25**(3), 285–301 (1991). https://doi.org/10.1016/0092-6566(91)90021-H

22. March, S., Day, J., Ritchie, G., Rowe, A., Gough, J., Hall, T., Yuen, C.Y.J., Donovan, C.L., Ireland, M.: Attitudes toward e-mental health services in a community sample of adults: Online survey. Journal of Medical Internet Research. **20**(2), (2018). https://doi.org/10.2196/jmir.9109

23. Jimmieson, N.L., Peach, M., White, K.M.: Utilizing the Theory of Planned Behavior to Inform Change Management: An Investigation of Employee Intentions to Support Organizational Change. The Journal of Applied Behavioral Science. **44**(2), 237–262 (2008). https://doi.org/10.1177/0021886307312773

24. Rogers, E.M.: Diffusion of Innovation Third Edition. Third Edit. Macmillan Publishing, New York (1983)

25. MacVaugh, J., Schiavone, F.: Limits to the diffusion of innovation: A literature review and integrative model. European Journal of Innovation Management. **13**(2), 197–221 (2010). https://doi.org/10.1108/14601061011040258

26. Woosley, J.M., Ashia, K.: Comparison of Contemporary Technology Acceptance Models and Evaluation of the Best Fit for Health Industry Organizations. International Journal of Computer Science Engineering and Technology. **1**(11), 709–717 (2011)

27. Carter, L., Belanger, F.: Citizen adoption of electronic government initiatives. System Sciences, Hawaii International: IEEE (2004). https://doi.org/10.1109/hicss.2004.1265306
28. Atkinson, N.L.: Developing a questionnaire to measure perceived attributes of eHealth innovations. American Journal of Health Behavior. **31**, 612–621 (2007). https://doi.org/10.5993/AJHB.31.6.6
29. Wainwright, D.W., Waring, T.S.: The application and adaptation of a diffusion of innovation framework for information systems research in NHS general medical practice. Journal of Information Technology. **22**(1), 44–58 (2007). https://doi.org/10.1057/palgrave.jit.2000093
30. Rogers, E.M.: Diffusion of innovations (1995). https://doi.org/citeulike-article-id:126680
31. Kante, M., Chepken, C., Oboko, R.: Methods for translating ICTs' survey questionnaire into French and Bambara. Knowledge and Innovation for Social and Economic Development. Egerton University, Njoro (2017)
32. Villar, A.: Agreement answer scale design for multilingual surveys: Effects of translation-related changes in verbal labels on response styles and response distributions. University of Nebraska (2009)
33. Kante, M., Chepken, C., Oboko, R.: Partial Least Square Structural Equation Modelling' use in Information Systems: An Updated Guideline of Practices in Exploratory Settings. Kabarak Journal of Research & Innovation. **6**(1), 49–67 (2018)
34. Khan, G.F., Sarstedt, M., Shiau, W.-L., Hair, J.F., Ringle, C.M., Fritze, M.P.: Methodological research on partial least squares structural equation modeling (PLS-SEM): An analysis based on social network approaches". Internet Research. **29**(3), 407–429 (2019). https://doi.org/10.1108/IntR-12-2017-0509
35. Hair, J.F., Ringle, C.M., Sarstedt, M.: PLS-SEM: Indeed a Silver Bullet. The Journal of Marketing Theory and Practice. **19**(2), 139–152 (2011). https://doi.org/10.2753/MTP1069-6679190202
36. Henseler, J., Hubona, G., Ash, P.: Using PLS path modeling in new technology research: updated guidelines. Industrial Management & Data Systems. **116**(1), 2–20 (2016). https://doi.org/10.1108/IMDS-09-2015-0382
37. Garson, G.D.: Partial Least Squares: Regression & Structural Equation Models. Statistical Associates Publishing, Asheboro (2016)
38. Hair, J.F., Risher, J.J., Sarstedt, M., Ringle, C.M.: When to use and how to report the results of PLS-SEM. European Business Review. **31**(1), 2–24 (2019). https://doi.org/10.1108/EBR-11-2018-0203
39. Carter, R.L.: Solutions for Missing Data in Structural Equation Modeling. Research and Practice Assessment. **1**(1), 1–6 (2006)
40. Urbach, N., Ahlemann, F.: Structural equation modeling in information systems research using partial least squares. Journal of Information Technology Theory and Application. **11**(2), 5–40 (2010). https://doi.org/10.1037/0021-9010.90.4.710
41. Kline, R.B.: Principales and practice of Strutural equation modeling. The Guilford Press, London (2013). https://doi.org/10.1017/cbo9781107415324.004
42. Hair, J.F., Hult, G.T.M., Ringle, C.M., Sarstedt, M.: Partial least squares structural equation modeling (PLS-SEM). Sage Publisher, Emerald Group Publishing Limited (2014). https://doi.org/10.1108/ebr-10-2013-0128
43. Moores, T.T., Chang, J.C.-J.: Ethical Decision Making in Software Piracy: Initial Development and Test of a Four-Component Model. Management Information Systems Research. **30**(1), 167–180 (2006)

Raising Students' Awareness of Unethical Information Technology Use

Ioana Boghian

Abstract This paper aims to approach issues related to unethical information technology use in higher education as a theoretical basis for providing practical suggestions on how academic teachers may raise students' awareness of unethical information technology use. The paper discusses the distinction between ethical and unethical information technology use in the academic teaching-learning-evaluation context; the impact of unethical information technology use on students' academic and personal life; practical suggestions on how academics may teach students about ethical versus unethical information technology use. Our findings revealed a significant amount of research on the issue of ethical/unethical information technology use. The practical suggestions on how academics may teach students about ethical versus unethical information technology use may be applied by teachers of all specializations, at the start of academic semesters.

Keywords Awareness · Students · Unethical information technology

1 Introduction

Today's society is characterized by the omnipresence of information technology, briefly defined as the use of computers and software to manage information. Information is managed, processed, stored, protected, transmitted, and retrieved. Progress in technology has been generally supported by a universal idea of hope for the better of humankind, and technological advancement has ensured solutions for some aspects of people's lives (e.g., innovative life-saving medical procedures; communication between people separated by large distances; education for vulnerable groups, etc.). However, it has not provided solutions to all of humanity's problems as society is constantly facing new challenges and problems, some of them emerging from the very ubiquity of information technology. With rapid information technology spread to influence most human activity domains (transport, health, energy, environment,

I. Boghian (✉)
Vasile Alecsandri University of Bacău, Bacău, Romania
e-mail: boghian.ioana@ub.ro

© The Author(s), under exclusive license to Springer Nature Singapore Pte Ltd. 2022
L. Mâță (ed.), *Ethical Use of Information Technology in Higher Education*,
EAI/Springer Innovations in Communication and Computing,
https://doi.org/10.1007/978-981-16-1951-9_4

oil, banking, entertainment, etc.), lifestyles have changed as a result, both at the personal and professional level: the information technology revolution has impacted personal, social, and work life globally.

In recent years, information technology has increased its impact on the activities performed in the domain of education and has begun to be viewed as irrevocably linked to teaching, learning, and research processes. Although in the beginning information technology has impacted the academic level and university life mostly, it has recently started to extend to primary and secondary education, as well as preschool education in the latest COVID-19 context. If there is one truth that has been reinforced by the online education that has been conducted in the COVID-19 context, this is the fact that learning, in general, as a social process based on the communication between teacher, student, and others cannot be replaced by technology; however, the same online education conducted during the coronavirus pandemic has almost fully revealed the potential of using information technology in education: enhanced communication and collaboration, problem-solving, research, transmission and presentation of learning content, all these performed with a touch of creativity and novelty based on the various possibilities provided by digital tools. Therefore, once the answer to whether information technology in education is efficient has been provided and demonstrated, there remains the issue of integrating information technology in education for the best outcomes in terms of teacher performance and efficiency, learner performance, and acquisition. Integrating information technology in education also concerns the ethics of using information technology for educational and research purposes: Knowing what is right or wrong in terms of information technology use has become a must considering the consequences of information technology arising from it being used by abusers. To maintain the stability and balance of human society, the availability of information technology must come with a user's guide on the associated ethical implications.

Information technology supports changes in education that affect both educators and learners: Educators have access to an increasingly numerous and diverse range of teaching, research, and evaluation tools and materials, as well as professional improvement platforms, whereas students are provided with a whole universe of information and applications for them to search and learn according to their needs and interests.

The ethical consequences of resorting to information technology for educational purposes that have been identified as harming others, such as plagiarism, inappropriate use of programs and applications, pirated software, using IT tools to cheat during exams, have generated discussions on ethical and unethical use of digital tools; also, such negative consequences of information technology use are growing along with the progress of technology itself all over the world [1, 2].

Previous studies have shown that the phenomenon of plagiarism among students and teachers is a national, as well as global issue [3, 4]. A study by Hamiti, Reka, and Baloghová [5] found that among the 225 students—10% of the students at the Faculty of Medical Sciences from the State University of Tetova in Macedonia—involved in the research, 47% of them were revealed to not have enough knowledge about the ethical use of the Internet. Also, other studies have shown that technology users knowingly undertake unethical information technology use for several so-perceived benefits, such as the easy accomplishment of information-based tasks (projects, speeches, learning assignments, financial opportunities, etc.) [1] as well as social norms, i.e., the desire to do like others do for reasons such as meeting one's need of belonging to a group.

For the arguments mentioned above, it is time to approach the distinction between ethical and unethical information technology use in the academic teaching-learning-evaluation context, the impact of unethical information technology use on academic and personal life to highlight the need to train academic teachers to raise their and the students' awareness of unethical information technology use and provide a series of practical suggestions on how every academic teacher may teach students about ethical versus unethical information technology use.

2 Method

This paper is based on a literature review type of research. The systematic literature review supports the identification, evaluation, and systematization of the studies and research relevant to our research topic. Our systematic literature search began in January 2020 and was completed in June 2020. The literature search was conducted in the databases EBSCO, Google Scholar, ProQuest, ResearchGate, and others, using the following keywords: "information technology use", "academic unethical information technology use by teachers/students", "academic ethical technology use by teachers/students". The selection of relevant studies consisted of covering by hand all the articles on one or several of our study's research objectives:

O1: to distinguish between ethical and unethical information technology use in the academic teaching-learning-evaluation context;

O2: to highlight the impact of unethical information technology use on academic and personal life;

O3: to provide practical suggestions on how every academic teacher may teach students about ethical versus unethical information technology use.

3 Results

We shall further present our findings synthesized for each of the research objectives. Regarding O1, distinguishing between ethical and unethical information technology (IT) use in the academic teaching-learning-evaluation context, there is a large number of articles on this topic. There has even emerged the term of cyberphilosophy that designates the intersection between philosophy and computing [6, 7]. Ethical and unethical use of IT is paralleled to the concepts of right and wrong: Acting ethically is a manifestation of people's desire to do good and avoid doing harmful behavior

[3, 8, 9]. Computer ethics, a concept coined by Walter Maner in 1970s [10], has grown as a branch of ethics as a philosophical field [11–15] as ethical issues in computing have begun to constitute one of the most important issues of computer scientists, scholars, and philosophers [16]; by some researchers, computer ethics is regarded as a subfield of information ethics that deals with information privacy in the infosphere [17]. Therefore, it should only be natural that teachers teach students about the possible risks resulting from unethical use of IT and raise their awareness of the ethical challenges associated with IT use in education. Unethical IT use in education has come across as a serious problem and irrespective of whether it is approached and discussed by areas designated as computer ethics, Information and Communication Technologies ethics, information ethics, cyberethics, it is clear that students should be instructed on the moral, legal, and social issues involving cyber technology [18–21]. First and foremost, "all educators who deal with technology need to understand the legal and illegal uses of intellectual property" to be able to pass such knowledge to their students and be ethical models in this respect [22, p. 15].

One of the most relevant definitions of what unethical means is that provided by Kuo and Hsu: An act can be defined as unethical when "one party, in pursuit of its goals, engages in a behavior that is harmful to the abilities for other parties to pursue their goals" [23]. Highly relevant for our distinction between ethical and unethical use of IT is Mason's PAPA model of IT use that comprises four ethical dimensions of the information age: *privacy* (the ability of individuals to personally control information about themselves when using IT), *accuracy* (the correctness of the information that is distributed on IT support), *property* (respecting intellectual property rights), and *access* (the ability to obtain online information from users) [24]. Whereas ethical IT use is the respect for and compliance with the rules of privacy, accuracy, property, and access, unethical usage of IT is the violation of privacy, property, accuracy, and access of any individual, group, or organization by any other individual, group, or organization. As academics and students resort to a wide range of technologies in teaching and studying, as well as concerning other aspects of their lives by using computers, laptops, tablets, and mobile phones daily to engage in content sharing, online learning, messaging, blogging, social networking, and more, the risk of unethical IT use becomes increasingly relevant [25, 26]. The unethical consequences that may result from consciously or unconsciously violating IT *privacy, accuracy, property*, and *access* rules include plagiarism, pirating software, inappropriate use of programs, unauthorized use and sharing of copyrighted content, and the use of IT devices to copy during exams.

Our literature review and content analysis revealed a series of studies highlighting the need for computer ethics education in educational institutions [19, 20, 27–32], as well as studies that proposed models on certain dimensions related to (un)ethical IT use, and some of them aimed at highlighting the mechanisms behind (un)ethical IT use [4, 33] and other proposing steps for controlling and reducing unethical IT use [34, 35] in the academic environment. The study by Akbulut et al. [36] aimed at investigating whether a program of study, gender, and PC experience impact the undergraduates' judgments regarding computer ethics in a faculty of education; the results revealed that there are significant differences between males and females,

males being more prone to unethical IT use behavior than females; the study also revealed a significant interaction between the program of study and gender.

Chatterjee [33] provides a model of unethical IT use based on Fishbein's and Ajzen's 1975 Theory of Reasoned Action, Mason's 1986 PAPA model, the concept of social norms and Zimbardo's 1969 definition of deindividuation, i.e., "a feeling of being estranged from others, leading to behavior violating appropriate norms", also drawing on ethical philosophy [33, p. 2892]. Chatterjee's model for understanding unethical IT use is comprehensive by the three dimensions included: individual, technological, and social.

Our previous study [4] aimed at exploring the ethical aspects of IT use in higher education and analyzing theories and models of (un)ethical IT use; based on the literature review and content analysis, the theories were categorized into general theories (the theory of reasoned action, theory of planned behaviour, and the theory of James Rest); decision-making models (the person-situation interactionist model, Bommer's ethical decision-making model, etc.); information technology models (IT ethical model, the model of unethical use of information technology, the model of ethical behavior in computer use, digital piracy attitude model, and hypothetical and actual information security compliance models). The general theories have supported the development of subsequent decision-making and information technology models and theories. The result of this study was to elaborate a model of factors influencing the attitudes of higher education teachers toward the unethical use of information technology.

Caldwell [34] proposed a ten-step model for academic integrity for business students and schools that is an academic integrity program. Caldwell's model may be helpful to administrators and business faculties but also to academics in other domains who could adapt the model to suit their domain particularities. Caldwell's model reflects Dufresne's (2004) idea that an integrity academic model involves all the actors participating in the educational process: students, faculty, and administrators.

In his article, suggestively entitled *Arresting student plagiarism: Are we investigators of educators?*, Davis [35] highlights the teacher's mission to educate students on ethical IT use which should be focused on training rather than punishing. According to Davis [35, pp. 160–161], information on plagiarism, cheating, and their consequences should be specified in the class syllabus given to students in the first class meeting, and there should be an open conversation on the topic. Like most problems, unethical IT use can be solved through communication. The author further describes the approach to raising business students, but the steps described can be applied to students from any study program: At the start of each semester, students are given an assignment on plagiarism for the completion of which they get credit. To do this, students are provided with a plagiarism tutorial by the university librarians; they complete a pretest on plagiarism, after which they receive materials on plagiarism to help them self-evaluate their knowledge and then a posttest. The results of the pre- and posttest are scores provided by the plagiarism tutorial program and stored to be printed or emailed, or simply accessed for documentation purposes. If there is no university tutorial on plagiarism available, any online platform designed for educational purposes may be used to test students' knowledge of unethical IT uses and raise their awareness.

Concerning O2, the impact of unethical IT use on academic and personal life, the consequences of committing plagiarism, pirating software, or copyrighted content are surely negative. Whether students unethically use IT consciously or unconsciously, the risks are [37–40]:

- *in terms of the student's academic life*: poor grades as a result of having one's act of unethical IT use discovered and sanctioned; being disqualified from exams and competitions; resitting tests or even graduation exams, also poor academic efficiency manifested mainly as wasting time in this case, losing a job opportunity; accusations of fraud and having to face legal and financial issues (court trials and fines); lack of professional development;
- *at the student's personal level*: poor self-image and low self-esteem; poor public image defined by the consequences of the accusations of fraud such as shame, guilt, loneliness, isolation, and self-isolation; lack of personal development.

In other words, raising students' awareness of unethical information technology use is, in fact, teaching them about respect: *respect for property* (system security issues, e.g., computer hacking, and intellectual property rights, namely copyrights); *respect for territory and privacy* (system security issues, dissemination and/or gathering of private information); *respect for others and common courtesy* (respectful communication, the avoidance of irresponsible speech, i.e., defamation, harassment, flaming/abusive language, spamming, e-mail forgery to disguise the source of disrespectful communication); *respect for institution* ("the use of a limited purpose Internet account in accord with its limited purpose", for example, limited purpose accounts provided by educational institutions and business or government employers that permit only a series of online activities); *respect for self* (respect for self issues refers to those activities that can be harmful to the self, e.g., addiction, personal safety, pornographic and unethical searches via the Internet) [41].

Concerning O3, practical suggestions on how every academic teacher may teach students about ethical versus unethical IT use, several articles highlight the educators' responsibility to instruct learners on what is right and what is wrong, on the ethical versus unethical IT use in education by focusing on the negative consequences, but also functions and benefits of IT [42, 43]. According to Meeder [44, p. 58], "classroom practitioners have a much better sense of what is best for their students than do a group of software engineers working for a corporate software manufacturer". Studies show that instruction on ethical IT use should be done at the beginning of the academic semester [45] and highlight the role of universities in transmitting social, cultural, and academic values, such as ethics [46, p. 91], as well as the idea that a course on computer ethics should be made compulsory to students from all study programs [21, p. 206].

Our literature review and content analysis enabled us to highlight several steps that all teachers may cover to raise students' awareness of unethical IT use. These steps are enumerated and described below:

(1) *Self-reflection and ethical conduct while elaborating the course*: Academics should follow standards and ethical behavior concerning their courses and academic work in general; while planning their academic course, teachers should ask themselves questions such as: What motivates students to give time and effort to achieving the learning objectives of the respective course?

According to some authors [47–49], teachers have the ethical responsibility to improve students' knowledge, skills and abilities, in other words, not to waste student's time, effort and money; such responsibility involves providing comprehensive course content and assigning interesting assignments that promote learner motivation which is a deterrent to such practices of copy-pasting and plagiarism.

(2) *Presentation of the institutional ethical code*: Teachers should make expectations for ethical behavior known to students by delivering brief presentations of the institutional ethical code that help build a climate that encourages ethical behavior [50].

Students' perception of their peers' behaviors is a highly relevant factor in their ethical or unethical behavior [34, 51–53]: Peer ethical behavior encourages ethical choices at students. Also, teachers should be supported in such initiatives by institutional programs aimed at familiarizing students with the ethical approach and conduct in the academic environment [34, 51, 54, 55]. Where such programs are yet unavailable, teachers may still approach the subject of (un)ethical IT use by resorting to various online resources: videos, tutorials, blogs, Web sites of various agencies that regulate IT use in education, and not only.

(3) *Ongoing, proactive prevention and discouragement of cheating*: Academic teachers should prevent and discourage cheating proactively: During tests, students should have their phones turned off, as well as other electronic devices that may provide them with learning content during the exam [49, 53, 56].

Also, students should not take or keep photos of exam sheets; the classical rules of sitting for an exam still apply: Students are not allowed to leave the room during the exam, multiple-choice questions may be provided in various scrambled versions, changing examination questions from one semester/year to another, etc. Online quizzes pose typical ethical problems; some suggestions to discourage unethically IT use during an online examination include applying a time limit for each question and randomly selecting questions from a larger sample of questions [57, 58].

(4) *Ongoing proactive prevention of plagiarism in designing assignments*: Sometimes plagiarism looks so frequent that teachers may start dreading the idea of assigning written homework [49].

Certain strategies support teachers in elaborating assignments that discourage plagiarism:

– thoroughly designed assignments: Teachers should provide students with comprehensively designed assignments that make plagiarism difficult; such assignments have clearly specified instructions that connect to the course content and learning goals; the assignment should reveal the teacher's effort to construct an interesting, learning task that the students may find motivating and challenging: Such a task invites students to put effort into solving it, studying, doing research and bringing their own contribution to the final result, unlike a poorly designed task that demotivates them and indirectly suggests that the task is not worth their effort, which further determines them to resort to unethical practices such as plagiarizing or even buying/borrowing assignments from their peers; also, the assignments should consider the students' level of understanding, time and effort needed to complete it, as it has been shown that students and academia are more likely to plagiarize a difficult passage than an easy one [59, 60] and also that plagiarism occurs more frequently with short deadlines [61];

– explanation and presentation: provide students with learning content and illustrations on (un)ethical IT use and the consequences that unethical IT use may have on their professional and personal lives, as well as on the professional and personal lives of others; teachers should not assume that students know what plagiarism is, but should make sure that they let students know about plagiarism and the different types of plagiarism and their standards regarding this issue; teachers may provide students with best practices on how to prevent unethical IT use with regard to their work: tutorials on how to avoid committing plagiarism and self-plagiarism; teach students techniques for accurate, correct referencing of the sources used; techniques for rendering copyrighted content belonging to other authors with proper citation [62, 63]; teachers can even have students complete assignments focused on avoiding plagiarism (e.g., proper citation techniques) [62, 64];

– storytelling: Highlight the human lives and interest behind the IT /online content: Tell students the fact that the authors of the digital content they are using in their learning and studies have been generated by human beings that have put effort, time, and hope with regards to their work and the various types of expectations and consequences regarding the respective work (copyright, financial matters); students may be provided with time, financial, resource estimations involved in the generation of certain online content;

– teaching students how to paraphrase: Studies have shown that providing students with instructions on paraphrasing generates less plagiarism among students [65–67];

(5) *Provide a personal example of ethical IT use*: Academics should illustrate practices of ethical IT use with examples from their courses and teaching materials, scientific research and studies, and in other words, teachers should be role models professionally and ethically;

(6) *Encouraging students to use anti-plagiarism software*: Students should check their assignments with anti-plagiarism software; academics should implement ethical reflection practices during the courses and seminars regularly;

(7) *Rewarding the students' ethical IT use*: rewarding the students' participation to activities, events on ethical IT use in education, as well as the proofs of their ethical IT use: for example, award 5–10 extra points on assignments that have been revealed as having low to zero scores of similarities [68–71].

Table 1 Suggestions on raising students' awareness of ethical versus unethical IT use

Stage of the educational process	Practice	Interaction
Course preparation and teaching	Self-reflection and ethical conduct while elaborating the course	Teacher
	Presentation of the institutional ethical code	Teacher–students
	Provide a personal example of ethical IT use	Teacher–students
Designing assignments	Ongoing proactive prevention of plagiarism in designing assignments	Teacher–students
	Encouraging students to use anti-plagiarism software	Teacher–students
Evaluation	Ongoing, proactive prevention and discouragement of cheating	Teacher–students
	Rewarding the students' ethical IT use	Teacher–students

We have systematized the practices identified and presented above according to the stage at which they may be applied in the educational process: course preparation and teaching, designing assignments and evaluation; the systematized organization is presented in Table 1.

The practices presented above on raising students' awareness of (un)ethical IT use may be applied by teachers and/or be included in training sessions with larger numbers of students organized by the university regularly, for example, at the beginning of each academic semester.

4 Conclusions

Academic (dis)honesty has been an issue ever since academia has existed. With the emergence of information technology and its progress touching upon all domains of human activity, the issue of (un)ethical IT use has come to generate a series of problems and concerns in scientific domains worldwide. With the temptation of achieving grades more easily by accomplishing learning tasks based on copy-paste and other similar practices that generate the phenomena of plagiarism, students need to be made aware of all the implications of such practices in terms of their personal and professional lives, as well as of the lives of others.

Assuming that academics are role models with respect to the ethical use of IT, we believe that today, one of their tasks is to build an ethical classroom climate. The best ways to create an ethical climate in the learning environment were described above. For this, academics must prove their ethical attitude by designing comprehensive courses and accurate learning tasks connected to the learning content; also, a relevant impact on students' awareness of (un)ethical IT use is achieved by providing them with examples of ethical practices extracted from the teacher's work.

Another high-impact strategy in raising students' awareness of (un)ethical IT use is to resort to storytelling: Teachers should tell the students the stories of the people behind the research, the studies, the inventions, the discoveries that they are using in their learning process. Storytelling helps build empathy and understanding and connect students with the authors of the learning content on a different level. In other words, it is like telling students: The author of this or that research is a human being, like you and me, with a personal and professional life, who has put a certain amount of effort and time in producing the respective scientific outcome; so why should we take the scientific content without giving the author the credit and sometimes the financial support for all the hard work; who would like to have his/her work stolen?

Acknowledgements "This work was supported by a grant of Ministry of Research and Innovation, CNCS—UEFISCDI, project number PN-III-P1-1.1-TE-2016-0773, within PNCDI III."

References

1. Phukan, S., Dhillon, G.: Ethical and intellectual property concerns in a multicultural global economy. EJISDC **7**(3), 1–8 (2001)
2. Özer, N., Uğurlu, C.T., Beycioglu, K.: Computer teachers' Attitudes toward Ethical use of computers in Elementary Schools. Int. J. Cyber Ethics in Educ. **1**(2), 15–24 (2011)
3. Ghiațău, R.M., Mâță, L.: Factors influencing higher education teachers' attitudes towards unethical use of information technology: A review. Revista Romaneasca pentru Educatie Multidimensionala. **11**(1), 287–300 (2009)
4. Mâță, L., Boghian, I., Poenaru, A.G., Ghiațău, R.M.: Models and theories of unethical use of information technology in higher education. Proceedings of the International Scientific Conference eLearning and Software for Education **1**, 138–144 (2019)
5. Hamiti, M., Reka, B., Baloghová, A.: Ethical use of information technology in high education. Procedia—Social and Behavioral Sciences. **116**, 4411–4415 (2014)
6. Beycioglu, K.: A cyberphilosophical issue in education: Unethical computer using behavior—The case of prospective teachers. Comput. Educ. **53**, 201–208 (2009)
7. Moor, J.H., Bynum, T.W.: Introduction to cyberphilosophy. Metaphilosophy **33**(1–2), 4–10 (2002)
8. Floridi, L.: What is the philosophy of information? Metaphilosophy **35**(1–2), 123–145 (2002)
9. Floridi, L.: Open problems the philosophy of information? Metaphilosophy **33**(4), 554–582 (2004)
10. Manner, W.: Heuristic methods for computer ethics. Metaphilosophy **33**(3), 339–365 (2002)
11. Adam, A.: Computer ethics in a different voice. Inf. Organ. **1**(4), 235–261 (2001)
12. Bynum, T.W.: Flourishing ethics? Ethics Inf. Technol. **8**(4), 157–173 (2006)
13. Ess, C.: Universal information ethics? Ethical pluralism and social justice. In: Rooksby, E., Weckert, J. (eds.) Information technology and social justice, pp. 69–92. Information Science Publishing, London (2007)
14. Tavani, H.T.: The state of computer ethics as a philosophical field of inquiry: Some contemporary perspectives, future projections, and current resources. Ethics Inf. Technol. **4**(1), 37–54 (2001)
15. Tavani, H.T.: Ethics and technology: Ethical issues in an age of information and communication technology. Wiley, New York (2004)
16. Van Den Hoven, J., Lokhorst, G.J.: Deontic logic and computer-supported computer ethics. Metaphilosophy **33**(3), 376–386 (2002)

17. Floridi, L., Sanders, J.W.: Artificial evil and the foundation of computer ethics. Ethics Inf. Technol. **3**(1), 55–66 (2001)
18. Baek, Y., Junk, J., Kim, B.: What makes teachers use technology in the classroom? Exploring the factors affecting facilitation of technology with a Korean sample. Comput. Educ. **50**(1), 224–234 (2008)
19. Brockhoff, M., Schmidt, G.: Ethics as applied to computer science students. (2004). Retrieved August 13, 2020, from http://www.micsymposium.org/mics_2004/Brockhof.pdf
20. Ki, H., Ahn, S.: A study on the methodology of information ethics education in youth. Int. J. Comp. Sci. Net. Sec. **6**(6), 91–100 (2006)
21. Namlu, A.G., Odabasi, F.H.: Unethical computer using behavior scale: A study of reliability and validity on Turkish university students. Comp. Educ. **48**(2), 205–215 (2007)
22. Johnson, D., Simpson, C.: Are you the copy cop? Learning and Leading with Technology. **323**(7), 14–20 (2005)
23. Kuo, F., Hsu, M.: Development and validation of ethical computer self-efficacy measure: The case of softlifting. J. Bus. Ethics **32**(4), 299–315 (2001)
24. Mason, R.O.: Four Ethical Issues of the Information Age. Manag. Info. Syst. Quarterly **10**(1), 5–12 (1986)
25. Browning, L., Gerlich, R., Westermann, L.: The new HD classroom: A Hyper Diverse approach to engaging with students. J. Instruc. Pedagogies, 1–10 (2011)
26. Cassidy, E., Britsch, J., Griffin, G., Manolovitz, T., Shen, L., Turney, L.: Higher education and emerging technologies: Student usage, preferences, and lessons for library services. Reference & User Services Quarterly **50**(4), 380–391 (2011)
27. Atjonen, P.: Effective studies of pedagogical ethics with computers? A quasi-experimental process–product study of two learning modes. Scandinavian J. Educ. Res. **49**(5), 523–542 (2005)
28. Kafai, Y.B., Nixon, A.S., Burnam, B.: Digital dilemmas: How elementary preservice teachers reason about students' appropriate computer and internet use. J. Techn. Teacher Educ. **15**(3), 409–424 (2007)
29. Nordkvelle, Y.T., Olson, J.: Visions for ICT, ethics and the practice of teachers. Education and Info. Tech. **10**(1–2), 19–30 (2005)
30. Siponen, M.: A pragmatic evaluation of the theory of information ethics. Ethics Inf. Technol. **6**(4), 279–290 (2004)
31. Woodward, B., Davis, D.C., Hodis, F.A.: The relationship between ethical decision making and ethical reasoning in information technology students. J. Infor. Syst. Educ. **18**(2), 193–202 (2001)
32. Yeaman, A.R.J.: The origins of educational technology's professional ethics: Part two—establishing professional ethics in education. TechTrends. **49**(2), 14–17 (2005)
33. Chatterjee, S.: A Model of Unethical Usage of Information Technology. AMCIS 2005 Proceedings. 51, 2891–2896 (2005)
34. Caldwell, C.: A ten-step model for academic integrity: A positive approach for business schools. J. Bus. Ethics **92**, 1–13 (2010)
35. Davis, L.: Arresting student plagiarism: Are we investigators of educators? Business Comm. Quart. **74**(2), 160–163 (2011)
36. Akbulut, Y., Uysal, Ö., Odabasi, H.F., Kuzu, A.: Influence of gender, program of study and PC experience on unethical computer using behaviors of Turkish undergraduate students. Comput. Educ. **51**(2), 485–492 (2008)
37. Cennamo, K.S., Ertmer, P.A., Ross, J.D.: Technology Integration for Meaningful Classroom Use: A Standards-Based Approach, 1st edn. Wadsworth Cengage Learning, Belmont, CA (2010)
38. Oxley, C.: Digital citizenship: Developing an ethical and responsible online culture. Access **25**(3), 5–9 (2010)
39. Jordan, A.E.: College student cheating: The role of motivation, perceived norms, attitudes, and knowledge of institutional policy. Ethics Behav. **11**, 233–247 (2001)

40. Pulvers, K., Diekhoff, G.M.: The relationship between classroom dishonesty and college classroom environment. Res. High. Educ. **40**, 487–498 (1999)
41. Isfandyari Moghaddam, A.: Some considerations on ethical and unethical issues originating from information technology revolution. LIS Department of Islamic Azad University, Hamedan Branch, Hamedan. (2007). Retrieved August 13, 2020, http://eprints.rclis.org/10236/
42. Baum, J.J.: CyberEthics: The new frontier. TechTrends **49**(6), 54–55 (2005)
43. Roh, Y.R.: Democratic citizenship education in the information age: A comparative study of South Korea and Australia. Asia Pacific Educ. Rev. **5**(2), 167–177 (2004)
44. Meeder, R.: Access denied: Internet filtering software in K-12 classrooms. TechTrends **49**(6), 56–58 (2005)
45. Bennett, L.: Guidelines for using technology in the social studies classroom. The Social Studies **96**(1), 38–40 (2005)
46. Brey, B.: Social and ethical dimensions of computer-mediated education. Infor. Comm. & Ethics in Soc. **4**(2), 91–101 (2006)
47. Davis, S.F., Ludvigson, H.W.: Additional data on academic dishonesty and a proposal for remediation. Teaching of Psyc. **22**, 119–121 (1995)
48. Prohaska, V.: Encouraging Students' Ethical Behaviour (2013). Retrieved July 30, 2020, from https://www.apa.org/ed/precollege/ptn/2013/05/ethical-behavior
49. Prohaska, V.: Teachers can have an effect: Strategies for encouraging ethical student behavior. In: Landrum, R.E., McCarthy, M. (eds.) Teaching ethically: Challenges and opportunities. American Psychological Association, Washington, DC (2012)
50. Whitley Jr., B.E., Keith-Spiegel, P.: Academic integrity as an institutional issue. Ethics Behav. **11**, 325–342 (2001)
51. Engler, J.N., Landau, J.D., Epstein, M.: Keeping up with the Joneses: Students' perceptions of academically dishonest behavior. Teaching of Psych. **35**, 99–102 (2008)
52. McCabe, D.L., Bowers, W.J.: The relationship between student cheating and college fraternity or sorority membership. National Asso. of Student Personnel Admin. J. **46**, 573–586 (2009)
53. McCabe, D.L., Butterfield, K.D., Treviño, L.K.: Academic dishonesty in graduate business programs: Prevalence, causes, and proposed action. Academy of Management, Learning and Education **5**, 294–305 (2006)
54. Macdonald, R., Carroll, J.: Plagiarism—a complex issue requiring a holistic institutional approach. Assessment & Evaluation in Higher Education **31**, 233–245 (2006)
55. Roig, M., Marks, A.: Attitudes toward cheating before and after the implementation of a modified honor code: A case study. Ethics Behav. **16**, 163–171 (2006)
56. Hollinger, R.C., Lanza-Kaduce, L.: Academic dishonesty and the perceived effectiveness of countermeasures: An empirical survey of cheating at a major public university. National Association of Student Personnel Administrators J. **46**, 587–602 (2009)
57. Brothen, T., Wambach, C.: Effective student use of computerized quizzes. Teaching of Psyc. **23**, 292–294 (2001)
58. Young, J.R.: High-tech cheating abounds, and professors bear some blame. Chronicle of Higher Educ. **56**(29), A1 (2010)
59. Roig, M.: When college students' attempts at paraphrasing become instances of potential plagiarism. Psychol. Rep. **84**, 973–982 (1999)
60. Roig, M.: Plagiarism and paraphrasing criteria of college and university professors. Ethics Behav. **11**, 307–323 (2001)
61. Starovoytova, D., Namango, S.S.: Viewpoint of Undergraduate Engineering Students on Plagiarism. J. Educ. Prac. **7**(31), 48–65 (2016)
62. Belter, R.W., du Pré, A.: Plagiarism: Ignorance is not bliss. Poster presented at the annual convention of the American Psychological Association, August 2007, San Francisco (2007)
63. Blum, S.D.: Academic integrity and student plagiarism: A question of education, not ethics. Chronicle of Higher Educ. **55**(24), A35 (2009)
64. Schuetze, P.: Evaluation of a brief homework assignment designed to reduce citation problems. Teaching of Psych. **31**, 257–259 (2004)

65. Barry, E.S.: Can paraphrasing practice help students define plagiarism? College Student J. **40**, 377–384 (2006)

66. Landau, J.D., Druen, P.B., Arcuri, J.A.: Methods for helping students avoid plagiarism. Teaching of Psyc. **29**, 112–115 (2002)

67. Walker, A.L.: Preventing unintentional plagiarism: A method for strengthening paraphrasing skills. J. Instructional Psyc. **35**, 387–395 (2008)

68. Vallor, S.: An Introduction to Cybersecurity Ethics. Markkula Center for Applied Ethics Website, February 7, 48–52 (2018). Retrieved July 30, 2020, from https://www.scu.edu/media/ethics-center/technology-ethics/IntroToCybersecurityEthics.pdf

69. Vallor, S.: An Introduction to Data Ethics. Markkula Center for Applied Ethics Website, January 23, 48–52 (2018). Retrieved July 30, 2020, from https://www.scu.edu/media/ethics-center/technology-ethics/IntroToDataEthics.pdf

70. Macer, D.: Computing ethics: Intercultural comparisons. Ethical pluralism and social justice. In: Rooksby, E., Weckert, J. (eds.) Information technology and social justice, pp. 1899–2204. Information Science Publishing, London (2007)

71. Mâță, L., Clipa, O., Tzafilkou, K.: The Development and Validation of a Scale to Measure University Teachers' Attitude towards Ethical Use of Information Technology for a Sustainable Education. Sustainability **12**(15), 6268 (2020). https://doi.org/10.3390/su12156268

Investigating the Relationship Between Internet Ethics and Motivational Orientations in Higher Education

Otilia Clipa, Nuri Balta, and Liliana Mâță

Abstract The study aimed to investigate the correlation between the students' type of motivation (extrinsic/intrinsic) and their attitude toward the ethics of the use of information technologies, as well as the individual differences in students' unethical Internet use concerning intrinsic and extrinsic motivational orientations. There was used the Internet-triggered Academic Dishonesty Scale to measure unethical behavior and the Work Preference Inventory to determine motivational orientations for university students. The results of this study indicate significant relationships between the motivational orientation factors and the Internet-triggered academic dishonesty behaviors. There are positive correlations between the dimensions of extrinsic motivation and the dimensions of unethical Internet use (reward and falsification, reward and misuse, recognition). As far as intrinsic motivation is concerned, there is only one positive correlation between pleasure and fraudulence. Depending on age, the research result shows that younger students are more prone to unethical behaviors on the Internet than older students. The study is expected to provide a significant contribution to the understanding of ethical Internet behaviors and to generate appropriate mechanisms for education and awareness of these issues by students and professors from higher education.

Keywords Internet ethics · Motivational orientations · Students

---

All authors had equal contributions to this chapter.

O. Clipa
Ștefan cel Mare University of Suceava, Suceava, Romania
e-mail: otiliac@usv.ro

N. Balta (✉)
Suleyman Demirel University, Kaskelen, Kazakhstan
e-mail: baltanuri@gmail.com

L. Mâță
Vasile Alecsandri University of Bacău, Bacău, Romania
e-mail: liliana.mata@ub.ro

© The Author(s), under exclusive license to Springer Nature Singapore Pte Ltd. 2022   65
L. Mâță (ed.), *Ethical Use of Information Technology in Higher Education*,
EAI/Springer Innovations in Communication and Computing,
https://doi.org/10.1007/978-981-16-1951-9_5

1 Introduction

The higher education system reveals a mission to develop the entire society and the changes that occurred at the social level are related to what is happening at the academic education level. The academic life of the university gives information, cognitive strategies, transversal skills, and deep values for life, attitudinal models, ethical principles for each part of academic activities. University teachers need to teach styles of being and becoming, and this is a reason why they must possess multiple competencies. The last period brings new challenges and dilemmas both for students and teachers in university education, from the perspective of ethical and stimulating use of technological resources. The teacher must adapt to new technology and integrate it in all activities and, by this, develop the cognitive level, motivate student learning, and respect all ethical issues for using information and communication technologies (ICT) in all activities [1]. The new technological tools are used by teachers in teaching–learning activities and evaluating student results, but also in research and innovation. On the other hand, students are increasingly using technological resources to participate in online courses and seminar activities. Also, students are evaluated predominantly through educational platforms, which determines new ethical implications on the use of technology [2]. Under these conditions, the question arises whether there is a link between students' motivation and ethical attitude toward the use of information technology in educational activities.

A recent international document on information and communication technologies in education [3, 4] underlines the necessity of developing the competencies of using digital instruments from educational policies to applying the curriculum, assessment strategies, management of education, and for professional development. Every competence has three levels of integration in the professional life of teachers: knowledge acquisition, knowledge deepening, and knowledge creation. For instance, a teacher who wants to possess the competence to use ICT in pedagogy must consider the following levels: at the level of knowledge acquisition to enhance teaching; at the level of knowledge deepening to solve complex problems; and, at the level of knowledge creation to achieve a very good self-management that involves intrinsic motivation for using technology.

Implementation of information and communication technologies in higher education could bring out the pedagogical point of view with some question marks: "What is the added value of technology in learning?; What is 'authentic and inauthentic' labor in the learning situation?; How can we measure the impact of ICT on learning and attainment?; Can we ever hope to demonstrate a causal relationship between ICT use and enhanced learning and attainment?; What effect has ICT had on the role of the teacher and the 'grammar of schooling'" [5]. Akgun [6] emphasizes some issues to support the usefulness of ICT in education such as: the power to improve retention, enhancing the learning interactivity, the potential to make learning active and interactive, the power to motivate, and also the improvement of class productivity. The added value consists of the fact that ICT can provide learning experiences besides other didactical uses. In the author's view "multimedia in science learning can provide differentiation, a variety of approaches, learning at the student's own pace, improved attitudes and motivation in learning, and (uniquely for science) improved visualization and understanding of abstract concepts" [6]. The authors [7, 8] noticed a positive effect of the technology on learning, which was related to the students' involvement and motivation. Whether teachers improve their practice with ICT depends on their knowledge [9] and educational beliefs about new technologies [8, 10, 11] that determine the motivation for using digital tools and a high level of motivation for the students. Stoyanov [12] declared that in the future, the major challenges for the field of education will be integrations of formal and informal training and rethinking the learning and teaching strategies [13] with adopting and using new technologies in the educational field and open resources for all university activities. The creative and responsible integration of technologies in educational activities in higher education contributes to improving students' motivation and encouraging teachers. Along with the positive effects of information technology on students' motivation, it is also interesting to investigate the correlation between their types of motivation and their attitude toward the ethical use of ICT in higher education.

2 Types of Motivational Orientations

Motivation provides the energy for action because it is "an internal state that energizes and drives action or behavior and determines its direction and persistence" [14]. Intrinsic motivation is defined as "the doing of an activity for its inherent satisfactions rather than for some separable consequence" [15]. Intrinsic motivation generates altruistic motives: being in the service of the people, community, and country [16]. In this report, there are many pieces of research in Australia, Belgium, Canada, France, the Netherlands, Slovakia, and the UK revealing that internal motivation was working with children and adults, desire for intellectual development, and making a social contribution.

Unlike intrinsic motivation, which underlies behaviors performed purely for interest and pleasure, extrinsic motivation underlies behaviors performed to obtain separable rewards or to avoid negative outcomes [17]. Extrinsic motivation thus contrasts with intrinsic motivation, which refers "to doing an activity simply for the enjoyment of the activity itself, rather than its instrumental value" [15]. According to Hennessey [18], extrinsic motivation is the motivation to learn or to do an activity for an external goal or meet some externally imposed constraint and intrinsic motivation is when doing something for its own sake, for the enjoyment of a task of learning. This motivation can be extrinsic, for example: marks, performance, grants, job guarantee, money, holidays, social security, appointment, and ease. Intrinsic motives as: interest for knowledge, curiosity, personal satisfaction, desire and love of professions, love for people, developing the personality of other people. Extrinsic motivation can be required for this, such as obtaining money, a grant for this or a high mark, and a high position in the students' hierarchy. The differences between intrinsic and extrinsic motivation are highlighted by Vallerand [19] in relation to three characteristic aspects (Table 1).

Some authors [15, 20] consider that it is important to use both kinds of motivation for learning and to stimulate the affective motivation (curiosity, enthusiasm, pleasure in learning) and cognitive (learning for knowing, for improving cognitive, deep understanding, to know how to know). This is specific to the self-determination theory. Six different types of motivation [21] vary along a continuum from lower levels to higher levels of self-determination, which are divided into autonomous motivation, controlled motivation, and amotivation (Fig. 1). The autonomous motivation is the most self-determined and is a combination of intrinsic motivation, integrated regulation, and identified regulation [14]. In contrast, controlled motivation is less self-determined and focuses on requirements that are formulated externally or internally. Controlled motivation is a combination of introjected regulation and external regulation. Finally, amotivation is at the end of the continuum and can be

Table 1 Characteristics of intrinsic and extrinsic motivation

| | Type of motivation | |
	Intrinsic	Extrinsic
Purpose of participation	Enjoyment in the process itself	Benefits derived from participating
Emotions experienced	Pleasant (enjoyment, freedom, relaxation)	Tension and pressure (social approval is not under their direct control)
Rewards	Affective rewards (enjoyment, pleasure)	Social or material rewards

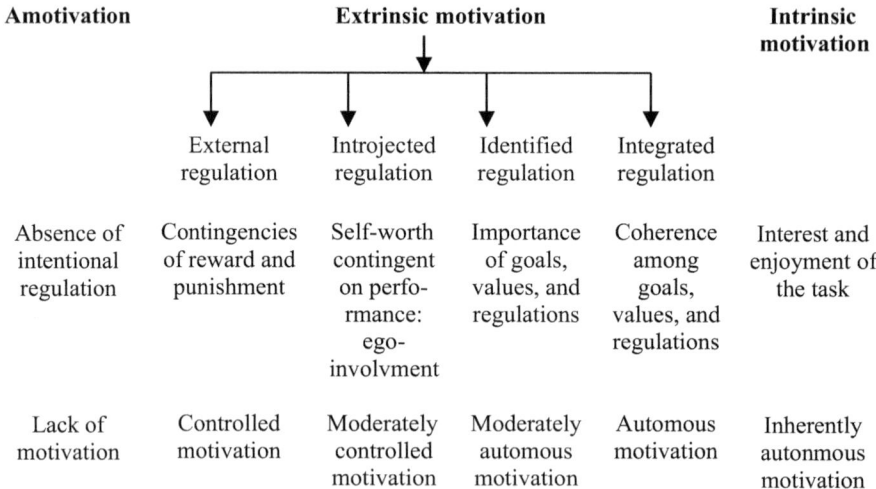

Fig. 1 Self-determination continuum

observed when an individual is neither intrinsically nor extrinsically motivated and therefore has no motivation and will to a certain behavior. Knowing a person's motivation along this continuum that evolves from motivation to extrinsic motivation to intrinsic motivation contributes to predicting a person's quality of commitment, performance, and well-being [22].

According to the self-determination theory [23, p. 14], "humans have the basic propensities to be intrinsically motivated, to assimilate their social and physical worlds, to integrate external regulations into self-regulations, and, in so doing, integrate themselves into a larger social whole." For a teacher who wants to use information and communication technologies in the teaching activity, the intrinsic motivation would be a desire to enrich or supplement the existing curriculum and to provide a different pedagogical approach [24, 25], availability for learning in professional development, whereas the extrinsic motivation would be to get paid for this or to achieve prestige. Everaert et al. [26] found that students who have a high intrinsic and extrinsic motivation tend to be more involved in deep learning. Therefore, an important role in higher education is for teachers to stimulate the intrinsic motivation of students, to provide them with opportunities for independent learning.

3 The Relationship Between Motivation and the Ethical Use of the Internet

It is important to understand what kind of motivation the students have because in a difficult situation, this may urge students to forward learning activity, being the most crucial component playing the role of an engine [27]. The motivation for learning and using the Internet in learning may be stimulated through the teaching activity that builds interest in learning, learning autonomy, complex competencies of students, relatedness or community of learning. All of this is possible to manage as objectives of teaching in higher education and be involved in the learning process. For students who use the Internet in learning activities, the intrinsic motivation would be curiosity for knowledge, desire for personal development, enriching the possibility for learning strategy, metacognition, and reflection in the learning process.

The relationship between motivation and the use of technologies is a current topic that is found in studies in recent years [28–36]. Oudeyer and Kaplan [33] described how motivations, in general, are conceived and used in computer and robotic architectures. López and Hidalgo [37] developed a set of indicators to create a useful model to "measure" both the intrinsic and extrinsic motivation potential and the quality of motivation of an installed technology. According to Heemskerk et al. [38], ICT contribute to "educational equality due to its motivating effects on students and the opportunities it offers for facilitating differentiation and individualization." In a few studies, it is underlined the link between altruism influencing the use of ICT and personal motivation, namely status status-seeking or reputation is very important for using new technology [39]. This status-seeking is an extrinsic motivation or economic benefit. These authors described social capital as a very important motivation for students to be active learners in a new environment of education. The social capital had three components: structural, cognitive (shared information), and relational (trust, norms, obligation, etc.). The ethical dimensions of using ICT are part of this attitude. Intrinsic motivation may be involved in the development of community and an article [40] found a significant correlation between the socio-emotional interpersonal knowledge and sense of community in higher education. The socio-emotional interpersonal knowledge is related to personal beliefs, values personality, and emotions and is similar to the concept of identification-based or knowledge-based trust. The results obtained by the present study revealed the influences of the social capital framework in predicting learner's online participation given the similarity in the conceptualization of trust and socio-emotional interpersonal knowledge.

If the relationship between motivational orientations and the use of technology has been little investigated, the correlation between motivation and ethical attitudes or behaviors has been even less researched. Bairaktarova and Woodcock [41] examined the relationship between the level of orientation of engineering students and their ethical responses to different scenarios. Matveeva [42] highlights the correlation between the three components, as a result of the impact of the teacher's ethical teaching skills with digital resources on students' motivation.

The basis of our study is the need to investigate the correlation between the type of motivation of students (extrinsic/ intrinsic) and the attitude toward the ethical use of the Internet. Moreover, the individual differences in students' unethical Internet use and intrinsic and extrinsic motivational orientations were another goal of this study. Given the strong correlations between types of motivation and ethical behaviors, the main aim of our study is to investigate the degree of unethical Internet use among university students and to explore the relationship between motivation and unethical Internet use among students in a higher education institution. In light of the above discussions, we thus consider the following research questions to reflect a set of inquiries for this study:

- Is there a relationship between unethical Internet use and intrinsic and extrinsic motivational orientations?
- Can intrinsic and extrinsic motivational orientations predict unethical Internet behaviors?
- Does students' unethical Internet use differ across student populations, e.g., by gender, grade level, age, discipline, and degree?
- Do students' intrinsic and extrinsic motivational orientations differ across student populations, e.g., by gender, age, degree, specialization, and study year?

4   Method

There was designed a quantitative methodology to measure the correlation between the type of motivation of students (extrinsic/ intrinsic) and the attitude toward the ethical use of the Internet. The quantitative approach is appropriate for the objective

Table 2 Demographic characteristics of participants

Variable	n (%)	Variable	n (%)
Gender		*Age*	
Males	40 (11.9)	21–32	269 (80.3)
Females	295 (88.1)	33–44	66 (19.7)
Degree		*Specialization*	
License	122 (36.4)	Natural sciences	110 (32.8)
Master	213 (63.6)	Social sciences	225 (67.2)
Study year			
I	50 (19.9)		
II	165 (49.3)		
III	120 (35.8)		

study of human phenomena [43]. The method of data collection is the question-naire, which allows obtaining quantitative data and their analysis using statistical information programs.

4.1 Participants

A total of 335 students from a state university from the north-eastern region of Romania participated in the research. The cluster sampling technique has been used, as it is based on the random selection of students. Table 2 further indicates the demographic characteristics of participants.

4.2 Research Instrument

Students' unethical Internet use was measured through the Internet-triggered Academic Dishonesty Scale (ITADS) by Karim et al. [44], adapted from Akbulut et al. [45]. Participants responded to 26 seven-point agree/disagree statements. The 26 items measured fraudulence (ten items), plagiarism (five items), falsification (three items), and misuse (eight items). All of the items were measured using the Likert scale 1–7, reflecting the degree or frequency of user engagement with these behaviors. The second instrument we used was the Work Preference Inventory (WPI) developed and validated by Amabile et al. [46]. The WPI was designed to assess individual differences in intrinsic and extrinsic motivational orientations. The items capture the major elements of intrinsic and extrinsic motivation. For intrinsic motivation, there are five components: self-determination (preference for choice and autonomy), competence (mastery orientation and preference for the challenge), task involvement (task absorption and flow), curiosity (preference for complexity), and interest (pleasure). For extrinsic motivation, there are also five components: evaluation concerns, recognition concerns, competition concerns, a focus on money or other tangible incentives (reward), and a focus on the dictates of others. For this part, the four-point Likert scale was used, from 1 (never or rarely true about me) to 4 (always or almost always true about me).

4.3 Data Analysis

All the statistical analyses were carried out using the Statistical Package for Social Sciences (SPSS), version 22 for Windows. We performed correlation analyses to identify possible relationships between the levels of ITADS and WPI. We also performed a regression analysis to predict unethical Internet use behavior from motivational orientations. Moreover, we ran a multivariate analysis of the variance (MANOVA) test with the dimensions of WPI as dependent variables and the age, gender, grade, degree, and specialization as independent variables. We ran a second MANOVA test to compare the age, city, gender, grade, degree, and discipline as independent variables on the categories of ITADS (fraudulence, plagiarism, falsification, and misuse) as dependent variables. There are several assumptions behind a MANOVA, including multivariate normality, the linearity of relationships, low influence of univariate and multivariate outliers, homogeneity of variance–covariance matrices, and an absence of multicollinearity [47]. Each assumption was tested, and no serious violations were noted.

5 Results

Cronbach's alphas for ITADS and WPI scales are presented in Table 3. The reliabilities for both scales were satisfactory. The reliability coefficients change between 0.91 and 0.95 for ITADS and range between 0.70 and 0.82 for WPI. Overall, while the internal consistency of the ITADS scale is very high, that of the WPI is moderate.

Table 3 Cronbach alpha values for the dimensions of ITADS and WPI

Scale	Fraudulence	Plagiarism	Falsification		Misuse	
Internet-triggered academic dishonesty	0.94	0.95	0.91	0.94		
	Intrinsic	Extrinsic	Challenge	Pleasure	Reward	Recognition
Work preference inventory	0.78	0.82	0.70	0.73	0.72	0.75

5.1 The Relationship Between Unethical Internet Use and Intrinsic and Extrinsic Motivational Orientations

The relationship between the intrinsic and extrinsic motivational orientations and unethical Internet use was explored using Pearson correlation analysis. The Pearson correlation analysis matrix between variables is presented in Table 4. There can be observed a correlation between the dimension pleasure (from intrinsic motivation) and fraudulence ($r = 0.149, p < 0.01$), between the dimension reward (from extrinsic motivation) and falsification ($r = 0.148, p < 0.01$), between the dimension reward (from extrinsic motivation) and misuse ($r = 0.168, p < 0.01$). Then, the analysis result indicated that several dimensions of extrinsic motivational orientations are significantly correlated with the dimensions of unethical Internet use variables. Moreover, the recognition dimension (from extrinsic motivation) had significant correlations with all dimensions of unethical Internet use at the 0.01 level (2-tailed) while the challenge dimension (from intrinsic motivation) was found to have no correlations with any of the dimensions of fraudulence, plagiarism, falsification, and misuse.

The positive correlations found in the analysis indicate that individuals high in the pleasure dimension (from intrinsic motivation) are more likely to engage in fraudulence behavior. Similarly, individuals high in the dimension reward (from extrinsic motivation) are more likely to engage in falsification behavior, and misuse. Likewise, individuals high in recognition dimension (from extrinsic motivation) are more likely to engage in activities involving fraudulence, plagiarism, falsification, and misuse. In a nutshell, except for intrinsic motivation/challenge, the result of the correlation analysis has provided signs of the presence of relationships among the intrinsic and extrinsic motivational orientations and unethical Internet behaviors. A stepwise multiple regression approach was used (Table 5) by handling the intrinsic and extrinsic motivational orientations as the predictor variables and the Internet-triggered academic dishonesty factors as dependent variables.

The findings indicated the presence of positive significant relationships between the motivational orientations factors as predictors and the Internet-triggered academic dishonesty behaviors as dependent variables. However, the possibility of forecast on the behaviors by motivational orientations factors is rather small with variances accounted for (R^2) of 4.3% for fraudulence, 4% for plagiarism, 5.9% for falsification, and 3.1% for misuse. The recognition dimension (from extrinsic motivation)

Table 4 Correlations among motivational orientations and unethical Internet use

	Fraudulence	Plagiarism	Falsification	Misuse
Intrinsic motivation/challenge	0.043	0.050	0.048	0.066
Intrinsic motivation/pleasure	0.149[a]	0.086	0.130	0.071
Extrinsic motivation/ reward	0.065	0.110	0.148[a]	0.168[a]
Extrinsic motivation/recognition	0.185[a]	0.208[a]	0.248[a]	0.185[a]

[a]Correlation is significant at the 0.01 level (2-tailed)

Table 5 Stepwise regression analysis of unethical Internet behaviors against the motivational orientation factors

Criterion	Predictors	Adjusted R^2	p
Fraudulence	Extrinsic motivation/recognition intrinsic motivation/pleasure	0.043	0.000
Plagiarism	Extrinsic motivation/recognition	0.040	0.000
Falsification	Extrinsic motivation/recognition	0.059	0.000
Misuse	Extrinsic motivation/recognition	0.031	0.001

appeared as predictors of four of the Internet-triggered academic dishonesty behaviors. On the other hand, the pleasure dimension (from intrinsic motivation) appeared only once while the challenge (from intrinsic motivation) and reward dimension (from extrinsic motivation) did not appear at all as possible predictors of the behaviors.

5.2   Work Preference Inventory Scale

A multivariate analysis of variance (MANOVA) was performed on the data using the four WPI dimensions as dependent variables and age, city, gender, grade, degree, and discipline as the grouping variables. The MANOVA output for significant results is displayed in Table 5. As illustrated (Table 5), a statistically significant multivariate main effect was found for gender, $F(4, 303) = 3.186, p = 0.014$; Wilks' $\lambda = 0.960$; $\eta^2 = 0.04$. The observed power to detect the effect was 0.822. Also, a statistically significant multivariate main effect was found for gender and discipline interaction, $F(4, 303) = 2.573, p = 0.038$; Wilks' $\lambda = 0.967$; $\eta^2 = 0.033$. The observed power to detect the effect was 0.723. Finally, a statistically significant multivariate main effect was found for grade and discipline interaction, $F(4, 303) = 2.526, p = 0.041$; Wilks' $\lambda = 0.968$; $\eta^2 = 0.032$. The observed power to detect the effect was 0.713. Among the effect of the variables age, city, gender, grade, degree, and discipline on the work preferences, we only represented the significant results in Table 6.

Because the MANOVA was significant for gender, gender and major interaction, and grade and major interaction, we then examined the univariate ANOVA results. To protect against Type I error, we used the Bonferroni correction and tested each ANOVA at the 0.0125 level (0.05 divided by the number of dependent variables). As

Table 6 MANOVA results for significant variables and significant interactions

Effect	Wilks' λ	F	df	p	η^2	power
Gender	0.960	3.186[b]	(4, 303)	0.014	0.040	0.822
Gender[a] Specialization	0.967	2.573[b]	(4, 303)	0.038	0.033	0.723
Grade[a] Specialization	0.968	2.526[b]	(4, 303)	0.041	0.032	0.713

[a]The adjusted alpha value [47] for ANOVA analysis was reduced to $\alpha = 0.0125$

Table 7 ANOVA results for WPI

Independent variables	Dependent variables	df	F	p^a	η^2	Power
Gender	Intrinsic motivation/challenge in solving problems	1	0.864	0.353	0.003	0.153
	Intrinsic motivation/pleasure to solve themes	1	0.512	0.475	0.002	0.110
	Extrinsic motivation/the need for reward	1	9.379	**0.002**	0.030	0.863
	Extrinsic motivation/the need for recognition	1	4.749	0.030	0.015	0.584
Gender[a] Specialization	Intrinsic motivation/challenge in solving problems	1	3.987	0.047	0.013	0.512
	Intrinsic motivation/pleasure to solve themes	1	4.605	0.033	0.015	0.571
	Extrinsic motivation/the need for reward	1	3.614	0.058	0.012	0.474
	Extrinsic motivation/the need for recognition	1	2.387	0.123	0.008	0.338
Study year[a] Specialization	Intrinsic motivation/challenge in solving problems	1	5.363	0.021	0.017	0.636
	Intrinsic motivation/pleasure to solve themes	1	0.860	0.355	0.003	0.152
	Extrinsic motivation/the need for reward	1	1.231	0.268	0.004	0.198
	Extrinsic motivation/the need for recognition	1	4.983	0.026	0.016	0.605

[a]The adjusted alpha value [47] for ANOVA analysis was reduced to $\alpha = 0.0125$

indicated in Table 7, there is no significant effect of the interaction of both gender and discipline, and grade level and discipline on students' intrinsic and extrinsic motivational orientations ($p > 0.0125$). However, there is a significant effect of gender on students' extrinsic motivation/ the need for reward. Male students' mean score for extrinsic motivation/ the need for reward was 2.15 and that of female students was 2.28. The ANOVA result showed that female students are significantly motivated extrinsically when a reward is introduced.

5.3 Internet-Triggered Academic Dishonesty Scale

For the ITADS, we constructed a MANOVA with six independent variables (age, gender, grade, degree, and specialization) and four dependent variables (four levels of ITADS); however, this MANOVA was not significant. We then checked the separate multivariate tests for each of the independent variables and their corresponding univariate tests to establish the extent to which each independent variable influenced the responses. Finally, we constructed our MANOVA with two grouping variables (age and degree) and four levels of ITADS as dependent variables. In other words, a 2×4 factorial MANOVA was used to compare students across age groups and degrees on unethical Internet use behaviors; fraudulence, plagiarism, falsification, and misuse. Results indicated a significant multivariate effect for age groups, Wilk's $\lambda = 0.940$, F (4, 328) = 5.198, $p = 0.000$, and degree, Wilk's $\lambda = 0.966$, F (4, 328) = 2.888, $p = 0.023$, but not for the interaction. Then, we looked at the univariate analyses (Table 8).

After the Bonferroni correction, results are significant for age groups at the $\alpha = 0.0125$ level, while it is not significant for degree groups at the same significance level. Table 7 shows that younger participants (21–32) showed significantly more unethical behavior than older participants (33–44) in all levels of ITADS. To be more specific, age groups' total scores on each dimension of ITADS are shown in Table 9. As seen in Table 8, participants between 21 and 32 years have higher scores than those between 33 and 44 years. However, compared to the seven-point scoring system, the overall scores of the participants are very low, which also shows that

Table 8 ANOVA results for ITAD

Independent variables	Dependent variables	df	F	p^{a}	η^2	Power
Age	Fraudulence	1	13.459	**0.000**	0.039	0.955
	Plagiarism	1	8.343	**0.004**	0.025	0.821
	Falsification	1	8.119	**0.005**	0.024	0.811
	Misuse	1	17.576	**0.000**	0.050	0.987
Degree	Fraudulence	1	4.885	0.028	0.015	0.596
	Plagiarism	1	1.754	0.186	0.005	0.262
	Falsification	1	0.082	0.775	0.000	0.059
	Misuse	1	0.088	0.767	0.000	0.060

[a]The adjusted alpha value [47] for ANOVA analysis was reduced to $\alpha = 0.0125$

Table 9 Descriptive statistics for age groups

Variable	Age group	M	SD	N
Fraudulence	21–32	3.187	1.523	269
	33–44	2.535	1.437	66
Plagiarism	21–32	3.708	1.860	269
	33–44	2.900	1.761	66
Falsification	21–32	3.476	1.724	269
	33–44	2.697	1.678	66
Misuse	21–32	3.601	1.756	269
	33–44	2.475	1.713	66

participants do not commit unethical behaviors at all. For a medium score of 3.5, except the score (3.708) of the 21–32 group on plagiarism, all other scores are below average.

6 Discussions

As motivated in the introduction of this article, unethical behaviors have generally been investigated without being explicitly linked to the technological context offered by the Internet. Although some authors have resorted to established motivation theories [48], the aim of the study was not to investigate the link between student motivation and ethical behavior in general but to identify the correlation between the type of student motivation and unethical behavior concerning the Internet. From the analysis of the research, one can find that no study directly highlights the correlation between the type of motivation of the university student and the academic dishonesty behaviors favored by the presence of the Internet. Although some studies [49, 50] have highlighted several internal or external factors, potentially triggering academic fraud, there are no studies based on a direct investigation into the motivational structure of students in higher education.

The objective of this study was to identify the correlation between the type of motivation and unethical behavior on the Internet. From the data provided by researchers so far, we can infer that people with intrinsic motivation are less likely than those with extrinsic motivation to engage in unethical Internet use. This has also been demonstrated in our study. Except for the pleasure dimension, there was no significant relationship between intrinsic motivation and unethical behavior. What happens with the dimension of pleasure? Why does the pleasure dimension correlate with fraudulent behavior? One possible explanation is that seeking pleasure not only leads to prosocial activities but also maladaptive activities such as Internet cheating [51].

In the case of extrinsic motivation, as expected, the relationship with unethical conduct is much stronger. The results indicate a positive relationship between the following dimensions of extrinsic motivation: reward and falsification, reward and misuse, recognition, and all dimensions of unethical Internet use. The recognition dimension of extrinsic motivation appeared as predictors of the Internet-triggered academic dishonesty behaviors.

A clear result of our research is that the younger generation (20–30 years) is more prone to unethical behaviors on the Internet than the mature generation. This result is extremely important, as these young people have grown up in a highly technologized environment, have had access to the Internet throughout their lives. Other authors [52, 53] have discovered the same thing, along with the fact that the general rate of dishonesty behaviors is increasing. It is not at all gratifying that young people may perceive as acceptable and normal unethical conduct on the Internet, not having the consciousness of the evil they do when they are fraudulent. All students must be trained in acquiring appropriate computer behavior, not just computer professionals.

It is a signal that preventive measures have so far had no effect and other approaches are needed.

7   Conclusions and Recommendations

This research attempts to investigate the relationship between students' motivational orientations and unethical behavior of using the Internet in academia. The results of this study indicate significant relationships between the motivational orientation factors and the Internet-triggered academic dishonesty behaviors. Depending on the type of motivation, the students who are motivated extrinsically are more likely to engage in fraudulence, plagiarism, falsification behavior, and misuse. There is also a positive correlation to a single dimension of intrinsic motivation, so students who have achieved a high level of pleasure are more likely to engage in fraudulent behavior. Another research result shows that younger students are more prone to unethical behaviors on the Internet than older students.

The study is expected to provide a significant contribution to the understanding of ethical Internet behaviors and in generating appropriate mechanisms for education and awareness of the issues. Educators and computer professionals alike play important roles in shaping and determining how computers and the Internet affect social lives and interactions among its users. Investigating motivational factors and reasons for using the Internet is very important to enhancing them concerning ethical principles. Therefore, the knowledge of appropriate computer behaviors should be well developed and identified through research and discussions, and further accommodated in the teaching of ethics to better equip them, as well as the general users, with the good moral values on its use. Not all universities have compulsory computer ethics courses and many syllabuses in computer ethics do not include the rightful use of the Internet among general users as a basis for the design and development of various information and information technologies policies.

Acknowledgements "This work was supported by a grant of Ministry of Research and Innovation, CNCS—UEFISCDI, project number PN-III-P1-1.1-TE-2016-0773, within PNCDI III."

References

1. Admiraal, W., Post, L., Lockhorst, D., Louws, M., Kester, L.: Personalizing learning with mobile technology in a secondary school in the Netherlands: Effects on students' autonomy support, learning motivation and achievement. Eur. Educ. Res. **3**(3), 119–137 (2020). https://doi.org/10.31757/euer.333
2. The Relationship Between U.S. High School Science Teacher's Self-Efficacy, Professionals Development, and Use of Technology in Classrooms. J. Res. Sci. Math. Technol. Educ. **4**(1), 45–62 (2021). https://doi.org/10.31756/jrsmte.414

3. Organisation for Economic Co-operation and Development: OECD skills outlook 2019. Thriving In a digital world. OECD, Paris (2019)
4. UNESCO: ICT competency framework for teachers harnessing open educational resources. The ICT Competency Framework for Teachers (ICT CFT) Version 3, (2020). https://en.une sco.org/themes/ict-eduction/competency-framework-teachers-oer
5. Wellington, J.: Has ICT come of age? Recurring debates on the role of ICT in education, 1982–2004. Research in Science & Technological Education. **23**(1), 25–39 (2005)
6. Akgun, O.E.: Technology in STEM project-based learning. In: Capraro, R.M., Capraro, M.M., Morgan, J.R. (eds.), STEM project-based learning. An integrated science, technology, engineering, and mathematics (STEM) approach, pp. 65–76. Sense Publishers, Rotterdam (2013)
7. Ceobanu, C.: Învățarea în mediul virtual [Learning in virtual environment]. Polirom, Iasi (2016)
8. Heitink, M., Voogt, J., Verplanken, L., van Braak, J., Fisser, P.: Teachers' professional reasoning about their pedagogical use of technology. Comput. Educ. **101**, 70–83 (2016)
9. Kafyulilo, A., Fisser, P., Pieters, J., Voogt, J.: ICT use in science and mathematics teacher education in Tanzania: developing technological pedagogical content knowledge. Australas. J. Educ. Technol. **31**(4), 382–399 (2015)
10. Prestridge, S.: The beliefs behind the teacher that influences their ICT practices. Comput. Educ. **58**(1), 449–458 (2012)
11. Moreira-Fontán, E., García-Señorán, M., Conde-Rodríguez, A., González, A.: Teachers' ICT-related self-efficacy, job resources, and positive emotions: Their structural relations with autonomous motivation and work engagement. Comput. Educ. **134**, 63–77 (2019). https://doi.org/10.1016/j.compedu.2019.02.007
12. Stoyanov, S. Hoogveld, B. Kirschner, P.: Mapping Major Chalanges to Education and Training in 2025. JRC Technical Note JRC59079 (2010)
13. Melnikova, J., Zascerinska, J., Ahrens, A., Hariharan, R., Clipa, O., Sawinska-Milewska, D., Andreeva, A.: A comparative study of educators views on advantages and disadvantages of open educational resources in Higher Education, Society. In: Integration. Education. Proceedings of the International Scientific Conference, vol. 1, 294–304 (2017)
14. Ryan, R.M., Deci, E.L.: Intrinsic and extrinsic motivation in exercise and sport. In: Hagger, M.S., Chatzisarantis, N.L.D. (eds.) Intrinsic motivation and self-determination in exercise and sport, pp. 1–19. Human Kinetics, Champaign, IL (2007)
15. Ryan, R.M., Deci, E.L.: Self-determination theory and the facilitation of intrinsic motivation, social development, and well-being. Am. Psychol. **55**, 68–78 (2000)
16. Organisation for Economic Co-operation and Development: Attracting, developing and retaining effective teachers—Final report: Teachers matter (2005). Retrieved from http://www.oecd.org/edu/school/attractingdevelopingandretainingeffectiveteachers-finalreportteachersma tter.htm
17. Levesque, C., Copeland, K. J., Pattie, M. D., Deci, E. L.: Intrinsic and Extrinsic Motivation. In Peterson, P., Baker, E., McGaw, B. (eds.), International Encyclopedia of Education, 3rd Edition (2010)
18. Hennessey, B., Moran, S., Altringer, B., Amabile, T.M.: Extrinsic and Intrinsic Motivation. In Wiley Encyclopaedia of Management, Vol. 11. Wiley (2015). https://doi.org/10.1002/978111 8785317.weom110098
19. Vallerand, R.J.: A hierarchical model of intrinsic and extrinsic motivation in sport and exercise. In: Roberts, G.C. (ed.) Advances in motivation in sport and exercise, pp. 263–319. Human Kinetics, Champaign, IL (2001)
20. Brophy, J.: Motivating students to learn, 3rd edn. Routledge, New York (2010)
21. Gagne, M., Deci, E.L.: Self-detemination theory and motivation. J. Organ. Behav. **26**, 331–362 (2005)
22. Deci, E.L., Ryan, R. M.: Motivation, personality, and development within embedded social contexts: An overview of self-determination theory. In: Ryan, R. M. (ed.), Oxford library of psychology. The Oxford handbook of human motivation, pp. 85–107. Oxford University Press (2012)

23. Ryan, R.M., Deci, E.L.: When rewards compete with nature: The undermining of intrinsic motivation and self-regulation. Academic Press, New York, NY (2000)
24. Clipa, O., Colomeishi, A.: University Teaching—The Use of Social Media in Teacher Education. In: Pătruț, M., Pătruț, B. (eds., Web 2.0 in Education and politics. The Social Media Revolution, pp. 187–203. Lambert Academic Publishing, Germany (2013)
25. Yüce, K., Şahin, E.Y., Koçer, Ö., Kana, F.: Motivations for choosing teaching as a career: a perspective of pre-service teachers from a Turkish context. Asia Pacific Education Review. 14(3), 295–306 (2013). https://doi.org/10.1007/s12564-013-9258-9
26. Everaert, P., Opdecam, E., Maussen, S.: The relationship between motivation, learning approaches, academic performance and time spent. Acc. Educ. 26(1), 78–107 (2017)
27. Csikszentmihalyi, M., Wolfe, R.: New conceptions and research approaches to creativity: Implications of a systems perspective for creativity in education. In: Heller, K.A., Monks, F.J., Sternberg, R.J., Subotnik, R. (eds.) The systems model of creativity, pp. 81–93. Elsevier, U.K. (2000)
28. Hashmi, Z.F., Dahar, M.A., Sharif, A.: Role of information and communication technology in motivating university undergraduate students towards a learning task in public sector universities of Rawalpindi City. Sociol. Criminol. 7, 196 (2019). https://doi.org/10.35248/2375-4435.19.7.196
29. Hung, S., Durcikova, A., Lai, H.-M., Lin, W.-M.: The influence of intrinsic and extrinsic motivation on individuals' knowledge sharing behavior. Int. J. Hum Comput Stud. 69(6), 415–427 (2011)
30. Kerner, C., Goodyear, V.A.: The motivational impact of wearable healthy lifestyle technologies: A self-determination perspective on fitbits with adolescents. Am. J. Health Educ. 48(5), 287–297 (2017). https://doi.org/10.1080/19325037.2017.1343161
31. Lee, Y., Lee, J., Hwang, Y.: Relating motivation to information and communication technology acceptance: Self-determination theory perspective. Comput. Hum. Behav. 51, 418–428 (2015)
32. Martens, R.L., Gulikersw, J., Bastiaens, T.: The impact of intrinsic motivation on e-learning in authentic computer tasks. J. Comput. Assist. Learn. 20, 368–376 (2004)
33. Oudeyer, P.-Y., Kaplan, F.: What is intrinsic motivation? A typology of computational approaches. Front. Neurorobotics 1, 1–6 (2007). https://doi.org/10.3389/neuro.12.006.2007
34. Peters, D., Calvo, R.A., Ryan, R.M.: Designing for motivation, engagement and wellbeing in digital experience. Front. Psychol. (2018). https://doi.org/10.3389/fpsyg.2018.00797
35. Shim, S., Chae, M., Lee, B.: Empirical analysis of risk-taking behavior in IT platform migration decisions. Comput. Hum. Behav. 25(6), 1290–1305 (2009)
36. Zarzour, H., Bendjaballah, S., Harirche, H.: Exploring the behavioral patterns of students learning with a Facebook-based e-book approach. Comput. Educ. 156, (2020). https://doi.org/10.1016/j.compedu.2020.103957
37. López, V.A., Hidalgo, A.: Technology and Motivation: are we able to measure its interaction? Dirección y Organización 49, 27–43 (2013)
38. Heemskerk, I., Volman, M., Admiraal, W., Dam, G.: Inclusiveness of ICT in secondary education: students' appreciation of ICT tools. Int. J. Incl. Educ. 16(2), 155–170 (2012)
39. Diep, N., Cocquyt, C., Zhu, C., Vanwing, T.: Predicting adult learners' online participation: Effects of altruism, performance expectancy, and social capital. Comput. Educ. 101, 84–101 (2016). https://doi.org/10.1016/j.compedu.2016.06.002
40. Nistor, N., Daxecker, I., Stanciu, D., Diekamp, O.: Sense of community in academic communities of practice: predictors and effects. High. Educ. 69(2), 257–273 (2015)
41. Bairaktarova, D., Woodcock, A.: The Role of Motivation in Engineering Students' Ethical Decisions. IEEE International Symposium on Ethics in Science, Technology and Engineering. Chicago, IL (2014)
42. Matveeva, N.V., Makar, L.V.: Ethics as a Motivation Indicator in Second Language Vocational Digital Teaching. Adv. Sci., Technol. Eng. Syst. J. 5(4), 776–782 (2020). https://doi.org/10.25046/aj050492
43. Parahoo, K.: Nursing research: Principles, process and issues. Palgrave Macmillan, London (2014)

44. Karim, N.S.A., Zamzuri, N.H.A., Nor, Y.M.: Exploring the relationship between Internet ethics in university students and the big five model of personality. Comput. Educ. **53**(1), 86–93 (2009)
45. Akbulut, Y., Şendağ, S., Birinci, G., Kılıçer, K., Şahin, M.C., Odabaşı, H.F.: Exploring the types and reasons of Internet-triggered academic dishonesty among Turkish undergraduate students: Development of Internet-Triggered Academic Dishonesty Scale (ITADS). Comput. Educ. **51**(1), 463–473 (2008)
46. Amabile, T.M., Hill, K.G., Hennessey, B.A., Tighe, E.M.: The Work Preference Inventory: assessing intrinsic and extrinsic motivational orientations. J. Pers. Soc. Psychol. **66**(5), 950–967 (1994)
47. Pallant, J.: SPSS survival manual. Open University Press, New York, USA (2013)
48. Ives, B., Alama, M., Mosora, L.C., Mosora, M., Grosu-Radulescu, L., Clinciu, A.I., Cazan, A.-M., Badescu, G., Tufis, C., Diaconu, M., Dutu, A.: Patterns and predictors of academic dishonesty in Romanian university students. High. Educ. **74**(5), 815–831 (2017)
49. Anderman, E.M., Murdock, T.B.: Psychology of academic cheating. Elsevier Academic Press, San Diego, CA, US (2007)
50. Murdock, T.B., Anderman, E.M.: Motivational perspectives on student cheating: Toward an integrated model of academic dishonesty. Educ. Psychol. **41**(3), 129–145 (2006)
51. Yang, Y., Li, P., Fu, X., Kou, Y.: Orientations to happiness and subjective well-being in Chinese adolescents: The roles of prosocial behavior and internet addictive behavior. J. Happiness Stud. **18**(6), 1747–1762 (2017)
52. Cizek, G.J.: Cheating on tests: How to do it, detect it, and prevent it. Lawrence Erlbaum Associates Inc, Mahwah, NJ (1999)
53. Newstead, S.E., Franklyn-Stokes, A., Armstead, P.: Individual differences in student cheating. J. Educ. Psychol. **88**(2), 229–241 (1996). https://doi.org/10.1037/0022-0663.88.2.229

Students' Attitude Toward the Unethical Use of Information Technology

Alexandra-Georgiana Poenaru

Abstract Nowadays, the phenomenon of plagiarism, unfortunately, is constantly growing. The chapter aims to analyze the attitude of students toward the unethical use of information technology as educational actors benefit from increasingly sophisticated technology. The issue of unethical use of information technology by students has attracted the attention of many researchers. In the educational field, the unethical use of IT refers to plagiarism, inappropriate use of programs, or piracy of software and others. The author initiated a quantitative sociological research, based on a questionnaire, among students. The questionnaire referred to various issues such as reading time and the Internet, the main sources of information and inspiration when they have to carry out a project for university, the reasons why students turn to the Internet for academic tasks, the issue of plagiarism and intellectual fraud through information technology as well as several one-off situations regarding the software. Information technology is present in students' lives, and they use various sources and resources online rather than using books or going to the library, and finally, convenience, lack of time, and lack of reading, in general, contribute to the development of a culture of plagiarism. In this context, teachers can play an important role in combating academic dishonesty by paying attention, detecting, and reporting incidents of deception and plagiarism.

Keywords Antiplagiarism programs · Higher education · Information technology · Modern devices · Plagiarism · Students

1 Introduction

The progress made in the field of information technology brings many scientific gains to humanity. One of the interesting and quite complex topics in the field of information technology is computer science ethics. Today, in the digital age, society is dependent on computers in almost all its fields, and the study of ethics in the field of

A.-G. Poenaru (✉)
Vasile Alecsandri University of Bacău, Bacău, Romania

L. Mâță (ed.), *Ethical Use of Information Technology in Higher Education*,
EAI/Springer Innovations in Communication and Computing,
https://doi.org/10.1007/978-981-16-1951-9_6

83

information and information technology must always be considered by researchers. One of the areas where information technology is ubiquitous is the educational one. As Adrian Hatos [1] argues, education can be understood as "a particular case of social processes, consisting of the intergenerational transmission and reproduction of a society's cultural content and instruments." In contemporary society, the education–information technology relationship is particularly highlighted, as new technologies have largely contributed to a change in education. The change lies in the fact that students are increasingly using the Internet in carrying out academic tasks over classical methods. In the educational environment, the right to technology is presently increasing, especially since this area is "one of the most important in a society" [2]. Plagiarism is a problem that has hit the world of education even harder since the establishment of the World Wide Web. With information available in electronic format on the Internet, students have found it easier to copy and paste the material into their assignments or reports and send it for classification as an original paper. The rise of information technologies has influenced students who have become digital natives. They can download different types of media, and this has an unintended consequence that there are a lot of materials that can be cut and pasted easily into their assignments. Plagiarism of online materials is a serious issue in all universities where students are concerned about the acceptable use of the Internet.

The ethics of information technology use is a common problem in higher education whether it is analyzed from the perspective of teachers or the perspective of students. Through this study, we aim to identify the attitude of students toward the unethical use of information technology in the context of educational actors benefiting from increasingly sophisticated technology that allows access to different sources of information and inspiration. At the same time, we are considering to determine which are students' perception of the sources of information and inspiration used in the achievement of academic tasks as well as the reasons why they are turning to the Internet. The author also aims to identify students' positions on various unethical practices developed in academia, referring to intellectual property, plagiarism, and software use. In this context, the trend of misuse of IT by students in academia is likely to arise, which can be seen as a way of school promotion, but with consequences difficult to appreciate.

The main objectives proposed in conducting this study are the following: making a brief presentation of the literature on this issue and designing and applying a questionnaire among students to address the ethical dimension of online information management and electronic resources.

This research is based on two premises: *the diversity of open-source educational sources and resources available online discourages students from using "printed" books in carrying out academic tasks* and *open access to a variety of educational resources through the Internet favors unethical behavior among students such as plagiarism and intellectual fraud.*

2 Theoretical Framework for University Students' Attitude Toward the Unethical Use of Information Technology

2.1 The Concept of Plagiarism: Definitions and Forms

A general definition of the concept of plagiarism aspects an "act of plagiarism," which means "to fit (ideas, passages, etc.) from another work or author" [3]. Plagiarism involves literary theft, theft by copying someone else's words or ideas and transmitting them as one's own, without mentioning the source. In the same direction, a definition of plagiarism by Carroll [4] states that it is a situation where someone presents the work of an author as if it were his work, "intentionally or unintentionally." Plagiarism is a "literacy practice" [5] and is something that people do with reading and writing. Plagiarism is part of a practice that involves the values, attitudes, and feelings of the participants, as well as the social relationships between them and the institutions in which they work.

Some authors consider that the basic activity of knowledge is the management of information and ideas from different sources, thus inevitably being able to plagiarize in the academic world. This concept appears in a variety of forms, including collaboration or cooperation between students working together [6]. There is extensive literature on plagiarism in higher education, in this case in North America and especially by students [7, 8]. But plagiarism itself must be understood as part of a more complex problem of fraud [9, 10]. Researchers analyzed plagiarism in different ways, talking about academic misconduct [11], academic dishonesty [12, 13], or academical integrity [14–17]. For others, it simply means unethical behavior [18, 19].

Plagiarism is not a new phenomenon of academic activity. Plagiarism has no borders. The cases of plagiarism could be found in students' written works all over the world, but more numerous cases could be met in countries having comparatively poor legal regulation on copyright and quality of studies as well as in higher education institutions missing ethical norms, policies, and procedures on plagiarism prevention. In higher education, plagiarism is seen as a sign of immorality. Rebecca Moore Howard [20] points out that plagiarism is connected to morality through university policies, even if it is defined as a textual practice: "university policies describe plagiarism in moral terms when they list it as a form of academic dishonesty." As Valentine [5] also stated, plagiarism is considered an ethical issue being highlighted in the ethical codes of universities which prescribed corrective behavior universally as though there is one set way to quote and document that good, honest, and ethical students will follow. Regarding such policies, students' choices are limited. They are often reduced to rule-following as a way of doing morality. This sense of morality is similar to what Zygmut Bauman [21] considered ethical morality. An ethical morality is one in which morality is a state of being that can be achieved by rule-following rather than by deciding and then acting on what one believes to be good in a given situation. In this context, people have no moral responsibility; they are only responsible for compliance with ethical rules. Ethics becomes "a code of law that prescribes universally correct behavior" [21].

The majority of the available literature on the subject references inquiries into the prevalence of such misconduct among students [22–25]. Indeed, plagiarism and academic fraud can be seen as reflections on the need to get good grades at all costs. These situations continue to be really serious problems in the academia [23, 26–31]. In the opinion of Gomez [32], many students tend to analyze fraud as a victimless crime, and some students relate to this phenomenon using the phrase "it is no big deal." According to McCabe's [23] studies, the idea is that students generally cheat at an alarming rate and students who follow a business profile cheat even more than others. If we refer to students, there are many forms of plagiarism. For Wilhoit [33], Brandt [34] and Howard [35], students plagiarize in four main ways: stealing material from another source and passing it off as their own; submitting a paper written by someone else (e.g., a peer or relative) and passing it off as their own; copying sections of material from one or more source texts, supplying proper documentation (including the full reference) but leaving out quotation marks, thus giving the impression that the material has been paraphrased rather than directly quoted; paraphrasing material from one or more source texts without supplying appropriate documentation. Students can also resort to "smart" forms of plagiarism by modifying words, grammatical structures, or using synonyms of the original words, instead of simply copying and pasting to hide their plagiarism [36]. Referring to the current possibilities and the diversity of ways in which information is gathered, as several sources claimed [37, 38], old-style plagiarism was difficult, required some degree of skill, and was relatively easy to spot by knowledgeable faculty. In the opposite direction, in contemporary society, the Internet has made cybercheating quite simple, like a mouse click, requiring a certain degree of skills and competencies for those who have to keep up with students who resort to such ways of accomplishing tasks. As Granitz and Loewy [39] stated, the Internet is seductive given the ease with which various information can be accessed, and for a student that is under the pressure of performing tasks, it is very tempting. Consequently, stealing or copying one's work no longer involves any effort and students may be careless of the ethical or legal consequences of such behavior since access to databases and publications through the Internet is more simple by making it much easier for students to give copy-paste much more easily.

2.2 Modern Plagiarism Devices

According to the literature, computers are part of the educational environment, and students from various specializations "use them as research tools and communicate with friends and colleagues" [40]. In the same context, according to one study, Swain and Gilmore [41] found that students were very informed about copyright laws and ethical problems regarding the use of computers in society.

Danielsen et al. [26], in their work, The Culture of Cheating: From the Classroom to the Exam Room, develop the concept of high-tech cheating. Thus, according to the authors, in the IT age, high-tech devices improved the learning environment and subsequent performance in many legitimate ways, but the same devices have also improved fraud through the existing technology. According to the authors, some of the most common devices that can contribute to fraud are:

- hand scanners and pens; a USB pen or portable scanner reads up to 1000 characters per second and can easily fit into a pocket;
- laptops and digital watches; portable computers using an infrared transmitter allow users to send and receive information. Digital watches can store data downloaded from a student's computer. Students can send lists, answers, and information to other students;
- pagers; students can preprogram these devices with all the information needed for a test. I can also send questions to someone outside the testing environment, requesting and receiving answers;
- headphones; many students are trying to wear headphones to listen to music during examinations. Students may have data, formulas, or other information between songs to play during the exam. iPods and other digital players may contain audio files with exam responses;
- other electronic devices; tiny and wireless cameras can be used to record each page and transmit images to someone outside the room. The outsider can send answers with a call or text message and then distribute the test to other students.

Besides, technology has created easier and easier ways to cheat [3, 23, 28, 29, 42–44]. Therefore, according to Rosamond [30], "academic sensitivity to the nature of plagiarism has increased in recent years by the development of web technology as well as the emergence of countless Internet offers involving the sale of scientific works" and the development of new devices has amplified and affected how students report to the idea of integrity [3, 23, 29, 45–47].

Bottom line is, the Internet, computers, smartphones, and other technology devices have made student fraud less difficult and more frequent than in previous years [26, 43, 46, 48, 49].

2.3   Studies Based on Students Attitude Toward the Unethical Use of Information Technology

Several studies on academic integrity and how students relate to the problem of using information technology in educational training are relevant to the Romanian academic environment. One of the recent studies on the desiderates of academic ethics among students was conducted by a group of professors from the University of Bucharest in 2018. The sample for this study consisted of students and professors from the University of Bucharest and was based on an online questionnaire. The questionnaire addressed the students, gathered information about "personal practice, representation of the practice of colleagues, and the perceived seriousness of certain behaviors that deviate from academic integrity" [50]. According to this study, 86% consider it serious or very serious to present a report written by someone else as a work of your own, and 81% produce fictitious data. Students are more relaxed in terms of text management and plagiarism. Only 61% consider it serious or very serious to quote the source incorrectly (without quotation marks), 59% not to clearly distinguish between their ideas and a translation, and 65% to take over from the Internet without indicating the source. Repeated use of the same material in different examinations is the most accepted behavior, with only 48% considering it serious or very serious.

Also, according to a study conducted in Turkey by [51] aimed at determining the ethical behaviors of students regarding the use of the Internet in the field of information technology as well as the factors influencing these behaviors, concludes that the age of students influences the unethical use of information technologies. Together with the transmission of basic skills in the use of the computer, teachers should raise student awareness of ethical issues arising in computer technologies and teach them how they should act regarding ethical issues.

Other studies on plagiarism among students have been concerned with how the behavior of the group leader influences the conduct of group members [52], to what extent there is a relationship between students' attitude toward cheating and demographics factors [53, 54] have tested the relationship between students' awareness and the violation of copyright. The reasons why young people plagiarize were explored by [55]. They are developing a strategy to combat digital plagiarism and strategies for teachers include the need to discuss what plagiarism means and teach students how to correctly quote references and how to use bibliographies. Besides, they recommend the use of antiplagiarism software packages. Other strategies include combining punishment with parents' responsibility to build an ethical model for their children and using the colleague's culture as a tool to combat digital plagiarism.

3 Methodology

3.1 Research Method

Starting from the problem highlighted in the theoretical part of this study, the author initiated a quantitative sociological research, based on a questionnaire, among students. The questionnaire made available to respondents was distributed in an online format through the Google app. Thus, the sample is a theoretical one, consisting of 100 female and male students, both from urban and rural areas, from various specializations. The sampling called was that of the "snowball."

This procedure refers to the "accumulation process as each localized subject suggests other subjects" [56]. So, as [56] suggests, snowball sampling is a non-probabilistic sampling method requiring each interviewee to indicate other people who might become respondents. Further to what has been said, the sample is not representative and cannot be generalized. The population is randomly selected, the condition is to be classified as a form of study within the afore-mentioned university. However, a gender field of study can be achieved by age-based quota, gender, the field of study. Students' attitudes toward the unethical use of IT were identified by a questionnaire involving 11 questions that referred to various issues such as reading time and the Internet, the main sources of information and inspiration when they have to carry out a project for university, the reasons why students turn to the Internet for academic tasks, the issue of plagiarism and intellectual fraud through information technology as well as several one-off situations regarding the software.

The questionnaire, as a research tool and technique in socio-human sciences, is not easy to define, being understood in different ways over time. If for [57], questionnaires "are tests consisting of a greater or lesser number of questions submitted in writing to subjects and refer to their opinions, preferences, feelings, interests, and behaviors in precise circumstances," for [58], the questionnaire is "a method of collecting data through questions to individuals or by questioning whether they agree or disagree with statements representing different points of view." Another, more recent definition, belongs to sociologist S. Chelcea [59] for whom the research questionnaire is "a technique and, accordingly, an investigative tool consisting of a set of written questions and possibly graphic images, logically and psychologically ordered, which, by being administrated by the investigation operators or by self-administration, determine from the persons investigated answers to be registered in writing." According to the Work Dictionary of Social Research Methods, coordinated by V. Jupp [60], the questionnaire contains "a set of carefully designed questions" that are administered to a group of people to collect data on the subject of interest for the researcher. Finally, questionnaires constitute "an excellent means of collecting quantitative data on a large scale."

3.2 Research Procedure

In the first phase, we designed a questionnaire based on various pioneering research made in Romania conducted by various specialists, including A. Netedu [61]. In the second phase, between the February 9 and 23, 2020, the questionnaire was distributed to students to be completed, using, as mentioned before, the snowball technique. The questionnaire entitled "The ethical dimension of online information management and electronic resources" contains 11 questions. The questions referred to the following aspects: the number of hours allocated per day to the use of the Internet, television, reading; the main sources of information in making a report; the main sources of inspiration available in the online environment, how many books they have read and bought in the last year in printed format, e-book; the reasons why students download certain content from the Internet without interfering with the information; if there have been situations in which some colleagues have been sanctioned for plagiarism; assessing the severity of internships among students; expressing agreement or disagreement on certain statements; requesting a point of view regarding the use of some software. The questionnaire was completed by 100 students stating that some respondents did not answer.

3.3   Results

Generally, the aspects related to the use of information technology are ubiquitous in the educational field, students using technology to fulfill academic tasks. Many times, the unethical use of technology is discussed. Phukan and Dhillon [62] point out that the unethical use of the technology of information is ubiquitous and developing as rapidly as the technology itself and such unethical behavior is prevalent in all countries. The majority of students who responded were female (96%) and only 4% of the male gender.

One reason for this difference is that the majority of respondents are enrolled in specializations such as primary and preschool education pedagogy, letters, communication, and public relations, as well as conversion into education sciences where there prevails the female population. Respondents are between the ages of 18 and 50, from both rural (41%) and urban areas (59%).

A first aspect of the questionnaire was related to the time spent browsing the Internet, reading (library and home), and television. According to the answers given by students, it is worrying that the time spent at the library is quite small compared to the time allocated to the Internet or television. Also, the main resources used by the respondents in making projects are: specialized sites in the field of study (71.8%), searching for keywords on Google (58.3%), Wikipedia (50.5%), Google Academics (35.9%). Only four respondents mentioned that they are using platforms such as CEEOL or the Cambridge base.

One of the questions contained in the questionnaire referred to the reasons why students turn to the Internet to carry out tasks, with the choice of several options. On the premise that Internet information can be downloaded quite easily increases accessibility but decreases interest in going to the library or searching for books. Therefore, convenience is the most common response (77%), followed by lack of time (51%), lack of readings in general (44%) as well as lack of creativity (43%). With the possibility to add other answers, some of the respondents highlighted laziness, as well as lack of interest.

Further, respondents were asked for their opinion on the seriousness of some practices among students, who, at least at a declarative level, were assessed as serious or very serious. They expressed their opinion on the following concrete situations: to help a colleague/pass an exam by fraud, copy to an exam, retrieve texts/information from the Internet without specifying this, taking passages from printed papers without indicating the source and presenting a reference written by someone else as their work. According to the results recorded, the situation that was considered the most serious was related to the presentation of a report written by someone else as a work of its own (46%) and 36% considered it quite serious to retrieve texts from the Internet texts or information without specifying this. As to whether a colleague can be helped to pass a fraud exam, 23 of respondents consider it somewhat serious, 31 consider the situation to be quite serious, and 32 as very serious.

As can be seen, the majority of respondents are aware of the seriousness of these practices but are quite permissive in terms of taking texts from the Internet without specifying what additional effort this implies or the extent to which some students know the criteria for scientific drafting.

Respondents considered that the practices mentioned above are rarely encountered in their specialization, which denotes scientific rigor and the non-tolerance of such behavior by teachers. Moreover, it can be noted that in the faculty or study group, unethical behaviors were noticed and sanctioned by teachers. Satisfaction with the quality of university studies and their relevance in the labor market is an important aspect and respondents expressed their opinion highlighting the quality of the teaching act. Thus, almost 70% of respondents declare themselves very satisfied with their studies in the faculty, and 57 of the respondents would enroll in the same faculty if they had the opportunity.

Another question contained in the questionnaire was related to the use of the software by students in their educational activity (Table 1). Therefore, students use both licensed and unlicensed software, a reason for this being their rather high cost (75 respondents consider software to be too expensive), preferring to use open-source software that does not involve certain fees. A rather important aspect would be that the university does not use unlicensed software, encouraging ethical behavior in this respect (94 of respondents appreciated that no licensed software is used in the university).

Finally, one of the questions had covered several aspects of plagiarism and how students relate to this phenomenon. Respondents expressed their agreement or disagreement on several claims, according to Table 2, and respondents' responses were also mentioned.

As can be seen in Table 1, respondents seek to justify intellectual theft by reference to what society promotes, in this case, dishonesty which inevitably leads to the

Table 1 Software that requires licensing

Items	Yes	No
Do you use unlicensed software?	46	54
Does the faculty use unlicensed software?	6	94
Are you willing to buy a license extension for Windows or other programs?	58	42
I prefer to use open-source software that does not require fees	73	27
I think there are millions of people who can not be prosecuted	61	39
I think that the original software is too expensive	75	25

Table 2 Student perception of various aspects of plagiarism

Items	Agree	Disagree
1. It is easier to plagiarize than to be original	37	63
2. Plagiarism is an easy way to achieve good results without too much intellectual effort	52	48
3. Intellectual theft is present because society promotes dishonesty	71	29
4. Plagiarism arose due to the improvement of the means of communication	53	47
5. The educational system allows the spread of plagiarism and does not cultivate authenticity and creativity	46	54
6. Plagiarism affects the degree of competence of future specialists	89	11
7. This phenomenon also occurred due to the elimination of university admission	43	57
8. Workplace dissatisfaction is one reason why teachers do not emphasize the originality of the texts offered by students	44	56

impairment of the competence of future specialists. At the same time, the development of the means of communication and, implicitly, free access to them, facilitates this unethical behavior. As for the educational system, respondents believe that it does not allow the development of plagiarism as evidence being the sanctions imposed in various contexts.

4 Discussions

Academic dishonesty at the university level is a common phenomenon among students of all ages and specializations. Nowadays, the widespread use of the Internet and the popularity of mobile and wireless devices have made it easier to access and transmit information illegally and dishonestly. As students have access to numerous academic publications and the fact that they can be downloaded quite easily and free of charge decreases interest in going to the library or searching for information in books. Besides, as it results from our study, convenience, lack of time, and lack of reading, in general, contribute to the development of a culture of plagiarism. Student plagiarism occurs in different forms, including incorrect citation and stealing someone else's ideas and work. Plagiarism also occurs from different sources. These include journals, books, the Internet, newspapers, and other students. However, Internet plagiarism has become more and more popular.

Today, the academic community pays particular attention to raising students' awareness of ethical issues and the use of information in the electronic age. Among the solutions implemented by universities would be the elaboration and publication of codes of ethics as well as the teaching of ethics and academic writing courses that can help combat the academic dishonesty that exists among students. [29] identified several practices to reduce the phenomenon of plagiarism. They correlated elements of education (by explaining to students what academic honesty is and what their expectations are) but instructional practice (use of codes of ethics). Research has shown that students plagiarize less when they know that faculties are using a plagiarism detection program. In this respect, as Stapleton [63] stated, if in 2012, the Turnitin program was available in 126 countries (in ten different languages), in 2016, Turnitin was used by 26 million students from 15,000 institutions in 140 countries. To combat plagiarism on the Internet, in addition to the various antiplagiarism programs, blocking, filtering, and rating systems can also be used [46].

Teachers can play an important role in combating academic dishonesty by paying attention, detecting, and reporting incidents of deception and plagiarism. Also, teachers can reduce the tendency to copy by engaging students in interesting, appealing, and relevant tasks for students to develop their creativity [55] as well as instruct them on how to document them. Last but not least, more specialists draws attention to the importance of academic institutions by developing codes of ethics to be presented to students and introducing ethics courses. As is apparent from the Honor Code of the University of Richmond [64], the penalties imposed on a student who has been found guilty of plagiarism may be: meeting with the dean (or a representative), written reprimand, honor probation, loss of academic credits, suspension and separation from the university and loss of credit in all the races in which the student was enrolled at the time of the violation, meeting with an academic writing consultant.

Alschuler and Blimling [65] say that if plagiarism is not eliminated, then the problem is not with the individual students who commit the offense, but with institutions that support it. All colleges must emphasize the importance of this issue to students and address it, according to Wilson [66]. Academic integrity should be the responsibility of all the stakeholders in education [16, 67].

5   Conclusions and Recommendations

Plagiarism is academic misconduct commonly found in educational institutions nowadays. This paper first defines the types of plagiarism and explains the typical reasons for university students to engage in plagiarism. Finally, information technology is present in students' lives, and they use various sources and resources online rather than using books or going to the library. The various unethical practices are appreciated as serious, in particular, to present a written report as their work, practices that are not tolerated by teachers. Intellectual theft seems to be justified by reference to what society promotes and dishonesty leads to an impaired level of competence of future specialists. Students use different software, both licensed and unlicensed, a problem being the too high cost of such programs.

There are many reasons why institutions need to fight plagiarism among students. Plagiarism affects not only individual students but also the integrity of the institution as a whole and the quality of its products. Therefore, each university must crack down on this problem for its own sake and the sake of the students. Also, apart from imparting academic knowledge to students, universities and colleges have a responsibility to impart moral and ethical values to students.

The first premise—the diversity of open-source educational sources and resources available online, discourages students from using "printed" books in carrying out academic tasks—is confirmed. According to the answers, the students prefer to use the information taken from the Internet rather than taking them from printed books. The main resources used by the respondents in making projects are: specialized sites in the field of study, searching for keywords on Google, Wikipedia, or Google Academics, and more than half of the respondents said that in the last year, they bought less than five books.

The second premise—open access to a variety of educational resources through the Internet favors unethical behavior among students such as plagiarism and intellectual fraud—is not confirmed because the majority of respondents are aware of the seriousness of these practices. Even if some students are quite permissive in terms of taking texts from the Internet without specifying this, respondents considered that some practices are rarely encountered in their specialization, which denotes scientific rigor and the non-tolerance of such behavior by teachers. Moreover, it can be noted that in the faculty or study group, unethical behaviors were noticed and sanctioned by teachers. A rather important aspect would be that the university does not use unlicensed software, encouraging ethical behavior in this respect (94 of respondents appreciated that no licensed software is used in the university).

Last but not least, the socio-demographic data included the following aspects: gender (96 females, 4 males), the age of the respondents is between 18 and 48 years, the environment of origin (urban-62 respondents, rural-38 respondents), the faculty where they are students, specialization and year of study, level of education (92 bachelors, 8 masters).

The literature [68, 69] highlights several strategies for reducing plagiarism, including: always acknowledge the contributions of others and the source of ideas and words, regardless of whether paraphrased or summarized, use of verbatim text/material must be enclosed in quotation marks, acknowledge sources used in the writing, when paraphrasing, understand the material completely and use your own words, when in doubt about whether or not the concept or fact is common knowledge, reference it, make sure to reference and cite references accurately.

6 Limitations and Future Work

The most important limitation of this study was the use of a smaller number of boy students than girl students as test material and the fact that data cannot be generalized. In this quantitative research, the author examined a sample of female and male undergraduate and master's students to highlight their position on plagiarism issues. Raising students' awareness of the seriousness of this practice is essential as is the transmission of essential information on academic writing and how technology can be used effectively in carrying out academic tasks. In the future, it would be interesting to conduct a comparative study on the level of plagiarism among undergraduates, masters, and doctoral students concerning the prestige of the university to which they belong.

Acknowledgements "This work was supported by a grant of the Ministry of Research and Innovation, CNCS—UEFISCDI, project number PN-III-P1-1.1-TE-2016-0773, within PNCDI III."

References

1. Hatos, A.: Educație [Education]. In: Vlăsceanu, L. (ed.) Sociologie [Sociology]. Polirom, Iași (2011)
2. Bigum, C., Kenway, J.: New information technologies and the ambiguous future of schooling—Some possible scenarios. In: Hargreaves, A. (ed.) Extending educational change. Springer, Dordrecht (2005)
3. Park, C.: In other (people's) words: Plagiarism by university students—literature and lessons. Assess. & Eval. High. Educ. **28**(5), 471–488 (2003)
4. Carroll, J.: A handbook for deterring plagiarism in higher education. Oxford Centre for Staff and Learning Development, Oxford, UK (2002)
5. Valentine, K.: Plagiarism as literacy practice: Recognizing and rethinking ethical binaries. Coll.E Compos. Commun. **58**(1), 89–109 (2006)
6. Wojtas, O.: Students asked for cheat alert. Times Higher Education. Supplement, 27 August, 36 (1999)
7. Brown, V.J., Howell, M.E.: The efficacy of policy statements on plagiarism: Do they change students' views. Res. High. Educ. **42**(1), 103–118 (2001)
8. Landau, J.D., Druen, P.B., Arcuri, J.A.: Methods for helping students avoid plagiarism. Teach. Psychol. **29**(2), 112–115 (2002)
9. Diekhoff, G.M., Labeff, E.E., Shinohara, K., Yasukawa, H.: College cheating in Japan and the United States. Res. High. Educ. **40**(3), 343–353 (1999)
10. McCabe, D.L.: Cheating: Why students do it and how we can help them stop. Am. Educ. **25**, 38–43 (2001)
11. Stern, E.B., Havlicek, L.: Academic misconduct: Results of faculty and undergraduate student surveys. J. Allied Health **15**(2), 129–142 (1986)
12. Caruana, A., Ramaseshan, B., Ewing, M.: The effect of anomie on academic dishonesty among university students. Int. J. Educ. Manag. **14**(1), 23–30 (2000)
13. Higbee, J., Thomas, P.: Preventing academic dishonesty. Res. Teach. Dev. Educ. **7**(1), 63–66 (2000)
14. Nuss, E.: Academic integrity: Comparing faculty and student attitudes. Improv. Coll.E Univ. Teach. **32**, 140–144 (1984)
15. Iovacchoni, E.V.: A comparative study of academic integrity at three different types of universities. Coll.E Stud. Aff. J. **9**(1), 35–43 (1989)
16. Cole, S., Conklin, D.L.: Academic integrity policies and procedures: opportunities to teach students about moral leadership and personal ethics. Coll.E Stud. Aff. J. **15**(2), 30–39 (1996)
17. Cole, S., McCabe, D.L.: Issues in academic integrity. New Dir. Stud. Serv. **73**, 67–77 (1996)
18. Anderson, R.E., Obenshain, S.S.: Cheating by students: findings, reflections and remedies. Acad. Med. **69**, 323–332 (1994)
19. Buckley, M.R., Wiese, D.S., Harvey, M.G.: An investigation into the dimensions of unethical behavior. J. Educ. Bus. **73**(5), 284–290 (1998)
20. Howard, R.M.: Plagiarisms, Authorships, and the Academic Death Penalty. Coll.E Engl. **57**, 788–806 (1995)

21. Bauman, Z.: Life in fragments: Essays in postmodern morality. Blackwell, Oxford (1995)
22. Batane, T.: Turning to Turnitin to fight plagiarism among university students. Educ. Technol. & Soc. **13**(2), 1–12 (2010)
23. McCabe, D.L.: Academic dishonesty in nursing schools: An empirical investigation. J. Nurs. Educ. **48**(11), 614–623 (2009)
24. Scanlon, P.M.: Student online plagiarism: How do we respond? Coll.E Teach. **51**(4), 161–165 (2003)
25. Walker, J.: Measuring plagiarism: Researching what students do, not what they say they do. Stud. High. Educ. **35**(1), 41–59 (2010)
26. Danielsen, R.D., Simon, A.F., Pavlick, R.: The culture of cheating: From the classroom to the exam room. J. Physician Assist. Educ. **17**(1), 23–29 (2006)
27. Fontana, J.: ursing faculty experiences of students' academic dishonesty. J. Nurs. Educ. **48**(4), 181–185 (2009)
28. Lipka, S.: Colleges sharpen tactics for resolving academic-integrity cases. Chron. High. Educ. **55**(31), A20 (2009)
29. McCabe, D.L., Butterfield, K.D., Trevino, L.K.: Academic dishonesty in graduate business programs: Prevalence, causes, and proposed action. Acad. Manag. Learn. & Educ. **5**(3), 294–305 (2006)
30. Rosamond, B.: Plagiarism, academic norms, and the governance of the profession. Politics **22**(3), 167–174 (2002)
31. Wilkerson, J.: Staff and student perceptions of plagiarism and cheating. Int. J. Teach. Learn. High. Educ. **20**(2), 98–105 (2009)
32. Gomez, D.: Putting the shame back in student cheating. Educ. Dig. **67**(4), 1–6 (2001)
33. Wilhoit, S.: Helping students avoid plagiarism. Coll.E Teach. **42**(4), 161–164 (1994)
34. Brandt, D.: Copyright's (not so) little cousin, plagiarism. Comput. Libr. **22**(5), 39–42 (2002)
35. Howard, R.: Don't police plagiarism: just teach! Educ. Dig. **67**(5), 46–50 (2002)
36. Howard, R.M.: The ethics of plagiarism. In: Pemberton, M.A. (ed.), The ethics of writing instructions: Issues in theory and practice. Stanford, USA (2000)
37. McKenzie, J.: The New plagiarism: Seven antidotes to prevent highway robbery in an electronic age: From now on. Educ. Technol. J. **7**(8) (1998)
38. McLafferty, C.L., Foust, K.M.: Electronic plagiarism as a college instructor's Nightmare— Prevention and detection. J. Educ. Bus. **79**(3), 186–189 (2004)
39. Granitz, N., Loewy, D.: Applying ethical theories: Interpreting and responding to student plagiarism. J. Bus. Ethics **72**(3), 293–306 (2007)
40. Ben-Jacob, M.G.: Integrating computer ethics across the curriculum: A case study. Educ. Technol. & Soc. **8**(4), 198–204 (2005)
41. Swain, C., Gilmore, E.: Repacking for the 21st Century: Teaching Copyright and Computer Ethics in Teacher Education Courses. Contemp. Issues Technol. Teach. Educ. **1**(4), 535–545 (2001)
42. Dehn, R.: Is technology contributing to academic dishonesty? J. Physician Assist. Educ. **14**(3), 190–192 (2003)
43. Maitland, R.: Disturbing trends in education. Oral Health **97**(9), 53–57 (2007)
44. Mayhew, M., Seifert, T., Pascarella, E.: A multi-institutional assessment of moral reasoning development among first-year students. Review of Higher Education. J. Assoc. Study High. Educ. **33**(3), 357–390 (2010)
45. Brown, B., Emmett, D.: Explaining variations in the level of academic dishonesty in studies of college students: Some new evidence. Coll.E Stud. J. **35**(4), 1–13 (2001)
46. Lathrop, A., Foss, K.: Student cheating and plagiarism in the Internet era: A wake-up call. Libraries Unlimited, Englewood (2000)
47. Szabo, A., Underwood, J.: Cybercheats: Is information and communication technology fueling academic dishonesty? Act. Learn. High Educ. **5**(2), 180–200 (2004)
48. Boehm, P., Justice, M., Weeks, S.: Promoting academic integrity in higher education. Community Coll.E Enterp. **15**(1), 45–61 (2009)
49. Choi, C.: The pull of integrity. ASEE. Prism. **18**(7), 29–33 (2009)

50. Vasile, M.: Practicarea integrității academice (IA) de către student [Practicing academic integrity by students]. In: Sandu, D., Vasile, M., Ilinca, C. (eds.) Integritatea academică la studenți [Academic integrity in students]. University of Bucharest Publishing House, Bucharest (2019)
51. Kürtüncü, M., Demirbağ, B., Yildiz, H.: Unethical computer using behaviors of Turkish high school students. J. Behav. Health **4**(2), 49–54 (2015)
52. Owunwanne, D., Rustagi, N., Dada, R.: Students perceptions of cheating and plagiarism in higher institutions. J. Coll.E Sci. Teach. **7**(11), 59–68 (2010)
53. Al-Qaisy, L.M.: Students attitudes toward cheat and relation to demographic factors. Eur. J. Soc. Sci. **7**(1), 140–146 (2008)
54. Marshall, S., Garry, M.: How well do students really understand plagiarism. In: 22nd Annual Conference of the Australasian Society for Computers in Learning in Tertiary Education, Brisbane, pp. 457–467 (2005)
55. Ma, H.J., Wan, G., Lu, E.Y.: Digital cheating and plagiarism in schools. Theor. Pract. J. **47**, 197–203 (2008)
56. Babbie, E.: Practica cercetării sociale [Practice of Social Research]. Polirom, Iași (2010)
57. Pichot, P.: Les Tests Mentaux. P.U.F, Paris (1954)
58. Babbie, E.: The practice of social research. Wadsworth Company, Belmont (1992)
59. Chelcea, S.: Metodologia cercetării sociologice [Methodology of sociological research]. Economic Publishing House, Bucharest (2001)
60. Jupp, V.: Dicționar al metodelor de cercetare socială [Dictionary of social research methods]. Polirom, Iași (2010)
61. Netedu, A.: Emoțiile, manipularea informației și frauda în mediul studențesc [Emotions, manipulation of information and fraud in the student environment]. In: Rusu, M. (ed.) Manifestarea și auto-reglarea emoțiilor [Manifestation and self-regulation of emotions]. Ars Longa, Iași (2013)
62. Phukan, S., Dhillon, G.: Ethical and intellectual property concerns in a multicultural global economy. Electr. J. Inf. Syst. Dev. Ctries. **7**(3), 1–8 (2001)
63. Stapleton, P.: Gauging the effectiveness of anti-plagiarism software: An empirical study os second language graduate writers. J. Engl. Acad. Purp. **11**(2), 125–133 (2002)
64. The Honor Code, University of Richmond. https://studentdevelopment.richmond.edu/student-handbook/honor/statutes.pdf.. Last accessed 7 September 2020
65. Alschuler, A.S., Blimling, G.S.: Curbing epidemic cheating through systemic change. Coll.E Teach. **43**(4), 123–126 (1995)
66. Wilson, R.: Colleges urged to better define academic integrity and to stress its importance. Chronicle of Higher Education, A 18 (1999)
67. Stovall, J.L.: Academic integrity: A joint responsibility of administrators, faculty and students. Carol. View **4**, 36–38 (1988)
68. Bahadori, M., Izadi, M., Hoseinpourfard, M.: Plagiarsim: concepts, factors and solutions. Iran. J. Mil.Y Med. **14**(3), 168–177 (2012)
69. Cicutto, L.: Plagiarism: avoiding the peril in scientific writing. Chest **133**(2), 579–581 (2008)

Ethical Rules of Online Communication Between University Teachers and Students

Liliana Mâță

Abstract The integration of social networking in the education process of universities raises more and more ethical issues. This study aims to explore the students' perceptions of the ethical issues involving online communication with the university professor. A qualitative research methodology based on the use of a semi-structured interview was designed. A total of 146 students from a state university in the northeastern part of Romania participated in the study. Preliminary results indicate that the most common ethical problems that arise in communication between students and teachers on social networks are those related to the use of inappropriate language, misunderstanding of information, failure to respect the teacher's private time. The analysis of the frequencies of the data obtained during the interview indicates that the norms to be respected by the teachers in the online communication with the student are: manifesting appropriate attitudes, offering the teacher's response on time to the students' requests, respecting the confidentiality of the content of the communication.

Keywords Ethical rules · Online communication · Qualitative research · Students

1 Introduction

The use of social media applications has created new ways of communicating around the world and has generated significant changes in people's lives [1]. Online communication has emerged as commonplace in everyday life because social media has changed the way people interact and their ability to share information with the rest of the world [2]. "We live in a digital environment in the sense that we look at reality within its possibility of being digital or its digitalization" [3]. In the field of education, new pedagogical paradigms have been developed that shape the views on the roles of teachers and students, as well as on the role of decision-makers and educational systems in general. Papandrea [4] believes that the use of online tools is essential for the future of education. Communication between students and teachers in higher

L. Mâță (✉)
"Vasile Alecsandri" University of Bacău, Bacău, Romania
e-mail: liliana.mata@ub.ro

© The Author(s), under exclusive license to Springer Nature Singapore Pte Ltd. 2022　　　99
L. Mâță (ed.), *Ethical Use of Information Technology in Higher Education*,
EAI/Springer Innovations in Communication and Computing,
https://doi.org/10.1007/978-981-16-1951-9_7

education is rapidly and radically changing, as a result of easy access to online learning resources [5]. The current modes of communication are based on interaction and collaboration, as opposed to traditional forms, in which the emphasis was placed on domination and authority. Therefore, Forkosh-Baruch, Hershkovitz, and Ang [6] observed that communication between students and teachers is reinvented as a result of the use of social networks.

The development of digital tools has led to new forms of communication and, at the same time, to the adoption of ethical rules that must be strictly respected by users. More and more teachers and students are familiar with the use of digital resources for communication in the academic environment. As electronic communication enters the university education system, it is necessary to establish ethical rules to protect students from those who could use digital resources for illicit purposes. However, there is a tendency to disregard ethical rules by both students and university teachers when using information technology, because the act of communication is less personal. A possible cause may be that while communicating with digital resources, the other person cannot be seen or heard. Hong and Jun [7] believe that the ethical and responsible training of students and teachers is a fundamental and effective way to reduce the occurrence of incorrect online behavior. According to Livingstone and Brake [8], moral and educational concerns regarding student–teacher communication based on the use of social networks must ensure the need to balance opportunities and risks at the political level.

Toprak et al. [9] highlighted that ethical behavior in e-learning derives from "communication ethics and instructional ethics". In this context, it is necessary to respect the moral imperatives of the Association for Computing Machines as a general framework for online ethical behavior. These imperatives signal the main ethical concerns that apply to all online users in academia, as follows: contributing to human and social well-being, avoiding harm to others, being honest and trustworthy, being fair and not taking discriminative action, respect for property rights, including copyright, the provision of adequate credit for intellectual property, respect for the confidentiality of others. Therefore, there is a need for mutual respect, justice, and goodwill in the behavior of students and teachers when engaging in online communication. It is recommended that students and university teachers avoid using derogatory, repulsive, or overly critical comments and support participants with information, feedback, and suggestions for locating online resources when engaging in online discussions [10]. Ethical responsibility in online communication involves a sense of camaraderie through positive exchanges that attract others to the discussion. Ethical behavior in online communication is guided by both existing institutional policies at the university level and the community agreement. Both students and teachers will follow the ethical norms of online communication established at the institutional level and by mutual agreement. When students and teachers cooperate and agree to abide by ethical rules, the conditions for effective online communication will be created.

2 Ethical Dimensions of Communication Between Students and Teachers in the Context of Using Online Resources

On the one hand, how online resources influence the communication between students and teachers is captured, and, on the other hand, the ethical issues that affect online communication are analyzed.

2.1 The Influence of the Online Resources on the Communication Between Teacher and Student

Higher education teachers are increasingly using social networks to connect with students beyond the educational environment. Several authors [11–13] have observed that social networks have gradually become a new communication tool between teachers and students, mainly in higher education. Forkosh-Baruch, Hershkovitz, and Ang [6] believe that teacher–student interactions should be carefully examined in the new context of the use of social networks, as they dramatically affect communication across time and space barriers. Therefore, the current model of communication between teachers and students goes beyond the traditional paradigms in which communication was limited and was based on traditional hierarchical roles.

The use of online communication resources offers multiple advantages, on the one hand [14], but it has also created potential problems, on the other hand [15]. Research results in the use of online learning resources highlight the improvement of student performance [16] and early intervention in learning and student behavior problems [17]. Also, with the help of these digital means, students become more independent [18]. The use of social networks gives communication new attributes, such as availability, contextuality, or the creation of learning experiences through several channels [6]. According to Huusimaki, Uusitalo-Malmivaara, and Tirri [19], digital communication is much more efficient than the traditional form of communication, because it facilitates the transmission of information online promptly and provides immediate feedback between students and teachers. Online communication offers the opportunity for teachers and students to be in constant contact [20]. Another advantage of social networks is the maintenance, development, and creation of interpersonal relationships [21]. Greenhow et al. [22] highlighted as facilities for online communication the freedom of expression of teachers and students, as well as the pedagogical potential of social networks. However, there are also several negative effects of using social networks, such as the use of violent language, the spread of harmful computer viruses, infringements of intellectual property, or privacy. Another disadvantage is that e-learning offers more possibilities for academic fraud because there is a predisposition to cheat online much easier than face to face [23]. According to Forkosh-Baruch et al. [6], the undesirable consequences of using social networks can range from wasting time to the existence of extreme cases of cyber-bullying. Asterhan & Rosenberg [24] drew attention to the fact that this new reality has generated debates on the topic of online communication between teachers and students, which has led some authorities to restrict or even prohibit such communication. Although there are potential threats and risks, electronic communication can be effective [25] if used with caution and professionalism.

The impact of accessing information online in academia has been investigated by researchers either at the student level or from the perspective of university teachers. There are several studies focused on investigating the impact of online resources on communication between teachers and students. Teclehaimanot and Hickman [26] showed that the possibilities for interaction between teachers and students improve as the number of teachers with a social network profile increases. Cunha et al. [27] investigated how the process of communication between students and teachers evolved in the online environment and how teachers perceived student involvement. Alshahrani et al. [28] explored the influence of online learning resources on personal and emotional aspects of the student–reader relationship in higher education. Froment, García González, and Bohórquez [29] analyzed the literature on the use of social networks as a communication tool between teachers and students based on a systematic review. Other research is conducted at the level of secondary education [6, 24, 30] and elementary education [31, 32].

However, it can be seen that there are few studies focused on investigating the influence of the use of online resources on the student–teacher relationship. It can also be seen that there is no research on the ethical use of digital resources for online communication in academia.

2.2 *Ethical Issues of Online Communication*

Communication that is based on the use of social networks changes the way teachers and students exchange information. This can affect mutual perceptions and beliefs [33], which changes the relationship between students and teachers. There may also be several ethical issues in online communication. Amichai-Hamburger and Vinitzky [34], Marwick and Boyd [35] highlighted the fundamental issues involved in online communication, such as self-exposure, intimacy, and self-expression. Several key ethical issues also arise in online communication research [3]: online identity, online language, online consent, and online privacy.

Regarding the approval of the use of online communication between teachers and students, O'Connor and Schmidt [36] note that some schools completely prohibit personal communication using social media between teachers and students, while others allow limited use of social networks. Often, online communication is restricted to be used only for instructional and educational purposes [37]. If a school organization fails to establish a policy for the use of online communication, teachers are allowed to use their judgment. It is very important to establish the rights of the use of social networks by teachers at the level of the employment contract [36]. Thus, teachers can use these ethical rules as a benchmark to guide the types of communication considered appropriate or inappropriate in their educational institutions.

According to Aragon et al. [15], the fundamental ethical principles provide a basis for creating the rules for the correct and responsible use of social networks in education. Severson [38] proposed four principles of the ethics of information communication: respect for intellectual property rights, respect for the privacy of the person, legal language, and non-provocation of harmful effects. A series of ethical rules can be formulated to guide online communication between students and teachers, based on the use of rules proposed by Capurro and Pingel [3] for online research:

- respect for the interests and values of students and teachers involved in online communication, giving them the opportunity for active cooperation;
- uncovering abuses regarding the misuse of online communication;
- creating an atmosphere of social responsibility of participants in online communication;
- awareness of one's prejudices related to gender or other ethnicities, cultures.

The Ontario College of Teachers [25] proposed a list of behaviors that would justify disciplinary action regarding the inappropriate use of digital resources in communication between students and teachers: inappropriate electronic communication with students, colleagues, sending inappropriate materials to students in digital format, the use of school equipment to access, view or download inappropriate materials, the enticement of students and non-students with the help of the Internet, according to the Criminal Code. There are also provided several ways to minimize risks and prevent unethical behaviors in teachers: interacting appropriately with students, understanding privacy issues, and how to act professionally. Teachers should always be aware that they can share information with students online, information that they can discuss appropriately in the institutionalized setting. Communication on social networks is useful to share various information that relates to the teaching activity and not aspects that concern personal life. Therefore, it is important to set the boundary between professional and personal communication so that communication is maintained at an optimal level.

Foxman [39] found that teachers often warn students about how to operate on online social networks and electronic communications to which they have safe and proper access, but the same advice is not so easily followed by teachers. Nemetz [40] provided several examples of inappropriate information that appears on the teacher's online profile: comments about piercings or tattoos, photos showing alcohol consumption, negative comments about other colleagues, comments of a political, racist, or religious nature. Based on the analysis of concrete cases of inappropriate behavior in terms of online communication, Foxman [39] urges representatives of educational institutions to try to educate teachers. In his view, teachers need to be careful when engaging in conversations with online students and avoid violating appropriate behavior.

2.3   Aim of the Research

This research aims to explore students' perceptions of the benefits of online communication with teachers and several ethical issues involved, as follows:

- the reasons for choosing this mode of communication;
- the ethical issues that may occur in online communication between teacher and student;
- the rules respected by students in online communication with teachers;
- the rules respected by teachers in online communication with students.

In this research, the ethical aspects involved in the new type of communication between students and teachers as a result of the increasing use of social networks in higher education are explored. The novelty of the research is the inclusion of ethical issues regarding the use of information technology to communicate online in academia.

3   Methodology

A qualitative research methodology is proposed based on the use of the interview as a way to explore students' perceptions of the benefits of using online communication with teachers, the ethical issues involved, and the rules respected by students and teachers in online communication.

3.1   Participants

The study was attended by 146 students from a state university in the northeastern part of Romania. Convenience sampling was used, which involves including accessible and available cases in the research group. As a variant of this, "snowball" (or "network") sampling was used [41], which involves two phases. In the first phase, a series of participants from the four specializations were identified, and in the second stage, they were asked to look for other participants who meet certain explicit criteria (use of information technology, specialization, year of study). The distribution of the research group is presented in Table 1, according to the independent variables.

3.2   Research Method

The interview is used in the present research because it is a suitable method to discover previously unknown trends and problems and to explore new topics of interest in the

Table 1 Distribution of the research group according to the independent variables

No.	Independent variables	Distribution of the research group
1	Frequency of use of digital tools in online communication	– Daily: 13 students (8.9%) – Weekly: 47 students (32.2%) – Monthly: 40 students (27.4%) – Per semester: 45 students (30.8%) – Never: 1 student (0.7%)
2	The types of technological resources used	– E-mail: 102 students – Facebook: 73 students – Messenger: 39 students – WhatsApp: 69 students – Facebook group: 5 students
3	Specialization	– Education sciences: 52 students (35.6%) – Sciences: 33 students (22.6%) – Physical education: 34 students (23.3%) – Philology: 27 students (18.5%)

research. The semi-structured interview, as a subcategory of the method, is part of the category of qualitative data collection techniques [42]. With the help of this type of interview, information is collected in detail based on the conversation [43]. The semi-structured interview is useful in conducting qualitative research to investigate students' views on the ethics of using online communication in-depth and to understand in detail the answers provided.

Several series of interviews were organized with a maximum of 8 students, depending on the specialization. All participants were informed about the objectives of the study and were also assured that the data are confidential and used for research purposes only. The interview data were recorded and then transcribed for processing and analysis of response frequencies for each category of ethical issues.

3.3 Data Analysis

All statistical analyses were achieved using the SPSS version 21.0 for Windows (IBM SPSS Statistics). The frequencies of student responses have been summarized using descriptive statistics. The responses were analyzed by using content analysis, as a systematic and objective means to achieve valid interpretations of verbal data [44] to describe and quantify issues related to the ethics of the use of digital resources in online communication between teachers and students.

4   Results

The first objective of the research was to identify *the reasons for choosing electronic communication* by students. The main benefits of using online communication by students, based on the frequencies obtained, are the following: speed of message transmission (52), time-saving (23), accessibility of communication (19), convenience, the efficiency of communication (17), obtaining information related to educational activities (15), overcoming barriers related to distance, ease of communication compared to face-to-face communication (8), the usefulness of online communication (6), simplicity, the discretion of communication, safety (5), overcoming barriers between student and teacher, the practical nature of the communication (3). Students also indicated other benefits that recorded the lowest frequency, as follows: adaptation to individual needs of students, fluency of communication, clarification of issues, the ability to respond to messages when the teacher has time, comfortable communication, sending information in different ways, such as files, text, the effectiveness of this mode of communication for economic reasons, which can be used by students when the credit ends, the use of the message as a reminder, providing feedback.

The second objective was to delimit the *ethical issues that can occur in online communication* between teachers and students. The prevailing ethical issues in electronic communication are varied: the use of inappropriate, informal language (29), misunderstanding of information, distortion of the message, subjective interpretation of information, the ambiguity of information (26), disrespect of the teacher's private time (22), breach of confidentiality (15), manifesting an inappropriate attitude (14), omitting messages or delaying the response of the teacher or students, overcoming the barrier in the student–teacher relationship (10), misuse of this form of communication (3), invasion of personal space, the incorrect transmission of information (2). Other problematic aspects mentioned less often by students related to online communication refer to the lack of rules for this type of communication, the use of messages by the teacher to the detriment of students, the subjectivity of the teacher toward certain students.

Regarding the existence of ethical rules in the university regulation regarding online communication, 137 of the students (93.8%) do not know explicit norms at the institutional level, while 9 (6.2%) state that there are such rules. The rules to be followed by students and teachers are presented in Table 2.

The appropriate attitudes that the teacher will show toward students are: respect for the integrity of the student, manifestation of understanding and openness to communication with the student, lack of discrimination, tolerance, fairness to all students, honesty, reciprocity in online communication. In the opinion of students, online communication must be based on respect and consideration. Both teachers and students will adopt an appropriate attitude. Students must first introduce themselves when addressing teachers and use the correct politeness formulas. The relationship between students and teachers in the online environment should not be confused with a friendly relationship. The teacher will maintain his professional status in the online environment. An important aspect that a student specified referred to

Table 2 Ethical rules observed by students and teachers in academia

Ethical rules observed by students	Ethical rules observed by teachers
– Use of appropriate, formal language (79) – Showing appropriate attitudes, such as respect for the teacher, seriousness (52) – Observance of the rules of moral conduct (35) – Observing the time interval for communication with the teacher (28) – Balanced use of this form of communication, without becoming insistent or disturbing (12) – Maintaining the optimal distance in the student–teacher relationship, maintaining strictly professional relationships, avoiding the formulation of personal questions (14) – Clear, explicit, and concise wording of the messages (11) – Respect for the confidentiality of the content of the communication (9) – Addressing topics related to the educational activity (6) – Correct transmission of information (4) – Respect for the private space of the teacher (2) – Giving up online communication during course and seminar activities (1) – Ensuring objective communication (1)	– The manifestation of appropriate attitudes (49) – Providing a timely response to student requests (33) – Respect for the confidentiality of the content of the communication (26) – Use of appropriate language (24) – Maintaining the optimal distance from the student and observing the rules of professional conduct (23) – Clear, concise, accurate, and accessible formulation of information (20) – Observance of the rules of moral conduct (6) – Correct transmission of information (6) – Observance of the time interval for communication with the student (4) – Ensuring objective communication, so that there is no interpretation of the content (3) – Observance of the student's personal space (2) – Addressing the topics related to the educational activity (2) – Keeping a balanced discourse, neither too close nor too far from the student (1) – Responsible use of online communication (1) – Behavioral constancy (1)

the manifestation by the teacher of the same attitude in the online environment as indirect communication. Also, another appreciation from the students aimed at serious treatment by the teacher of the subject approached by the student. The use of appropriate language by the teacher means not using threats or insults and even preventing certain conflicts, in the sense of not using irony. The information will be communicated as clearly as possible by the teacher, without deviating from the subject.

Respecting the confidentiality of the content of the communication is one of the important ethical rules that students appreciate in university teachers. Lack of the rule on confidentiality may lead to the public transmission of private information. Regarding the observance of the time interval for communication with the teacher, the students mentioned that no messages should be sent after 8 pm and during the resting period (2–4 pm). The students also specified that teachers should not have access to private conversations that take place inside different virtual groups of students on topics unrelated to the pedagogical act or the discipline taught.

In general, students appreciate that this mode of communication is useful because it facilitates problem-solving, does not interrupt the activity, or can be used in urgent situations, such as the situation when certain schedule changes occur. Also, online communication is much more efficient, both for sending messages and for transferring data and documents.

5 Discussions

The study aimed to investigate students' perceptions of the benefits of online communication between students and teachers and the ethical issues involved. Regarding the benefits that online communication offers, the data of the present research demonstrate that this type of communication determines the breaking of barriers between teachers and students, as shown by the results of other studies [45, 46]. Among the advantages listed by students are those related to the rapid transmission of information and providing immediate feedback, as shown by data obtained by Huusimaki et al. [19].

The *ethical issues* of using social networks in communication between students and teachers were diverse. One of these refers to the fact that this form of communication is appreciated by students as intrusive, which has been found in other research [46, 47]. Another ethical issue frequently mentioned by students was the one related to the erroneous transmission of messages, a problem also indicated in the study conducted by Au-Yeung [48].

Regarding the *ethical rules* that must be observed by both students and teachers, the research data show that this type of communication on social networks should be professional, focused mainly on educational topics, as indicated by the results of some studies on the same topic [13, 20, 49]. The rules that teachers must follow when communicating with students on social media refer to the fact that they must not harass students, use unauthorized information, spread false information, or transmit disturbing information, as indicated by data from other studies in the field [50]. Students also specified rules on how teachers can respond within an acceptable time frame. To provide equal access for all students, Au-Yeung [48] considers that teachers should respond to all messages, although this could affect the private time of the educator. Students have also highlighted the need to maintain the confidentiality of information discussed with the teacher, one of the ethical rules frequently addressed by the authors [51].

The research results strengthen some data obtained in other studies, but also provide new data on the causes underlying the choice of online communication by students in academia. The novelty element that the present research brings consists of the usefulness of the rules proposed by the students for the realization of online communication in adequate conditions. The observance of confidentiality by the teacher of the subject discussed with the students through different electronic sources is one of the rules frequently mentioned by the students. Also, another norm that must be the basis of online communication is the provision of a timely response by the teacher. The rules must be followed by both students and teachers for proper online communication.

6 Conclusions and Recommendations

The specialized works on the subject of online communication from an educational perspective are quite limited. Along with the benefits of this new way of communication, the risks it can determine at the level of interaction between students and teachers, but also at the organizational level were highlighted. An increasing number of problems affect the communication between students and teachers, as a result of transferring educational activities to the online environment.

The results of qualitative interview-based research reflect students' perceptions of the reasons behind using online communication, the ethical issues that may arise, and the rules that must be followed by both students and teachers. First of all, the main reasons that determine students to choose this mode of communication are the speed of message transmission, time-saving, accessibility of communication, convenience, the efficiency of communication. Secondly, the most important ethical issues that can affect the conduct of dialogue in the online environment can be the use of inappropriate language, misunderstanding of information, non-compliance with the private time of the teacher. Thirdly, ethical rules are perceived differently by students. The rules that must be observed by students when communicating online with the teacher are the use of appropriate language, the manifestation of appropriate attitudes, compliance with the rules of moral conduct. On the other hand, the ethical rules that must be observed by teachers in online communication with the student are: manifesting appropriate attitudes, providing a timely response by teachers to student requests, respecting the confidentiality of the content of the communication.

Implementing measures is a safe way to reduce the harmful effects that online communication can cause. In this new context, there are growing concerns for the ethical education of students and teachers in academia. Decision-makers in higher education must take a position at the institutional level regarding the regulation of the use of digital resources in communication between students and teachers. At the level of educational institutions, a formal policy on the responsible use of technology by students and teachers must be established and followed, which will be continuously reviewed and updated. Observance of the rules adopted at the level of higher education institutions, as well as those established by mutual agreement by students and teachers, will ensure the efficiency of online communication.

7 Limitations and Future Work

There are several limitations to the research. One of them refers to the fact that the interviewed students come from a single state university in the northeastern part of Romania, which cannot lead to the generalization of the results. Another limitation stems from the use of a single research method to investigate students' perceptions of ethical issues that arise in online communication in higher education. The use of a single research method provides a simple perspective on the issue of online communication in higher education.

To overcome these limits, future innovative research directions will be established. First of all, the elaboration of a questionnaire based on the topics proposed in the qualitative research will be followed to identify the attitude of the students and teachers from the academic environment toward the rules of online communication. Secondly, the questionnaire-based research will be combined with the research involving the use of the focus group, to develop a mixed methodology for investigating the issue of online communication in academia. Thirdly, research will be proposed involving students and teachers from different universities both in the country and in other countries, to conduct a comparative analysis of perceptions of how to achieve online communication in higher education.

Acknowledgements "This work was supported by a grant of Ministry of Research and Innovation, CNCS—UEFISCDI, project number PN-III-P1-1.1-TE-2016-0773, within PNCDI III".

References

1. Mioduser, D., Nachmias, R., Forkosh-Baruch, A.: New literacies for the knowledge society. In: Knezek, J., Voogt, J. (eds.) International handbook of information technology in education, pp. 23–42. Springer, New York, NY (2008)
2. Gómez, M., Roses, S., Farias, P.: El uso académico de las redes sociales en universitarios. Comunicar. **19**(38), 131–138 (2012)
3. Capurro, R., Pingel, C.: Ethical issues of online communication research. Ethics Inf. Technol. **4**, 189–194 (2002)
4. Papandrea, M.: Social media, public school teachers, and the First Amendment. N. C. Law Rev. **90**, 1597–1642 (2012)
5. Freeman, H., Patel, D., Routen, T., Ryan, S., Scott, B.: The virtual university: The internet and resource-based learning. Routledge, London (2013)
6. Forkosh-Baruch, A., Hershkovitz, A., Ang, R.P.: Teacher-student relationship and SNS-mediated communication: Perceptions of both role-players. Interdiscip. J. E-Ski. Life-Long Learn. **11**, 273–289 (2015)
7. Hong, S.-K., Jun, W.: The Development and Application of a Web-Based Information Communication Ethics Education System. In: Laganá, A., Gavrilova, M. L., Kumar, V., Mun, Y., Tan, C. J. K., Gervasi, O. (eds.), Computational science and its applications—ICCSA 2004. Lecture Notes in Computer Science, vol. 3044, pp. 902–912. Springer, Berlin, Heidelberg(2004). https://doi.org/10.1007/978-3-540-24709-8_95
8. Livingstone, S., Brake, D.R.: On the rapid rise of social networking sites: New findings and poli-cy implications. Child. Soc. **24**, 75–83 (2009)
9. Toprak, E., Özkanal, B., Aydin, S., Kaya, S.: Ethics in e-learning. Turk. Online J. Educ. Technol. **9**(2), 78–86 (2010)
10. Camuse, R.: Code of Ethics: Online learners and teachers (2010). Accessed March 14, 2020 from https://www.slideshare.net/rcamuse/code-of-ethics-for-online-learners-and-teachers
11. Akcaoglu, M., Bowman, N.D.: Using Instructor-led Facebook Groups to Enhance Students' Perceptions of Course Content. Comput. Hum. Behav. **65**, 582–590 (2016)
12. Albayrak, D., Yildirim, Z.: Using social networking sites for teaching and learning: Students´ involvement in and acceptance of Facebook as a course management system. J. Educ. Comput. Res. **52**(2), 155–179 (2015)

13. Chromey, K.J., Duchsherer, A., Pruett, J., Vareberg, K.: Double-edged Sword: Social Media Use in the Classroom. Educ. Media Int. **53**(1), 1–12 (2016)
14. Rezende da Cunha Jr, F., Van Kruistum, C., Van Oers, B.: Teachers and Facebook: using online groups to improve students' communication and engagement in education. **30**(4), 228–241 (2016)
15. Aragon, A., AlDoubi, S., Kaminski, K., Anderson, S.K., Isaacs, N.: Social networking: Boundaries and limits part 1: ethics. TechTrends **58**(2), 25–31 (2014)
16. Jones, J., Gaffney-Rhys, R., Jones, E.: Social network sites and student–lecturer communication: an academic voice. J. Furth. High. Educ. **35**(2), 201–219 (2011)
17. Heath, D., Maghrabi, R., Carr, N.: Implications of information and communication technologies (ICT) for school-home communication. J. Inf. Technol. Educ.: Res. **14**, 363–396 (2015)
18. Moore, J.L., Dickson-Deane, C., Galyen, K.: E-Learning, online learning, and distance learning environments: Are they the same? J. Inf. Technol. Educ.: Res. **14**, 129–135 (2011)
19. Huusimaki, A.-M., Uusitalo-Malmivaara, L., Tirri, K.: The role of digital school-home communication in teacher well-being. Front. Psychol. **10**, 1–8 (2019)
20. Ean, L.C., Lee, T.P.: Educational use of Facebook by undergraduate students in Malaysia higher education: A case study of a private university. Soc. Media Technol. **1**(1), 1–8 (2016)
21. Kwon, O., Yixing, W.: An Empirical Study of the Factors Affecting Social Network Service Use. Comput. Hum. Behav. **26**(2), 254–263 (2010)
22. Greenhow, C., Robelia, B., Hughes, J.H.: Web 2.0 and classroom research: what path should we take now? Educ. Res. **38**, 246–259 (2009)
23. Nagi, K.: Solving ethical issues in eLearning. Special issue of the International Journal of the Computer, the Internet and Management **14**, 71–76 (2006)
24. Asterhan, C., Rosenberg, H.: The promise, reality and dilemmas of secondary school teacher–Student interactions in facebook: The teacher perspective. Comput. Educ. **85**, 134–148 (2015)
25. Ontario College of Teachers: Professional Advisory: Use of Electronic Communication and Social Media (2011). Accessed June 3, 2020 from http://www.otbud12.com/media/OCT-Advisory-on-Social-Media.pdf
26. Teclehaimanot, B., Hickman, T.: Student-teacher interaction on Facebook: What students find appropriate. TechTrends **55**(3), 19–30 (2011)
27. Cunha Jr., F.R., van Kruistum, C., van Oers, B.: Teachers and Facebook: using online groups to improve students' communication and engagement in education. Comm. Teacher **30**(4), 228–241 (2016)
28. Alshahrani, S., Ahmed, E., Ward, R.: The influence of online resources on student–lecturer relationship in higher education: a comparison study. J. Comput. Educ. **4**(2), 87–106 (2017)
29. Froment, F., García González, A.J., Bohórquez, M.R.: The use of social networks as a communication tool between teachers and students: A literature review. Turk. Online J. Educ. Technol. **16**(4), 126–144 (2017)
30. Boyd, D.: It's complicated: The social lives of networked teens. Yael University Press, New Haven, CT (2014)
31. Aydin, S.: Foreign language learners' interactions with their teachers on Facebook. System **42**, 155–163 (2014)
32. Göktas, Z.: Physical education and sport students' interactions with their teachers on Facebook. Anthropologist **21**(1–2), 18–30 (2015)
33. Mazer, J.P., Murphy, R., Simonds, C.J.: The effects of teacher self-disclosure via Facebook on teacher credibility. Learn. Media Technol. Media Technol. **2**, 175–183 (2009)
34. Amichai-Hamburger, Y., Vinitzky, G.: Social network use and personality. Comput. Hum. Behav. **26**, 1289–1295 (2010)
35. Marwick, A.E., Boyd, D.: I tweet honestly, I tweet passionately: Twitter users, context collapse, and the imagined audience. New Media Soc. **13**, 96–113 (2010)
36. O'Connor, K.W., Schmidt, G.B.: "Facebook Fired": Legal Standards for Social Media–Based Terminations of K-12 Public School Teachers. Sage Open, 1–11. (2015). https://doi.org/10.1177/2158244015575636

37. Di Marzo, G.M.: Why can't we be friends? Banning student teacher communication via social media and the freedom of speech. Am. Univ. Law Rev. **62**, 123–166 (2012)
38. Severson, R.J.: The principles of information ethics. Sharpe (1997)
39. Foxman, S.: Can we be friends? Professionally speaking (2009). Accessed June 3, 2020 from http://professionallyspeaking.oct.ca/june_2009/online_friends.asp
40. Nemetz, P.: Faculty social networking interactions: Using social domain theory to assess student views. J. Instr. Pedagog. **8**, 1–13 (2012)
41. Huck, S.W.: Reading Statistic and Research. Pearson Education Inc. (2004)
42. Jamshed, S.: Qualitative research method-interviewing and observation. J. Basic Clin. Pharm. **5**(4), 87–88 (2014)
43. Harrell, M.C., Bradley, M.A.: Data collection methods. Semi-Structured Interviews and Focus Groups. RAND National Defense Research Institute, U.S. (2009)
44. Downe-Wamboldt, B.: Content analysis: method, applications, and issues. Health Care Women Int. **13**(3), 313–321 (1992)
45. DeGroot, J.M., Young, V.J., VanSlette, S.H.: Twitter use and its effects on student perception of instructor credibility. Comm. Educ. **64**(4), 419–437 (2015)
46. Rambe, P., Ng´ambi, D.: Learning with and from Facebook: Uncovering Power Asymmetries in Educational Interactions. Australas. J. Educ. Technol. **30**(3), 312–325 (2014)
47. Al-Dheleai, Y.M., Tasir, Z.: Facebook and education: Students´ privacy concerns. Int. Educ. Studies. **8**(13), 22–26 (2015)
48. Au-Yeung, A.: Let Us Be Friends: Integration of Electronic Communication in Elementary Schools and Ethical Considerations. Master Thesis. University of Toronto, Canada (2015)
49. Nemetz, P., Aiken, K.D., Cooney, V., Pascal, V.: Should faculty use social networks to engage with students? J. Adv. Mark. Educ. **20**(1), 19–28 (2012)
50. Deveci, A., Kolburan, A.: Unethical behaviours preservice teachers encounter on social networks. Educ. Res. Rev. **10**(14), 1901–1910 (2015)
51. Simshaw, D.: Ethical implications of electronic communication and storage of client information. Comput. & Internet Lawyer **33**(8) (2016). Accessed July 18, 2020 from https://ssrn.com/abstract=2814313

Ethics and Privacy in Learning Analytics: The Rise of Chief Privacy and Chief Ethics Officers

Roxana S. Timofte

Abstract Some of the most popular goals of learning analytics are the retention of students, optimization of learning, and data-driven decision making. However, ethics and privacy are among the challenges of learning analytics. Although a few ethics and privacy guidelines were developed along the time, there is still a shortage of leadership necessary to ensure the strategic planning and monitoring of learning analytics. A discussion regarding the role of the chief privacy and chief ethics officers at the university is provided.

Keywords Chief ethics officers · Learning analytics · Privacy · University

1 Learning During Covid-19 Pandemic

Nowadays, the traditional face-to-face education is replaced by computer-based educational systems (e.g., the widely used MOOC) or blended learning systems (hybrid learning). Since the lockdown rules came into effect in 2020, in most countries across Europe, there could be observed a significant increase in the use of online training [1]. The free tools include Zoom, Moodle, Google Classroom, Quizlet, Kahoot, FlipGrid, Ed Dojo (ClassDojo) [2].

In the context of the Covid-19 pandemic, the potential and limitations of online learning could be tested. Hence, the Organization for Economic Co-operation and Development (OECD) defined a few key lessons: the need to develop basic digital skills, to motivate online learners, to develop effective testing and certification methods, to broaden the range of online courses, to train online teachers, to establish quality assurance mechanisms, and to strengthen the digital infrastructure [1]. Furthermore, Nordmann et al. [3] proposed ten rules to handle online education in higher education during the Covid-19 pandemic (Fig. 1).

R. S. Timofte (✉)
Faculty of Psychology and Education Sciences, Department of Science and Mathematics Education, Babeş-Bolyai University, Cluj-Napoca, Romania
e-mail: roxana.timofte@ubbcluj.ro

© The Author(s), under exclusive license to Springer Nature Singapore Pte Ltd. 2022   113
L. Mâță (ed.), *Ethical Use of Information Technology in Higher Education*,
EAI/Springer Innovations in Communication and Computing,
https://doi.org/10.1007/978-981-16-1951-9_8

1) 'A temporary online pivot is not the same as emergency remote teaching or a specialized online course
2) Provide asynchronous content
3) Provide synchronous and asynchronous contact and communication
4) Set and communicate clear expectations about engagement
5) Design appropriate assessments and communicate expectations clearly
6) Monitor and support engagement
7) Review the use and format of recorded content
8) Focus on achievable learning outcomes for field, laboratory, & performance work
9) Ensure resources are available, accessible, and signposted
10) Create a community for staff and students'

Fig. 1 Ten rules to handle online education at university [3]

Most researchers, practitioners, and policy officers in the education field focus nowadays on the strategies to foster e-learning, on improving teachers' digital skills, and on the policies which must be adopted to make e-learning equitable and accessible for all learners [4, 5].

Nevertheless, the importance of adopting ethics and privacy rules when using learning platforms should not be underplayed. Ethics is a moral code comprising rules for the good of the individual and society and can have different connotations across time and cultures [6]. Every human has the basic right to privacy and the legal systems in developed countries include this human right [6].

2 Learning Analytics

2.1 Data Mining and Learning Analytics

Two distinct communities have emerged, with the common goal of using data to assist the learning process and the science of learning [7]: educational data mining (EDM) and learning analytics (LA). Romero and Ventura [7] suggested the following definitions for EDM and LA (Fig. 2).

'**Educational Data Mining (EDM)** is concerned with developing methods for exploring the unique types of data that come from educational environments [...]
Learning Analytics (LA) can be defined as the measurement, collection, analysis, and reporting of data about learners and their contexts, for purposes of understanding and optimizing learning and the environments in which it occurs [...]. There are three crucial elements involved in this definition [...]: data, analysis, and action.'

Fig. 2 Educational data mining and learning analytics: definitions [7, p. 2]

The focus of EDM is on the development of new tools, for the identification of patterns in data, while the focus of LA is on applying the tools and the techniques, aiming at educational challenges [7]. LA is an instrument which can be used for data-driven decision making. Once a pattern was discovered in the data, a prediction could be made, followed by a suitable action [8]. An example of an educational data mining/learning analytics public dataset is the MOOC-Ed Dataset provided by *Harvard Dataverse*. The most used educational data mining/learning analytics methods are causal mining, clustering, the discovery with models, the distillation of data from human judgment, knowledge tracing, nonnegative matrix factorization, outlier detection, prediction, process mining, recommendation, relationship mining, statistics, social network analysis, text mining, visualization, nonnegative matrix factorization [7].

2.2 Why Use Learning Analytics?

Learning analytics stands on the theories and methods from machine learning and data science, statistics, computer science, education, cognitive psychology, neuroscience, and social and learning sciences [9]. The research was undertaken for understanding the interaction of students, by using social network analysis and for understanding the communication of students, by using discourse analytics [5]. There were recently proposed methodologies for bridging the gap between learning analytics and learning design, by using the ADDIE [**A**nalysis, **D**esign, **D**evelopment, **I**mplementation, **E**valuation] approach to learning design [10].

Implementation of learning analytics in higher education can affect: acquiring students (market understanding, personalized recommendations, and community engagement), promoting learning (adaptive support, proactive retention management, personalized communication), offering timely relevant content (adaptive curriculum, scalable delivery, industry integration), delivery methods (world-leading pedagogy, adaptive assessment, managed outcomes framework), supporting alumni networks (strategic employment, alumni and lifelong learning communication, targeted recruitment into research) [11]. The Society for Learning Analytics Research [12] defined the goals of learning analytics (Fig. 3).

'Some of the most popular goal of learning analytics include:
1. Supporting student development of lifelong learning skills and strategies
2. Provision of personalized and timely feedback to students regarding their learning
3. Supporting the development of important skills such as collaboration, critical thinking, communication, and creativity
4. Develop student awareness by supporting self-reflection
5. Support quality learning and teaching by providing empirical evidence on the success of pedagogical innovations'

Fig. 3 Goals of learning analytics, as defined by the Society for Learning Analytics Research [12]

- 'Better institutional decision making and resource use.
- Improved learning for at-risk students.
- Increased institutional transparency.
- Transformative change to teaching methods.
- Better insight into networked knowledge.
- Data-driven experimentation for administrative problems (e.g., enrollment and retainment).
- Increased "organizational productivity and effectiveness."
- Value-ranking of faculty activity.
- Comparative learning metrics for students (e.g., how a student compares to her or his peers in a particular area).'

Fig. 4 Goals of learning analytics [13, p. 145]

Another perspective on the goals of learning analytics is presented in Fig. 4 [13].

2.3 Data-Informed Decision Making in Education

Although it appears that there is space for improvement in evidence-based decision making in education [14], data analytics offers valuable information at different stakeholder levels, from learners' level to governments' level [15, 16], being a potential aid in data-informed decision making [17]. Data can be obtained at different levels of granularity [7].

Triangulation of data is advisable, as the following type of data could be collected [17]: formal data, informal data, research results, big data. Concerning learning analytics, the interaction between instructors, students, the educational or administrative data, demographic data, or data regarding students' affective states are recorded [7, 18]. The benefits of the holistic learning analytics framework proposed by Ifenthaler [16] are depicted in Table 1 for different stakeholder levels, from learner to governance.

The summative perspective refers to information obtained after the completion of a learning phase, while the real-time perspective makes use of ongoing information, the aim being the improvement, through direct interventions. The predictive perspective is advantageous when planning for future strategies and immediate actions [16]. The utilization of student data in learning analytics should take into account the ethics and privacy principles.

3 Ethics and Privacy in Learning Analytics

Higher education institutions (Nottingham Trent University, UK, The Open University, UK, Charles Sturt University, Australia, the University of Sydney, Australia), as well as support organizations and research consortiums (Jisc, LACE, LEA's Box,

Table 1 LA benefit matrix [16, p. 236]

Stakeholder	Perspective		
	Summative	Real time	Predictive
Governance	Apply cross-institutional comparisons Develop benchmarks Inform policymaking Inform quality assurance processes	Increase productivity Apply rapid response to critical incidents Analyze performance	Model impact of organizational decision making Plan for change management
Institution	Analyze processes Optimize resource allocation Meet institutional standards Compare units across programs and faculties	Monitor processes Evaluate resources Track enrolments Analyze churn	Forecast processes Project attrition Model retention rates Identify gaps
Instructional design	Analyze pedagogic models Measure the impact of interventions Increase the quality of the curriculum	Compare learning designs Evaluate learning materials Adjust difficulty levels Provide resources required by learners	Identify learning preferences Plan for future interventions Model difficulty levels Model pathways
Facilitator	Compare learners, cohorts, and courses Analyze teaching practices Increase the quality of teaching	Monitor learning progression Create meaningful interventions Increase interaction Modify content to meet cohorts' needs	Identify learners at risk Forecast learning progression Plan interventions Model success rates
Learner	Understand learning habits Compare learning paths Analyze learning outcomes Track progress toward goals	Receive automated interventions and scaffolds Take assessments including just-in-time feedback	Optimize learning paths Adapt to recommendations Increase engagement Increase success rates

National Union of Students UK), played an important role in the development of learning analytics policies [19]. Ethics, privacy, lawful terms, and data protection are legal challenges of learning analytics [20]. A few frameworks for ethics and privacy in learning analytics were published. However, a thorough discussion of every framework was not the objective of this material.

3.1   Ethics in Learning Analytics

Along the time, researchers strived to develop the ethics framework for good practices in learning analytics [for example, 21]. Schwartz [22] argued that different ethical principles are applicable at different stages in learning analytics.

3.1.1   A *Socio-critical* Perspective on Learning Analytics

Slade and Prinsloo [23] proposed a framework of six principles to tackle ethics and privacy issues in learning analytics, proposing a *socio-critical* perspective on learning analytics:

- **Learning analytics as moral practice**: learning analytics should follow the moral necessities and should not focus only on what is effective. The role of learning analytics is understanding, not measuring.
- **Students as agents**: Students should be treated as collaborators and co-interpreters.
- **Student identity and performance are temporal dynamic constructs**: Data is dynamic, providing information of a student in a particular context and a particular point in time.
- **Student success is a complex and multidimensional phenomenon**: Student success is complex and data used in learning analytics is not complete, and it may be that learning analytics leads to bias or misinterpretation.
- **Transparency**: Universities should offer students information regarding the purpose of data usage and data controllers/processors. Furthermore, data should be protected. Information regarding benchmarks and success indicators should also be made transparent.
- **(Higher) education cannot afford not to use data**: Universities should not ignore the data.

3.1.2   Ethics in Learning Analytics

In 2019, the International Council for Open and Distance Education published a global guide regarding the ethics in learning analytics [24]. A description of the key issues is presented underneath.

Data ownership and control should be controlled by national and international legislation. Exceptional attention should be addressed to the way data is retrieved, deposited, used, or shared with third parties. It is considered that students are "constituted by their data" [24, p. 7], not that they only own the data. Personal and sensitive data should be treated as a special case, and the students should be able to control the collection and usage of such data. Institutions should allow students to correct or add context to their raw data.

Transparency—institutions should inform students and other stakeholders of the purpose of learning analytics, and that most of the time the utilization of learning analytics is more beneficial for the institution than for each student. Transparency should be addressed regarding how data is collected, analyzed, and used to optimize students' learning. Stakeholders should be informed on what data is collected and on what assumptions are made about the data (when data is incomplete, for example).

Accessibility of data can refer to students' capacity to access and correct their data, as well as to the establishment of who can have access to raw and analyzed data. Data is accessed by staff according to their role and on the necessity to access that data.

Validity and reliability of data—when collected and analyzed, data should be correct and representative. Proxy measures should be undertaken with prudence, and generally speaking, datasets should be complete, for robust statistical analyses to be made.

Institutional responsibility and obligation to act—the question which can be raised is: *Since the institution gains information on how students learn, is there also a moral responsibility to take action?* If support intervention is a choice for a student, then the institution should make the intervention transparent and comprehended by all stakeholders.

Communications—predictive analytics is often based on the analysis of past data of students and their results. Considering this, it is important not to overlook the fact that predictive analytics are only that, probabilities generated by a computer. Hence, the recommendation would be that communication with students in such cases to be undertaken in general support terms rather than in probabilistic terms. Furthermore, the staff should be made aware of the fact that the data and its interpretation may have limitations.

Cultural values—understanding and interpreting data should consider the specific context in which the students habituate and perform.

Inclusion—based on learning analytics, some students may be identified as students at risk. This may lead to students' exclusion. However, learning analytics should be used for student support, not exclusion.

Consent is required at the time of registration. However, the use of learning analytics and how this could support their performance is not known to students at this point. If consent is required at registration, students should be informed transparently on how their data is used. Furthermore, the possibility of withdrawing consent should be presented as a possibility for students.

Student agency and responsibility—it is advisable that students are treated as equal participants in the way their data is used. Institutions should involve students in applications of learning analytics. If students are involved in the development and implementation of learning analytics, the following benefits appear:

- University is sure that students are aware of the fact that they should regularly update their information on the learning analytics platform.
- Data regarding the interpretation of students' behaviors is more correct.

- University comprehends to a higher extent what type of intervention and support students need.
- A personalized approach to learning could be implemented, in the university's endeavor to understand how to shape students' learning path, to meet their needs and circumstances.
- Use learning analytics to advise them if it is advisable and in their best interest to continue studying a specific degree or not.

3.1.3   Tensions in the Practical Ethics in Learning Analytics

Kitto and Knight [25] argue that there are a few "tensions" regarding the practices of LA and the continuous interest in ethics and privacy issues associated with the use of LA:

- Overcautious use of LA may lead to its underuse; hence, a balance between the possible subsequent risks of harm and benefits of learning should be found.
- Frameworks are implemented differently in different contexts, for example, during the research activities designed to further develop learning analytics and during its use for institutional objectives.
- There are blurred lines between learning analytics as research and learning analytics as an institutional intervention.

Hence, further developments in the area of practical ethics in LA are necessary [25].

3.2   Privacy in Learning Analytics

"We're being tracked at all times': this is the perception of students on their privacy regarding the utilization of learning analytics" [26]. The lack of an unequivocal conceptualization of students' rights regarding learning analytics in education may be linked to the multifaceted and complex nature of privacy [26]. Some researchers address transparency, consent, and data ownership, while others consider fairness and justice [26].

3.2.1   Origin of Data

Big data generally uses observed, derived, or inferred data, rather than provided data [21]. This may be a concern for the privacy of students, as they may not be aware that data is collected and processed.

Personal data can be classified based on its origin [27]: provided data, observed data, derived data, and inferred data. A description of these types of data is provided according Fig. 5 [21].

'**Provided data** – consciously given by individuals e.g. when filling in an online form
Observed data – recorded automatically e.g. by cookies, sensors, or facial recognition from CCTV pictures
Derived data – produced from other data e.g. calculating customer profitability from the number of items purchased in a store and the number of visits
Inferred data – produced using analytics to find correlations between datasets to categorize or profile people e.g. predicting future health outcomes'

Fig. 5 Classification of personal data according to its origin [21, p. 16]

3.2.2 Privacy in e-Learning Platforms

In 2013, the OECD [28] provided a set of privacy principles, comprising of: collection limitation, data quality, purpose specification, use limitation, security safeguards, openness, individual participation, and accountability. We further present a resolution regarding privacy concerning e-learning platforms [29], a resolution issued at the 40th International Conference of Data Protection and Privacy Commissioners in 2018. A list of actions was established, aimed especially at e-learning platform providers and manufacturers, and Educational authorities (Fig. 6).

3.2.3 The DELICATE Framework

Privacy is one big concern for institutions using analytics on students' data. Drachsler and Greller [30] published the legal frameworks and codes of practice, as well as international ethics and privacy workshops, and proposed a framework, for a trustworthy way of using learning analytics. The components of the DELICATE framework [30] are explained underneath:

- **Determination**: What is the added value of using learning analytics?
- **Explain**: What data will be collected, what will be the purpose of collected data, how long will the data be stored, and who has access to the data?
- **Legitimate**: Why should you collect the data? Is the data already collected not enough?
- **Involve**: All the stakeholders and data subjects should be involved, subjects should have access to their data, and staff should be qualified and trained.
- **Consent**: A contract should be signed with the data subjects, for consent. Clear consent questions should be included in the contract, and the possibility to opt-out should be given.
- **Anonymise**: For as much as possible, the data should be anonymized. Data should be aggregated, for creating metadata models.
- **Technical**: Privacy should be guaranteed, by adopting specific procedures such as regular monitoring of who has access to data, and updating privacy regulations when analytics change.

'The actions required to educational authorities were:
- Ensure they have authority and expertise to engage the services of e-learning platforms
- Develop policies and procedures to evaluate, approve and support the use of e-learning platforms and, were feasible or required, conduct data protection/privacy impact assessments
- Work with other educational authorities and, in cooperation with local data protection authorities, agree on common standards for engaging on e-learning platforms
- Where required or appropriate, seek valid, informed, and meaningful consent from individuals
- Consistent with domestic law, implement a policy for individuals who access the e-learning platform with their electronic devices

Educational authorities and e-learning platform providers and manufacturers are advised to:
- Ensure that e-learning platforms appropriately safeguard users' data and meet the appropriate data protection standards
- Make sure that the purposes for which personal data are being collected, processed, and used are legitimate, suited to the context, and authorized by law.
- Minimize the amount of personal data to be processed.
- Before collecting personal data, notify individuals about the personal data to be processed by the e-learning platform and the reasons for processing
- As far as possible, allow individuals to use the e-learning platform with de-identified data.
- As far as possible, avoid the use of personal data per se, and particularly data on learning behavior, for predictive purposes, profiling, or automated decision-making.
- Embed and employ tools that enable individuals to control their data and effectively exercise their privacy rights, including their right to access, correction, erasure, and, where applicable, data portability.
- Set and respect retention periods for different categories of personal data

E-learning platform providers and manufacturers should consider:
- Be transparent about their data processing practices to both educational authorities and the individuals using the e-learning platforms
- Limit the purposes for collecting personal data as appropriate to the context, and specify in their terms of services or other legal contracts when personal data may be disclosed
- Be clear, specific, and consistent in their terms and conditions of services.
- Adopt Privacy Enhancing Technologies and apply the principles of Privacy by Design and by Default
- Ensure that personal data is stored in compliance with local data protection legislation.'

Fig. 6 Actions required for assuring privacy on e-learning platforms [29]

- **External**: In case the institution works with external providers, it should ensure that they fulfill the national and organizational rules and that data is not used for other purposes than the intended services. A contract should be signed, for data security.

3.3 Staff Awareness and Training

Although there are codes of practice for learning analytics, inevitably institutions could potentially adopt different ethical approaches [21]. Learning analytics will be applied differently, according to the institution's key drivers [21, 23]. The universities' targets for widening participation, for rising the completion rates of disadvantaged students, or maximizing profits may conflict with the findings of learning analytics [21, 31]. Codes of practice suggest that training is given to staff, concerning ethical and legal issues [21].

4 Ethics and Privacy Officers at University: To Hire or Not to Hire?

4.1 Strategic Planning and Policy

Tsai and Gasevic reviewed the learning analytics policies developed by eight institutions and concluded that there are some challenges related to strategic planning and policy [19]. Among them is the shortage of leadership necessary to assure the strategic planning and monitoring of learning analytics.

4.2 The Rise of Chief Ethics and Privacy Officers at University

In early 2020, higher education leaders identified privacy as the second most-critical IT issue [32]. Since the widespread use of blended learning and e-learning, the necessity to sustain strong data privacy and to develop and implement appropriate governance policies and protocols has grown [33]. Neale and Tryniecki [33] argue that the position of the chief privacy officer at university should change from the back-office role to a visible campus ambassador, adopting leadership roles in relation to different stakeholders.

In their article regarding the post-pandemic evolution of student's data privacy, Neale and Tryniecki [33], stated that

> Forward-thinking colleges and universities will embrace this new frontier in higher education by building a robust infrastructure to support ethical data usage, privacy education, and innovation.

Not so long ago, the chief privacy officer (CPO) was employed [34] in the private sector rather than at university. Only recently interest from American universities has grown toward employing personnel to deal with the concerns regarding privacy and data protection [34]. The responsibilities of the chief privacy officers can differ according to the institutional needs, academic missions, and individual styles [34]. Some institutions address privacy in an ad hoc fashion. Other institutions, employing well-established CPOs, are developing strategic plans and privacy principles, playing an important role in the fulfillment of the institution's mission and values [34]. According to a CPO from an American university,

The role of the CPO is evolving as the profession itself has matured, in no small part due to any number of data breaches, in addition to the ever-increasing amount of personal data that is collected by services and devices and the evolution of Big Data. [34]

Another CPO from an American university has proposed to:

see the role as going from virtually nonexistent to one that is playing an increasing[ly] large role in helping the university manage its wealth of data. [34]

An article published in Forbes from 2019 highlighted the fact that a 2018 survey carried out by Deloitte revealed that 32% of the participants rated ethical issues as one of the top three risks of artificial intelligence [35]. Since as early as 2003, Bennett [36] reflected on the necessity of the ethics officers at universities and colleges. Still, in 2020 O'Brien [37] appreciated that

We must come to grips with digital ethics, which I define simply as "doing the right thing at the intersection of technology innovation and accepted social values"

Nowadays, e-learning activities are ubiquitous and the importance of the ethics and privacy officers at universities is indubitable. Furthermore, the employment of chief privacy and chief ethics officers at universities that are using learning analytics may fill the gap of leadership necessary to tackle the learning analytics privacy and ethics issues.

References

1. OECD: The potential of online learning for adults: early lessons from the Covid-19 (2020). Accessed September 15, 2020, from OECD Publishing: https://read.oecd-ilibrary.org/view/?ref=135_135358-ool6fisocq&title=The-potential-of-Online-Learning-for-adults-Early-lessons-from-the-COVID-19-crisis
2. Reimers, F., Schleicher, A., Saavedra, J., Tuominen, S.: Supporting the continuation of teaching and learning during the COVID-19 Pandemic. Annotated resources for online learning (2020). Accessed September 15, 2020 from OECD Publishing, Paris: http://www.oecd.org/education/Supporting-the-continuation-of-teaching-and-learning-during-the-COVID-19-pandemic.pdf
3. Nordmann, E., Horlin, C., Hutchison, J., Murray, J.-A., Robson, L., Seery, M.K., MacKay, J.R.D.: 10 Simple Rules for Supporting a Temporary Online Pivot in Higher Education. PsyArXiv, April 27 (2020)
4. Williamson, B., Eynon, R., Potter, J.: Pandemic politics, pedagogies and practices: digital technologies and distance education during the coronavirus emergency. Learn., Media Technol. **45**(2), 107–114 (2020)
5. Seale, C.: Distance learning during the coronavirus pandemic: equity and access questions for school leaders. Forbes (2020). Accessed September 15, 2020 from Forbes: https://www.forbes.com/sites/colinseale/2020/03/17/distance-learning-during-the-coronavirus-pandemic-equity-and-access-questions-for-school-leaders/#41cf9ca31d4d
6. Drachsler, H., Greller, W., Griffiths, D., Hoel, T. Kickmeier-Rust, M.: Is privacy a show-stopper for learning analytics? A review of current issues and their solutions. Learn. Anal. Rev. **6** (2016). Accessed September 15, 2020 from LACE: http://www.laceproject.eu/learning-analytics-review/files/2016/04/LACE-review-6_privacy-show-stopper.pdf
7. Romero, C., Ventura, S.: Educational data mining and learning analytics: An updated survey. Wiley Interdiscip. Rev. e1355 (2020)

8. Bienkowski, M., Feng, M., Means, B.: Enhancing teaching and learning through educational data mining and learning analytics: An issue brief, pp. 1–57. US Department of Education, Office of Educational Technology (2012)
9. Joksimović, S., Kovanović, V., Dawson, S.: The journey of learning analytics. HERDSA Rev. High. Educ. **6**, 37–63 (2019)
10. Nguyen, A., Gardner, L., Sheridan, D.: A design methodology for learning analytics information systems: Informing learning analytics development with learning design. In: Proceedings of the 53rd Hawaii International Conference on System Sciences, 7–10 January 2020, Hawaii, United States (2020)
11. Gibson, D.C., Ifenthaler, D.: Adoption of learning analytics. In: Ifenthaler, D., Gibson, D.C. (eds.) Adoption of data analytics in higher education learning and teaching, pp. 3–20. Springer, Cham (2020)
12. https://www.solaresearch.org/about/what-is-learning-analytics/
13. Rubel, R., Jones, K.M.L.: Student privacy in learning analytics: An information ethics perspective. Inf. Soc. **32**(2), 143–159 (2016)
14. Gorard, S., Huat See, B.; Siddiqui, N.: What is the evidence on the best way to get evidence into use in education? Review of Education (2020). Accessed September 15, 2020, from https://bera-journals.onlinelibrary.wiley.com/doi/10.1002/rev3.3200
15. Nguyen, A., Gardner, L. A., Sheridan, D.: A multi-layered taxonomy of learning analytics applications. In: Proceedings of the Twenty-First Pacific Asia Conference on Information Systems, 16–20 July 2017, Langkawi Island, Malaysia (2017)
16. Ifenthaler, D., Widanapathirana, C.: Development and validation of a learning analytics framework: Two case studies using support vector machines. Tech. Know Learn. **19**, 221–240 (2014)
17. Schildkamp, K.: Data-based decision-making for school improvement: Research insights and gaps. Educ. Res. **61**(3), 257–273 (2019)
18. Romero, C., Romero, J.R., Ventura, S.: A Survey on Pre-processing Educational Data. In Peña-Ayala, A. (ed): Educational Data Mining: Applications and Trends, Springer Series Studies in Computational Intelligence, pp. 29–64. Springer International Publishing (2014)
19. Tsai, Y.-S., Gašević, D.: Learning analytics in higher education—challenges and policies: A review of eight learning analytics policies. In: Proceedings of the 7th International Conference on Learning Analytics and Knowledge, 13–17 March 2017, Vancouver, BC, Canada (2017)
20. Peña-Ayala, A.: Learning analytics: A glance of evolution, status, and trends according to a proposed taxonomy. WIREs Data Mining Knowl Discov. (2018)
21. Sclater, N.: Code of practice for learning analytics. A literature review of the ethical and legal issues (2014). Accessed September 15, 2020, from Jisc: https://repository.jisc.ac.uk/5661/1/Learning_Analytics_A-_Literature_Review.pdf
22. Schwartz, P.M.: Privacy, ethics, and analytics. IEEE Secur. Priv. **9**, 66–69 (2011)
23. Slade, S., Prinsloo, P., 2013. Learning Analytics: Ethical Issues and Dilemmas. Am. Behav. Sci. **57**(10), 1510–1529 (2013)
24. Slade, S., Tait, A.: Global guidelines: Ethics in learning analytics (2019). Accessed September 15, 2020, from International Council for Open and Distance Education: https://www.icde.org/knowledge-hub/the-aim-of-the-guidelines-is-to-identify-which-core-principles-relating-to-ethics-are-core-to-all-and-where-there-is-legitimate-differentiation-due-to-separate-legal-or-more-broadly-cultural-env-5mppk
25. Kitto, K., Knight, S.: Practical ethics for building learning analytics. Br. J. Edu. Technol. **50**(6), 2855–2870 (2019)
26. Jones, K.M.L., Asher, A., Goben, A., Perry, M.R., Salo, D., Briney, K.A., Robertshaw, M. B.: "We're being tracked at all times": Student perspectives of their privacy in relation to learning analytics in higher education. Journal of the Association for Information Science and Technology, 1–16. (2020)
27. ICO (Information Commissioner's Office): Big data and data protection (2014). Accessed September 15, 2020, from Council of Europe (COE): https://rm.coe.int/big-data-and-data-protection-ico-information-commissioner-s-office/1680591220

28. OECD: OECD guidelines on the protection of privacy and transborder flows of personal data (2013). Accessed September 15, 2020, from OECD Publishing, Paris: http://www.oecd.org/sti/ieconomy/oecdguidelinesontheprotectionofprivacyandtransborderflowsofpersonaldata.htm
29. Office of the Information and Privacy Commissioner, Alberta, Canada, Office of the Information and Privacy Commissioner, Ontario, Canada, Office of the Privacy Commissioner of Canada, Office for Personal Data Protection, Czech Republic, Commission Nationale de l'Informatique et des Libertés, France: Resolution on e-learning platforms. In: 40th International Conference of Data Protection and Privacy Commissioners, 23 October 2018, Brussels, Belgium (2018)
30. Drachsler, H., Greller, W.: Privacy and Analytics—it's a DELICATE issue. A Checklist to establish trusted Learning Analytics. In: 6th Learning Analytics and Knowledge Conference, 25–29 April 2016, Edinburgh, UK (2016)
31. Prinsloo, P., Slade, S., Galpin, F.: Learning Analytics: Challenges, Paradoxes and Opportunities for Mega Open Distance Learning Institutions. In: Proceedings of the 2nd International Conference on Learning Analytics and Knowledge, 29 April 2012, Vancouver British Columbia, Canada (2012)
32. Grajek, S.: The 2019–2020 EDUCAUSE IT issues panel: Top 10 IT issues, 2020: The drive to digital transformation begins. EDUCAUSE Review Special Report (2020). Accessed September 15, 2020, from EDUCAUSE Review: https://er.educause.edu/articles/2020/1/top-10-it-issues-2020-the-drive-to-digital-transformation-begins
33. Neale, M., Mryniecki, M.: The post-pandemic evolution of student data privacy. EDUCAUSE review (2020). Accessed September 15, 2020, from EDUCAUSE Review: https://er.educause.edu/articles/2020/8/the-post-pandemic-evolution-of-student-data-privacy
34. Vogel, V.: The chief privacy officer in higher EDUCATION. EDUCAUSE Review (2015). Accessed September 15, 2020, from EDUCAUSE Review: https://er.educause.edu/articles/2015/5/the-chief-privacy-officer-in-higher-education
35. Insights team: Rise of the chief ethics officer. Forbes (2019). Accessed September 15, 2020, from Forbes: https://www.forbes.com/sites/insights-intelai/2019/03/27/rise-of-the-chief-ethics-officer/
36. Bennett, J.B.: Do colleges and universities need ethics officers? Acad. Lead.Ship: Online J. 1(2), Article 4 (2003)
37. O'Brien, J.: Digital Ethics in higher education: 2020. EDUCAUSE Review (2020). Accessed September 15, 2020, from EDUCAUSE Review: https://er.educause.edu/articles/2020/5/digital-ethics-in-higher-education-2020

Evaluation of Text Entities for Redundancy Detection on Written and Multimedia Contents

Cosmin Tomozei

Abstract This study focuses on the determination of intrinsic and extrinsic redundancy on text entities for the study of information replication. Redundancy presumes on the one hand that different entities behave in the same way when we talk about software and on the other hand, it contains the same information when we talk about data structures. Text entities are practically large data structures that have been formally evaluated. Nowadays, while taking into account the ethics in the utilization of information technology, it is essential to establish whether a certain number of texts, written or listened to, contain similar ideas, which may not be appropriated ethically. Actions should be taken such as the addition, modification, or deletion of data according to the results of the evaluation procedure. The evaluation procedure should be done either partially or completely in an automatic way, technology allowing both methods. This study intends to present a way to proceed in the evaluation of content, by implementing a set of metrics on text entities, which have to lead to the evaluation conclusion, should any modifications or updates be necessary to achieve a level of desired originality.

Keywords Ethics · Evaluation · Multimedia content · Redundancy

1 Text Analytics Technologies for Content (Re)structuring

In the field of computer science, text analytics is defined as a process of meaning extraction from verbal (multimedia) or written communication. In [1] text mining, it is also defined as a domain of science relating to natural language processing, which aims at gathering knowledge and information from a collection of large text documents. The text mining [2] process aims to build data relations and ontologies based on the written or multimedia data retrieved from documents.

C. Tomozei (✉)
Vasile Alecsandri University of Bacau, Bacau, Romania
e-mail: cosmin.tomozei@ub.ro

© The Author(s), under exclusive license to Springer Nature Singapore Pte Ltd. 2022   127
L. Mâță (ed.), *Ethical Use of Information Technology in Higher Education*,
EAI/Springer Innovations in Communication and Computing,
https://doi.org/10.1007/978-981-16-1951-9_9

The data is analyzed by patterns and contexts. Sometimes, when taking into consideration the customer experience, software applications analyze through automatic procedures the text that was uploaded by customers on online stores, such as reviews and informative messages. Patterns are to be identified and certain actions are taken to solve particular problems and increase the level of customers' satisfaction. Text analytics involves the restructuring of textual information to create data structures, such as lists, trees, files, databases, or ontologies, from which the information is processed in a technically reliable way. This approach consists of the structuring of unstructured data, from which dependable information may be further extracted and reliable decisions may be further taken.

Sound files may easily be transformed into text, with the help of software applications such as Speech–to–Text (Dictation) available in Office 365 or Speechnotes [3]. Automatic procedures of evaluation are also built as well for reading emails and for chatbots user text interaction, based on certain keywords or sentences of interest. The users often get automatic replies from robots or chatbots, which are as accurate as if they were texting, or talking to human persons. In this way, a scientist may deduct additional meanings and information based on user-generated content, but in many cases, the amount of redundancy becomes higher and almost impossible to control.

In this paper, we intend to study the intrinsic redundancy of user-generated content, to keep it within acceptable limits, and to use the redundant information if necessary, in other contextual situations. We intend to define a procedure of analyzing the textual amount of data for the elaboration of best user recommendations, based on the written information. Unlocking the meaning of unstructured written information sometimes becomes problematic in terms of formalization. It is difficult to create a set of indicators that are accurate in 100% of the situations. We do not intend to go to such a higher level of precision or accuracy, but to underline that certain statistical indicators could be utilized for textual analysis scenarios.

Other economic sectors, such as recruitment or retail often make use of automated textual analysis using text mining and text engineering technologies. In [4] the screening and evaluation processes, they are applied to unstructured sets of resumes uploaded by employment candidates on professional networks. This process becomes efficient by reducing the time and the costs of manual evaluation of thousands of profiles, while decreasing the number of errors is generated by manual information processing. In this case, the analysis also considers elaboration of recommendations through recommender systems intending to bring the right person in the right place and cover three "types of fits: person-job, person-team, and person-organization". In our study, we intend to reflect on the method that should be employed to construct a set of dependable indicators for text analysis or user-generated content analysis.

We intend to determine whether patterns and themes are to be identified and what steps should be taken forward in exploiting such patterns and themes to create a framework for text redundancy analysis. Having a clear image of the level of text redundancy will permit a more effective data management strategy. The level of data multiplication of text components, paragraphs, or phrases may lead to the increase of the level of text complexity and dimension, while the number of expressed ideas and the amount of valuable information stays the same. Consequently, automatic actions are to be taken to reduce the dimension of text and to extract the valuable information which is to be stored and processed for the decision-making process.

Some significant features of text analytics and text mining software [5] highlight the role of textual information in a data-driven digital world that is permanently increasing, as well as the need for processing unstructured content and user-generated information that is also constantly increasing and the need for extraction of numerical data (numerical indicators). The paper [5] reflects the development of a textual analysis software—Heracles, based on JAVA programming language that relies on object-oriented programming principles.

In our study, we briefly present some preliminary software development elements, including source code for the TextEngEval—Text Engineering and Evaluation software, which were developed in .NET Framework with the Visual C#.NET programming language. This framework is very well documented and also comprises a large set of libraries and classes for working with text elements. The .NET Framework provides many functionalities for the development of user-friendly graphical interfaces as and for the use of WCF or RESTful services. The platform also supports the development of productive and accurate algorithms and numerical functions. This approach allows deriving information from a text and supports working with many formats of text documents, from simple text (.txt) documents to word databases, XML formats, and Office documents (Word Automation). The C# programming language and the .NET classes have the necessary instruments to work with string objects.

One of the most important text analysis procedures consists of data information retrieval. Based on particular words, inferences are made to determine the presence of certain words in the text and certain groups of words or sentences. These patterns are further studied in an attempt to identify their frequency and distribution within the text. Once identified, the elements of interests, annotations, and associations are transferred to a certain context to proceed to predictions. Algorithms and methods of natural language processing achieve the interpretation of the gathered information. In the case of information redundancy, the text must be restructured to reduce the level to the minimum. For example, in Fig. 1 we show a sequence of source code in C# in which we want to express that each member of the group (array) of people (names) goes home at 10 pm.

The initial text included four sentences, indicating that each person intends to go home at 10 pm. The procedure of analysis has led to the construction of an array of four persons static string[] names = {"Alex", "John", "Diana", "Cristina"}; and a rule which states that for each member of the group a parameterized string is being built, with the sentence "{0} is going home at 10 pm." Where { } represents the parameter substituting the name of each person and 0 is the position of each person's name in the sentence. In this way, instead of storing several sentences that were essentially the same, we proceeded to the construction of a rule that applies to each person from the group.

In [6], the concepts and technologies regarding sentiment analysis are described concerning the opinion extracted from texts, aiming at determining the writer's opinion about a particular event, product, service, idea. Based on sentiment analysis,

```
using System;
namespace Strings
{ class String1
    {
        static string[] names = {"Alex", "John", "Diana", "Cristina"};
        static void Main(string[] args)
        {
            Console.BackgroundColor = ConsoleColor.White;
            Console.ForegroundColor = ConsoleColor.Blue;
            Console.WriteLine("Working with strings!");
            foreach (string sname in names)
            {
                string str1 = String.Format("{0} is going home at 10 pm.",
sname);
                Console.WriteLine(str1);
            }
            Console.ReadKey();
        }
    }
}
```

Fig. 1 Strings simple application in C#

the results could be either positive, negative, or neutral. However, sentiment analysis relies on machine learning algorithms and powerful natural language processing algorithms.

Sentiment analysis is often named as opinion mining or emotion artificial intelligence and intends to conclude numerically about subjective textual information. In other words, it intends to quantify the affective states based on subjective information. We have to keep in mind that all public texts that any particular author publishes online or offline may be subjected to sentiment analysis. Social media posts are sometimes analyzed [7] as well to find out how users feel about certain events or certain products or services. Contextual and customized recommendations related to shopping for products or to attend to certain events are then automatically offered to the user.

We believe that sentiment analysis involves profiling and provides to companies asymmetric information about the customers. The customers and the users, in general, should have the power to decide whether they admit being profiled based on their feelings and preferences or not. In any case, the user has the right not to be subject to any decision based only on the automatic decision-making process.

Figure 2 shows how text analytic works and how the Azure sentiment analysis [8] may be implemented either as a web application or as a JSON service.

When visiting the https://azure.microsoft.com/en-us/services/cognitive-services/ text-analytics/ URL, the user can test the sentiment analysis application and obtain the result either as a table or as JSON. A text related to the user preference for salads has been written online. The language has been automatically detected as English, with a confidence degree of 100%. Practically, the application identified the language as English without any doubt. The text has been parsed, and the key phrases have

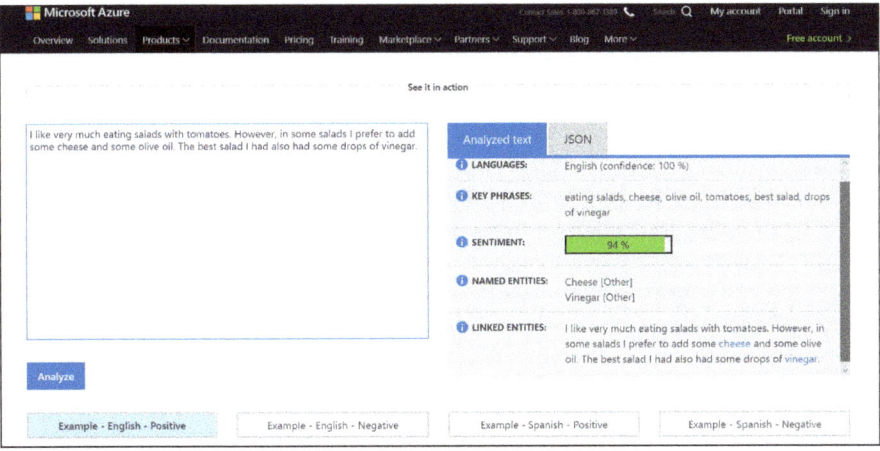

Fig. 2 Azure sentiment analysis

been extracted. A set of keywords resulted containing the following idioms: eating salads, cheese, olive oil, tomatoes, best salad, drops of vinegar.

The analysis went forward and associated the preference for the salad with the terms "cheese" and "vinegar" which have been extracted as named entities and the logical links of these entities to the other phraseological structures have been further analyzed. It resulted that the user-generated text has shown a positive feeling of 94% about adding cheese and vinegar to the salad.

This example has been defined in a very straightforward way, not a very technical one. It shows the power of Cloud Artificial Intelligence and text analytics APIs for the development of intelligent software applications.

This Cloud-based API then reflected the following structural elements:

- sentiment analysis, which shows whether the feeling of the user about a certain subject is either positive, negative, or neutral; in our case, it has been positive with a certainty level of 94%;
- key phrase extraction, such as the elements identified in Fig. 2, eating salads, cheese, olive oil, best salad, drops of vinegar;
- language detection, which in our case is English, identified with a level of precision of 100%;
- entity recognition that has shown the most important elements of our text, namely cheese and vinegar.

Azure Cognitive Services API provides a set of tools and technologies that analyze the text through powerful machine learning and artificial intelligence algorithms for many types of projects in various use-case scenarios. Cognitive services are also involved in the detection of intrinsic redundancy of text entities and user-generated content.

2 Text Processing Applications Engineering and Reengineering Concepts

This section aims at creating a framework for text entities' evaluation and transformation, using software engineering and reengineering methodologies. In [6], the process of text entities reengineering is presented. By analogy, the concept of reengineering of software applications involves the following practical aspects.

At first, we proceed to the definition of a new objective that should be achieved. The new objective differs significantly from the initial objective of the application. It should make a qualitative leap in input data and the level of the results it returns the application distributed as an output of reengineering processes. In other words, we need to adapt the existing text to a new objective and try to achieve the new objective with a higher level of quality and accuracy.

The process of reengineering also presumes the existence of a text entity to be subjected to the transformation process, so that the components remaining in the structure link with the new components are determined. New modules are introduced into the structure that the resulting application or text entity should become a finished, well-built product with a normal level of redundancy and a higher level of coherence.

The process of choosing a technology to make new modules text entity involves new architectures, diagrams, object classes, databases, relational tables, which are included in the new application. The resulting structure together with the items from the previous steps that remained in the application allows the creation of a new construction that is unified and does not show any weaknesses in terms of architecture.

Text entities reengineering also imply the establishment of practical ways of measuring the quality of each iteration result within the engineering processes. The process of reverse engineering starts from the existing implementations and goes up to the abstract architectural level. The process of reverse engineering presumes successive transformations until the result reaches the desired level of quality. The management of risks takes into consideration the amount of time and budgets which should not be exceeded. The estimates of the durations and costs of the software reengineering process for distributed applications to ensure that high-quality final results are achieved.

The following concepts take into consideration the reengineering of a text analytics distributed application. The process of reengineering entails the radical transformation of the existing application to achieve new functionalities in text analytics. We call that process information-driven add-on reengineering. It consists of a process based on the new objectives of the software application, and depending on them the need for information to be added to the system is determined. Switching from monolithic architecture to three-level modular architecture involves redefining the data distribution problem and software on each level of the application, as well as adding the database level.

To start the transformation process, we have to identify the situations where the software application in the original form becomes not operational or unusable. This is the reason why the reengineering operations need to be carried out and certain actions have to be taken to remove structural deficiencies.

The list of operations for the TextEngEval text analysis application shall be considered before making any transformations generated by the reengineering process are to be made.

Oper01—the reading of data entered by the users;
Oper02—user-generated content validation and data validation;
Oper03—the construction of text objects based on the user-generated content;
Oper04—the writing of texts on specialized controls, such as text boxes or rich text boxes;
Oper05—the definition of indicators, e.g., redundancy indicators;
Oper06—the text process algorithms instance creation;
Oper07—extraction of the main text ideas by machine learning and natural language processing algorithms;
Oper08—determination of the degree of redundancy;
Oper09—determination of the level of originality.

The requirements of the user are added to the structure of the application through the reengineering process, to implement the new requirements.

Oper11—reading the data from text files and word documents;
Oper12—data storage and serialization;
Oper13—the computing of the textual relations among entities (words) and phrases using machine learning algorithms;
Oper14—the elaboration of sentiment analysis;
Oper15—the computing of session durations;
Oper16—the graphical representation of textual relations between entities and the linked entities;
Oper17—the JSON representation of the textual data.

The list of operations is generalized without difficulty and still binds with multitudes of operations with nproper components.

The original ES^{init} application is to be considered, with operations that were implemented before the reengineering process.

$$ES^{init} = < Oper_1^0, Oper_2^0, Oper_3^0, \ldots Oper_i^0 \ldots Oper_{nroper-1}^0, Oper_{nroper}^0 > \quad (1)$$

where

$Oper_i^0$—the operation i, of the application ES^{init}, before the process of reengineering;

nroper—the number of operations of the initial application ES^{init}.

In the structure of the application, a lot of new operations are added, presented in the relationship:

$$ES^{nou} = < Oper^0_{j1}, Oper^0_{j2}, Oper^0_{j3}, \ldots Oper^0_{j1} \ldots Oper^0_{jnroper-1}, Oper^0_{j\,nroper1} >$$

$$(2)$$

where

$Oper^1_{ji}$—the operation i from the set of operation added through reengineering ES^{nou};

nroper1—the number of new operations that were added through the process of reengineering.

The set of operations implemented by the application ES^{Fin} obtained by reengineering is gathered by the reunion of the two previous sets of operations ES^{init} and ES^{nou}.

$$ES^{fin} = ES^{init} \cup ES^{nou}$$

$$(3)$$

In relation (4), the elements of the ES^{fin} set are presented as a result of the completion of architectural transformations, through the reengineering process:

$$EES^{init} = < Oper^0_1, Oper^0_2, Oper^0_3, \ldots Oper^0_3 \ldots Oper^0_i, Oper^0_{ji} \ldots Oper^0_{nroper}, Oper^1_{j\,nroper1} >$$

$$(4)$$

The realization of two new reengineering operations adds two elements to the set of operations performed on the structure of the computer application.

The specific of the application requires measures of reengineering process such as:

- the adding of classes that include existing functions;
- the adding of classes of objects with completely new methods in which machine learning algorithms are implemented for working with text;
- the adding of interface classes to give clarity to the model and architecture of the distributed application;
- the mechanisms for the authentication and authorization process;
- the invoking of web services to perform machine-to-machine communication;
- the addition of relational tables to store data on new entities of distributed application structure;
- adding stored procedures for better management of transactions on databases within distributed applications;
- adding methods for automatic collection of test data;
- adding procedures for assessing the quality of the software entity resulting from the reengineering process.

The ED set of operations that are eliminated by the reengineering process and the set ESR of elements remaining in the software application structure shall be considered. In relationship (3), the set of remaining elements in the structure is presented, as the difference between the set of existing elements of ES^{fin} and the set of removed elements.

$$ESR = ES^{fin} - ED \tag{5}$$

The modification of components in the structure of the original software application is carried out in three steps. The first step is to extract modules from the set. In the second step, the extracted items are updated by removing, adding, or modifying lines of code, and will be reintegrated into the software application structure in the third step.

Modified operations belonging to the *ESM* set are extracted from the application structure, being updated in terms of implemented algorithms that are subsequently reintegrated into the structure of the application.

$$ES^{fin} = \left(ES^{init} - ED\right) \cup ESM \tag{6}$$

Switching to new versions of distributed applications is mainly achieved through reengineering with information-driven addition.

The host of the modules of the original application, *EM*^{init} consisting of modules:

$$EM^{init} = < M_0, \ M_1, \ M_2, \ M_3, \ M_4, \ M_5, \ \ldots, \ M_k, \ \ldots M_{nrmod-1}, \ M_{nrmod} \tag{7}$$

The set of new modules E^{Nou}, added in the structure of the application is shown in (8)

$$E^{Nou} = < N_1, \ N_2, \ \ldots, \ N_k, \ \ldots N_{nrmod1} > \tag{8}$$

The final version of the text processing application EM^{Fin} is obtained through the reunion of the sets EM^{init} and E^{Nou}.

$$EM^{fin} = EM^{init} \cup E^{Nou} \tag{9}$$

The evolution for the final version of the application presumes the guided addition of information to:

- insert the module N_0 between the module M_2 and M_3;
- insert the modules N_1 and N_2 between the modules M_4 and M_5;
- By adding modules, the M_3 becomes M_3' and the M_5 becomes M_5';
- The *Nnrmod1* element is added after the last item.

The version resulting from the process of reengineering with directed information addition is:

$$EM^{fin} = < M_0, \ M_1 M_2, \ N_0 M_3', \ M_4 N_1, \ N_2 M_5' \ \ldots, \ M_k, \ldots M_{nr\,mod\,+1}, \ M_{nr\,mod\,+2}, \ N_{nr\,mod\,1} > \tag{10}$$

The transformation of the application to achieve new objectives by guided addition of information is a very demanding process requiring much attention and an appropriate allocation of resources by the development teams.

3 Indicators for Automation in Working with Text Entities

The process of automation of working with text is very demanding as well and requires the definition of a set of indicators or metrics for text entities evaluation. The more user-generated content evolves, the more we'll have a permanent image about the size and the structure of the text at any moment.

The index of user-generated text, ID_{txt} is given by the relation (11)

$$ID_{txt} = \frac{DTxt_R}{DTxt_{init}} \tag{11}$$

where

$DTxt_R$—the dimension of the transformed text

$DTxt_{init}$—the dimension of the initial text.

When the value of the ID_{txt} indicator is overunit, the dimension of the user-generated text increased in time. If the value is underunit, then the size of the text was reduced, probably because of rephrasing or reduction of redundancy.

The indicator IWS of words structure is based on the following relation (12)

$$IWS = \frac{Frecv_i}{NumWords} \tag{12}$$

where

- $Frecv_i$—the frequency of word i within the text
- Numwords—the total number of words from the text

In Sect. 4, the development of TextEngEval application is analyzed. The application takes into account both indicators ID_{txt} and IWS, presented in the relations (11) and (12). Both indicators are relevant for the construction of text processing applications and the process of software transformation.

4 TextEngEval—A .NET Application for Text Engineering and Automation

The TextEngEval application has been developed on the .NET Framework with the Visual C#.NET programming language aiming at showing to the users and researchers a simple intuitive way of automatically working with text. This type of application may be used for the validation of abstracts and scientific papers in terms of structure. In Fig. 3, the main screen of the application is presented.

The application has an intuitive top menu that specifies the facility of parsing both simple text files (.txt) and word documents. Figure 4 shows the method implemented by the top menu for opening the text files.

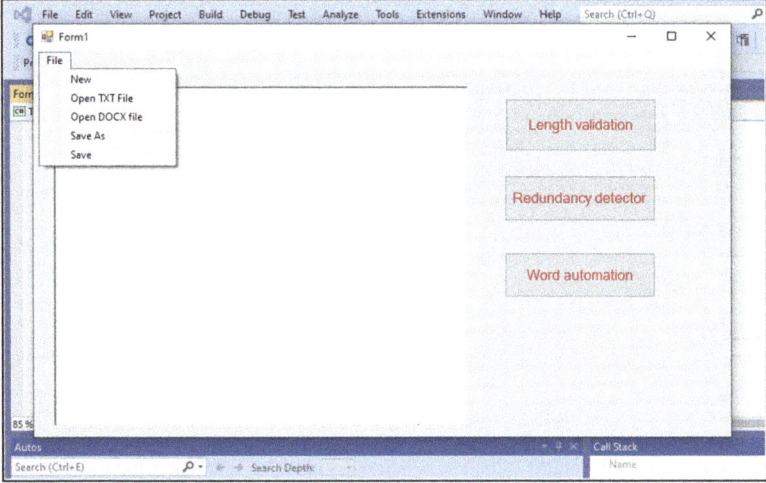

Fig. 3 TextEngEval main screen

```
private void openToolStripMenuItem_Click(object sender, EventArgs e)
    {
        try
        {
            OpenFileDialog ofd = new OpenFileDialog();
            ofd.Filter= "Text files (*.txt)|*.txt";
            if (ofd.ShowDialog() == DialogResult.OK)
            {
                var path1 = ofd.FileName;
                var texstream = ofd.OpenFile();
                var textread = string.Empty;
                using (StreamReader reader = new StreamReader(texstream))
                {
                    textread+= reader.ReadToEnd();
                    richTextBox1.Text = textread.ToString();
                    dimens = textread.Length;
                }

                richTextBox1.Text += Environment.NewLine;
                richTextBox1.Text += string.Format("Dimension is {0} characters",dimens);
            }
        }
        catch (Exception exc)
        {
            MessageBox.Show(exc.Message);
        }
    }
```

Fig. 4 Method for opening the text files

The main component of this method is the OpenFileDialog control, from the .NET Framework. The object is practically an instance of the OpenFileDialog class [9], which is defined by the framework in the following manner: public sealed class OpenFileDialog: System.Windows.Forms.FileDialog (Fig. 5).

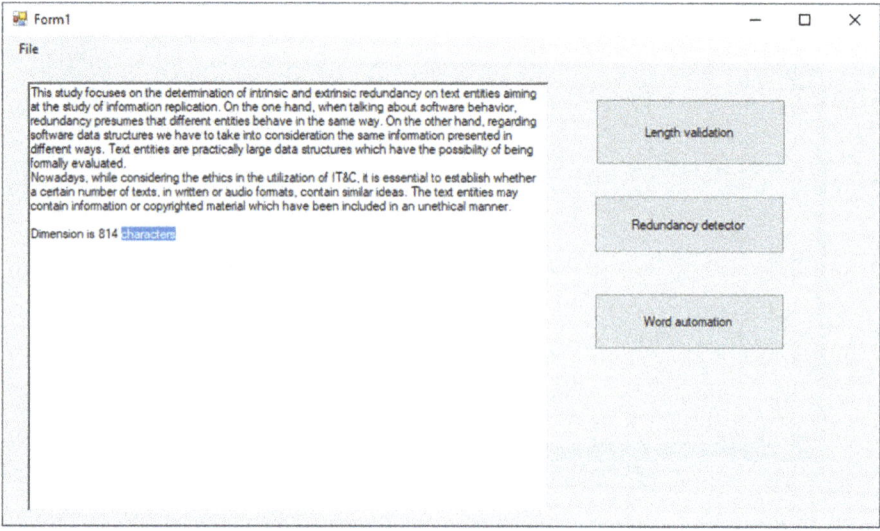

Fig. 5 Abstract length

The control is filtered, meaning that the only types of files that could be open are the text files. Another essential component of the method from Fig. 4 is the StreamReader [10]. The StreamReader allows the reading of the text files data as a stream of bytes and provides the length property, meaning that we may determine straightforwardly the length of the text written by the users. This approach will help us in the validation of paper abstracts, from Fig. 6.

```
private void LenVal_Click(object sender, EventArgs e)
        {
            switch (dimens)
            {
                case int dim when (dim > 0 && dim <=1000) :
                    MessageBox.Show ("Text is short!", "Text is
short!",MessageBoxButtons.OKCancel,MessageBoxIcon.Information); break;

                case int dim when (dim > 1000 && dim <= 2000):
                    MessageBox.Show("Text is almost OK in size!", "Text is
almost OK! in size", MessageBoxButtons.OKCancel,
MessageBoxIcon.Information); break;

                case int dim when (dim > 2000 && dim <= 2500):
                    MessageBox.Show("Text is OK!", "Text is OK!",
MessageBoxButtons.OKCancel, MessageBoxIcon.Information); break;
                default:MessageBox.Show("Please enter some text!");break;
            }
        }
```

Fig. 6 Abstract validation method

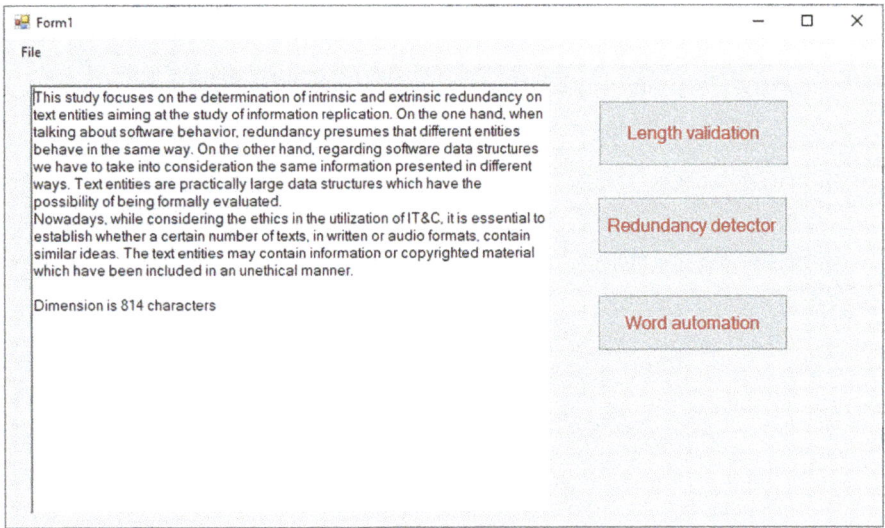

Fig. 7 Reformatted text

The method LenVal studies the length of the text inserted by the user. If the entered text is greater than zero characters and less or equal to 1000 characters, a message box will appear, notifying the user that the text is too short (Fig. 7).

If the length of the text is greater than 1000 characters and less than 2000 characters, then a message is sent to the user that the dimension of the abstract is almost OK. If the length of the submitted abstract is between 2001 and 2500 characters, the users receive a message that the length of the abstract is OK (Fig. 8).

The reformatted text in Fig. 7 is realized due to the method Form1_Load which enables the font by the object System.Drawing.Font. The constructor of the font object has two parameters, the font name and the font size (Fig. 9).

When the user clicks on the redundancy detector button, it is redirected to the second form. In the second form, Form2 has two components. The first component consists of a list box. The list box contains the distinct words appearing in the abstract in alphabetic order.

Each click on a particular word from the list calculates the frequency of appearance of the selected word in the abstract. The user has the possibility of defining thresholds,

```
        private void Form1_Load(object sender, EventArgs e)
        {
            richTextBox1.Font = new System.Drawing.Font("Microsoft
Sans Serif", 10);
        }
```

Fig. 8 Form_Load method

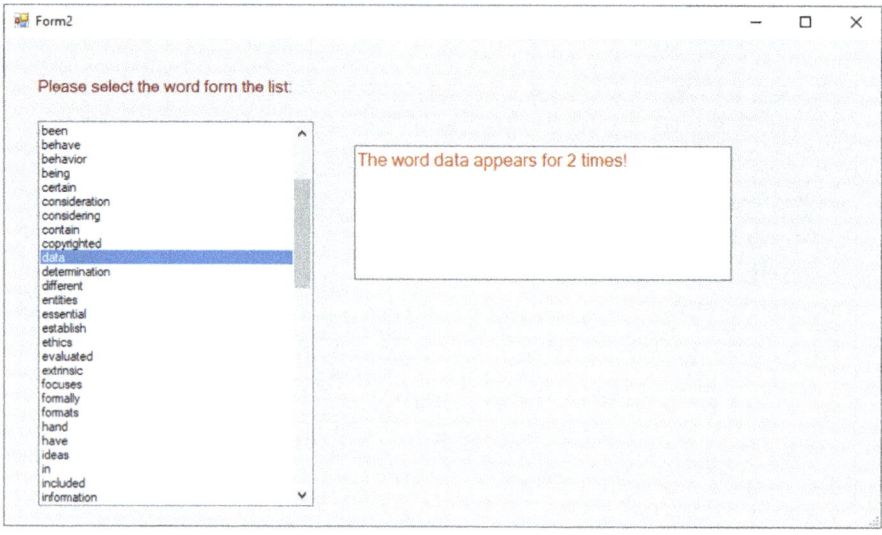

Fig. 9 Word frequency

meaning that a certain word, if repeated several times, leads to the redundancy of the text.

Figure 10 shows the frequency of the word "at" in the abstract. It appears just once, meaning that it is not redundant. The value of the indicator is 0.7%.

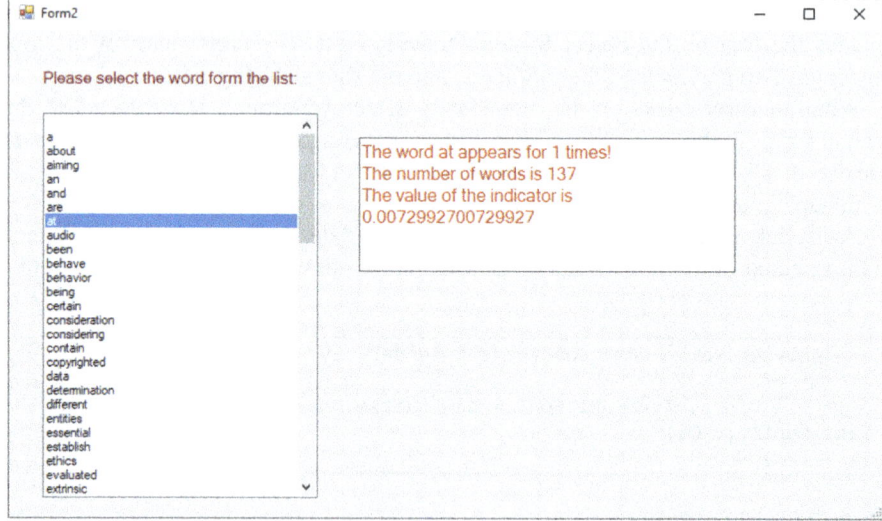

Fig. 10 "at" word frequency with indicator value

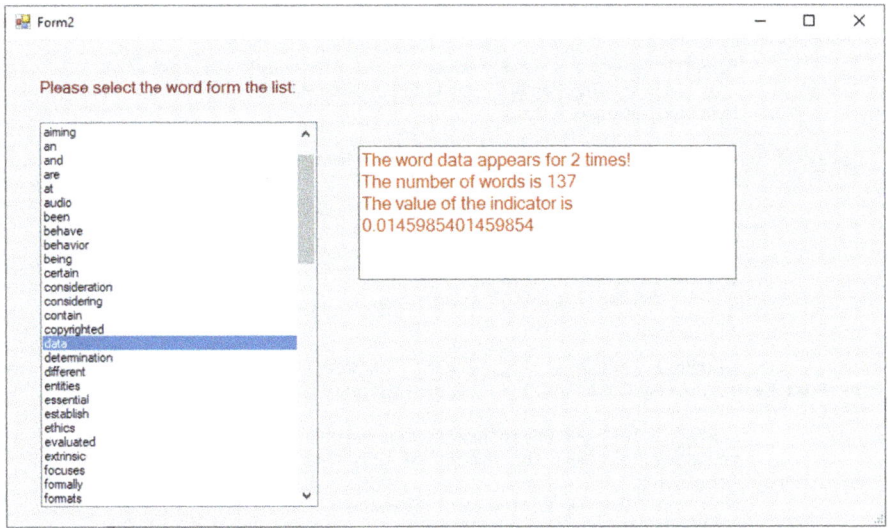

Fig. 11 "data" word frequency with indicator value

Figure 11 shows the frequency of the word "data" in the abstract. It appears twice, meaning that it is not redundant. The value of the indicator is 1.45%.

Figure 12 shows the frequency of the word "in" in the abstract. It appears five times, meaning that it might be redundant. The value of the indicator is 3.64%.

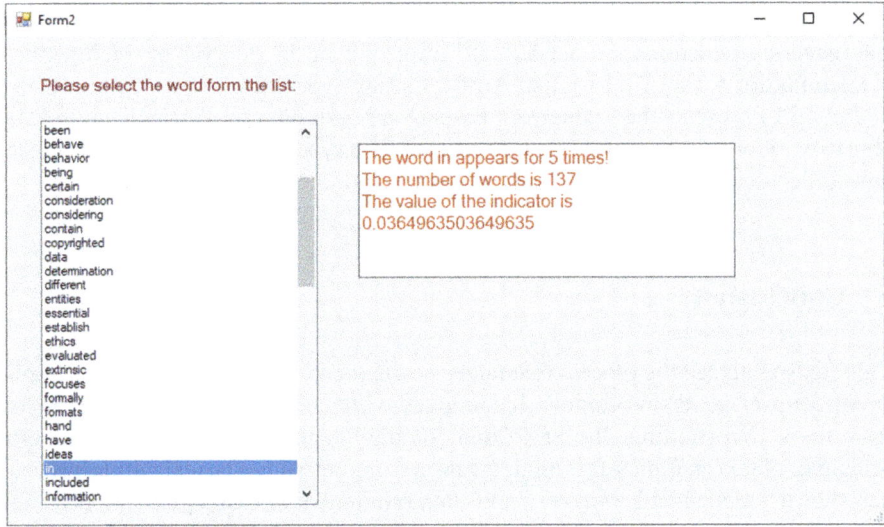

Fig. 12 "in" word frequency with indicator value

```
private void Form2_Load(object sender, EventArgs e)
    {
            foreach (string s in Form1.arrayList.ToArray().Distinct())
                if (s!=string.Empty)  listBox1.Items.Add(s);
            listBox1.Sorted = true
    }
  private void listBox1_SelectedIndexChanged(object sender, EventArgs e)
    {
            string buff = listBox1.SelectedItem.ToString();
            int counter=0;
            foreach (string s in Form1.arrayList)
            {
                if (s.Equals(buff)) counter++;
            }

            textBox1.Text = string.Format("The word {0} ",
listBox1.SelectedItem.ToString() + " appears for " +counter.ToString()+  "
times!" );
            textBox1.Text += Environment.NewLine;
            textBox1.Text += "The number of words is " +
Form1.arrayList.Count;
            textBox1.Text += Environment.NewLine;
            double indicator = (double)counter / Form1.arrayList.Count;
            textBox1.Text += "The value of the indicator is " +
indicator.ToString();
            }
```

Fig. 13 Source code for the redundancy application

Considering that the word is a preposition, it should not affect the redundancy of the text.

In Fig. 13, the source code of the application is presented, displaying the algorithm that calculates the indicators and the subsequent controls used for user interaction. The generic collections are needed and implemented as queryable. Such generic collections are ArrayList, List, and Array of string-type data.

Figure 14 presents the Framework Extension possibility, for the application to be able to work with Microsoft Office documents. The process of automation can create new Office documents and automatically work with them.

5 Conclusions

This study analyzed the process redundancy on text entities for the information replication for user-generated content. It continued with a process of meaning extraction from the verbal (multimedia) or written communication and followed the general principles of text analytics, text mining, and text engineering. The text mining process has shown a dependable way to build data relations and ontologies based on the written or multimedia data retrieved from documents, either simple text documents or more complex Office documents.

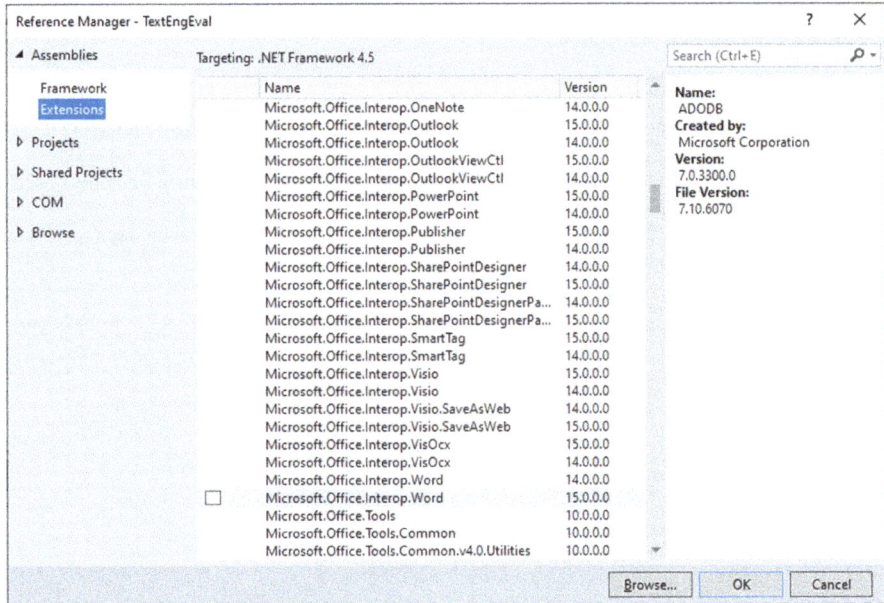

Fig. 14 .NET Framework extensions

The TextEngEval application has been developed on the .NET Framework with the Visual C#.NET programming language. The purpose of the application is to show to the users and researchers a simple and intuitive way of working with text automatically. This type of application may be further implemented for the validation of abstracts and scientific papers as well as for other types of documents, in terms of structure.

Acknowledgements "This work was supported by a grant of the Ministry of Research and Innovation, CNCS—UEFISCDI, project number PN-III-P1-1.1-TE-2016-0773, within PNCDI III".

References

1. Laplante, P.A.: Encyclopedia of computer science and technology. Taylor Francis (2017)
2. Greco, F., Polli, A.: Emotional text mining: Customer profiling in brand management. Int. J. Inf. Manag. (in press)
3. https://play.google.com/store/apps/details?id=co.speechnotes.speechnotes&hl=en_US
4. Enăchescu, M.-I.: Screening the candidates in IT field based on semantic web technologies: Automatic extraction of technical competencies from unstructured resumes. Inform. Econ. J. **23**(4), 51–65 (2019)
5. Schouten, K., Frasincar, F., Dekker, R., Riezebos-Heracles, M.: A framework for developing and evaluating text mining algorithms. Expert Syst. Appl. **127**, 68–84 (2019)

6. Ivan, I., Popa, M., Tomozei, C.: Reingineria entităţilor text. Rev. Română Inform. Şi Autom. **15**(2), 15–28 (2005)
7. Batrinca, B., Treleaven, P.C.: Social media analytics: a survey of techniques, tools and platforms. J. Knowl., Cult. Commun. AI & SOCIETY. **30**(1), 89–116 (2015)
8. Sentiment analysis based on microsoft Azure cloud technology. https://azure.microsoft.com/en-us/services/cognitive-services/text-analytics/
9. OpenFileDialog Class. Microsoft docs. https://docs.microsoft.com/en-us/dotnet/api/system.windows.forms.openfiledialog?view=netframework-4.8
10. StreamReader Class. Microsoft docs. https://docs.microsoft.com/en-us/dotnet/api/system.io.streamreader?view=netframework-4.8

Critical Media Literacy: A Comprehensive Approach Enabling Students (as Citizens) To Use ICT in the Quest for a Just Society

Lefkios Neophytou

Abstract Computers have considerably changed people's lives. Ever since the development of the first computer, many opinions have been expressed echoing different, even unbridgeable, standpoints concerning Information and Communication Technologies (ICT) and their implications on human ecology. Reviewing the benefits and perils associated with ICT in contemporary society, it becomes clear that education should focus both on the technical skills necessary for media production and the critical analytical skills that could help students uncover the politics underpinning the digitized world. In this context, Critical Media Literacy (CLM) becomes a necessity. The chapter aims to shape, via a narrative literature review, a theoretical framework that could help toward the development of educational approaches that would contribute to the development of the skills and attitudes that would help students uncover the politics underpinning the digitized world, empower them to resist to media manipulation, but also enable them to learn from media and to use it in constructive ways.

1 Introduction

Modern computers, ever since their discovery in the early twentieth century, evolved from simple calculators to sophisticated machines that significantly changed the manufacturing industry and revolutionized, almost, every aspect of life; civic, professional, and personal. Information and Communication Technologies (ICT) penetrated the reality of "ordinary" people, fundamentally altering and regulating it. Nowadays, we value computers as specialized machines for, more or less, every purpose and for every person [1].

Echoing the domination of ICT in contemporary societies, major issues have been raised concerning their implications on human ecology. Many opinions have been

L. Neophytou (✉)
The Cyprus Agency of Quality Assurance and Accreditation in Higher Education (CYQAA), Lefkosia, Cyprus

L. Mâță (ed.), *Ethical Use of Information Technology in Higher Education*,
EAI/Springer Innovations in Communication and Computing,
https://doi.org/10.1007/978-981-16-1951-9_10

expressed, on a continuum ranging from highly technophilic to extremely technophobic. This chapter presents a summary of the scientific and philosophical body of literature about the topic, reviewing the benefits and perils associated with ICT in contemporary society, and discusses the necessity for the development of Critical Media Literacy and its inclusion in educational programs.

2   Method

The chapter aims to refine, focus and shape a theoretical and conceptual framework that could help toward the development of educational approaches that would contribute to the development of the skills and attitudes that would help students uncover the politics underpinning the digitized world, empower them to resist to media manipulation, but also enable them to learn from media and to use it in constructive ways.

Narrative or traditional literature review [2–4] was used to analyze and summarize the body of literature about the topic. Available literature was selectively researched to highlight significant areas of discourse on the use of ICT in the context of participation in contemporary democratic societies and the multiple ways that ICT has influenced people's attitudes and perspectives in terms of active citizenship with a particular emphasis on education.

Two questions were, initially, set: How ICT usage diachronically influenced people's life and their participation in society? What are the implications of ICT usage for education? This was followed by inductive reasoning analysis [5] to facilitate the development of conclusions from available literature by weaving together new information into theories. Literature was analyzed to identify meaningful subjects answering the research questions. Nevertheless, the seminal works of Illich [6] on conviviality and Freire's [7] on critical pedagogy significantly shaped the interpretive framework of the study.

Findings were organized in qualitative content themes, making it possible to draw interpretations of the results. Both manifest and latent analyses were used [8, 9]. The manifest analysis was used to describe what the sources recorded, in close connection to the text. The latent analysis allowed an extension to an interpretive level seeking to find the underlying meaning of the text. Themes and categories were identified based on the evolution of the initial two questions. Accordingly, themes were organized based on categories reflecting four, new, questions:

1. How have computers been used diachronically?
2. How is ICT related to human equality and creativity?
3. What skills and attitudes are required in terms of ICT usage in contemporary societies?
4. How can education help toward the development of the necessary skills and attitudes to help students become active citizens in a digitized world?

The results of this deliberation were organized into separate sections presented in the following parts of the chapter:

- Computers as Tools for Productivity, Conviviality, and Democratization (question 1)
- Computers as Suppressors of Human Equality and Creativity (question 2)
- ICT: Help or Hindrance? (questions 1 and 2)
- Critical Media Literacy (questions 3 and 4)
- Conclusions (questions 3 and 4).

3 Results and Discussion

3.1 Computers as Tools for Productivity, Conviviality, and Democratization

The term computer, in the 1640s, designated a person performing calculations.[1] Many things have changed following this first record of the word. This meaning changed into a "calculating machine" (of any type) in 1897, while in 1946 we came to define computers as a programmable digital electronic machine hence allocating to the device a meaning more or less similar to its contemporary meaning.[2] Yet, even though modern computers are smaller in size and tremendously bigger in capabilities the fact remains that everyone who taps at a keyboard, opening a spreadsheet or a word-processing program, is working on an incarnation of the Turing machine the simplest form of the computer invented by Alan Turing in 1936 [9, 10].

Along with the definition, computer usage has also changed. Computers as basic arithmetic machines evolved to be sophisticated military devices assisting in code-breaking (e.g., the Colossus in England in 1943) and ballistic research (i.e., the ENIAC, in the USA in 1946) while nowadays computers have become an essential asset in every laboratory, business, and household. According to Eurostat, in 2017, in the 27 countries of the EU 83% of males and 80% of females aged 16–74 years old have used a computer in 12 months, while the proportion of households in the EU with access to the Internet reached 84%.

Contemporary computer usage has been aligned with productivity and effective time management. Computers are more efficient, convenient, and more reliable tools than the older ways of doing things, such as calculators, scales, typewriters, and conventional mail. They can be customized to meet specific needs of specific enterprises, large (i.e., major accounting firms) or small (i.e., the grocery store around the corner). Thus, people use computers as they make their jobs easier. However,

---

[1] Computer. (n.d.). Oxford English Dictionary. Retrieved April 10, 2009 from http://www.oed.com/.

[2] Computer. (n.d.). Online Etymology Dictionary. Retrieved May 3, 2012, from http://dictionary.ref erence.com/browse/computer.

computer literacy is not just an additional set of knowledge and skills. As under-standing and knowledge of computer applications become increasingly important in working life, computer knowledge becomes an inescapable necessity in a large majority of professions.

Nevertheless, people are not using computers only because they have to. They use computers because they enjoy using them. Gaming, Internet surfing, chatting, watching movies, or listening to music are just some of the many entertainment capacities that modern personal computers (PCs) have. In this sense, computers encapsulate Ivan Illich's notion of convivial tools [6] "Tools foster conviviality to the extent to which they can be easily used, by anybody, as often or as seldom as desired, for the accomplishment of a purpose chosen by the user" (ibid., p. 23). Checking for the name of a song you have listened to on the radio, finding overnight pharmacies, playing chess in Cyprus with a stranger in Brazil, speaking with your spouse when away on a business trip, paying bills or writing essays and reports, posting photographs on Facebook are some examples that indicate how a PC can foster conviviality. Hence, computers as convivial tools "give each person who uses them the greatest opportunity to enrich the environment with the fruits of his or her vision" (ibid., p. 22). Computers, and the subsequent globalized cyberspace, bring down the barriers associated with the "tyranny of the place" and the restraints on where people can live and go, what to buy, eat, read, hear or see. One can live in England but eat Thai food, read the New York Times on the Internet, buy books from Amazon.com in Seattle, and visit Egyptian pyramids without changing money or having a passport. Thus, people now enjoy increased freedom in shaping their identities, in a way that their ancestors could not have possibly imagined.

Computers, as convivial tools in a household, do not require that people having them should use them. Their existence does not impose any obligation to use them [6] nor does it require a specific type of use. In this sense, people may use a computer 24 h a day for work and/or recreation, they may just use them as a decorative item-showing off to house guests or just stack them in a pile among many other things. Moreover, "the use of such tools by one person does not restrain another from using them equally" (ibid., p. 23). Billions of people may be simultaneously working, playing, surfing the Internet, or listening to music.

Following the development of the first personal computer, the infusion of Infor-mation and Communication Technologies (ICT) into everyday life was also consid-ered as a medium for democratization [11–13]. Computers are no longer just large mainframes owned by large enterprises; they are small devices and handy gadgets accessible to and affordable by many people. To this extent, we may argue that the PC allocated power directly into the hands of the individual. The advance and expan-sion of ICT can be associated with Habermas's [14] notion of the "public sphere": A context in which there is minimum domination or manipulation, where the force of the better argument prevails. A forum that enhances the voluntary and active engagement of individuals and enables them to exchange their ideas openly and reach consensus in the "universal speech situation". As Kellner and Kim [15] suggest, the innovation of information and communication technologies has provided ordinary people with unprecedented opportunities to take on the ruling educational power structure. It challenged the uncontested monopoly of knowledge and the institutionalization of education making it possible for decentralized and interactive communication and a participatory model of culture and democracy to flourish. The emergence of the Internet and social networking sites enhanced the individual right of access to information and opened a space for individuals to realize Benjamin's [16] belief that a "reader is at all times ready to become a writer". Multiple voices in an expanded flow of information, dialogical two-way communication, and collective "many-to-many" communication have been widely implemented amplifying individual, voluntary participation in mutual education.

Kellner and Kim [15] utilizing the example of Zakgeorge21 (the nickname of an anonymous YouTube user) provide many convincing arguments about how ordinary people can get significant attention from others in the world of the Internet. Zakgeorge21 posted his video clip to initiate a thought-provoking discussion during a relatively early stage of YouTube's (UT's) development. Posing several discursive questions such as "Why do you tube? "Why do you make a video for UT?", "What is the future of UT and how is it going to impact the world globally?" "What do you think about the implications of UT and what can be beneficial about it?" he introduced a thematic investigation topic that made fellow UTers reconsider their motives and purposes in UTing. The response rate was enormous. By March 5, 2007, 700,183 UT users had watched Zakgeorge21's video posting and there were 4062 text comments and 80 video responses after his initial videos post on January 9, 2007.

Recognizing the power embedded within the social media, large and small enterprises, NGO's, even politicians are now using UT and other social networking tools to inform the public and especially the young. What is interesting, however, is that all these stakeholders are competing in the informational flow arena, with anyone, no matter how "insignificant he/she might be". It can be therefore argued that the president of the USA has the same privileges as a schoolboy from Cyprus. Consequently, conventional relationships between the producers and the consumers of knowledge have been challenged and a new, more active, and participatory model for civic engagement emerged [15].

3.2 Computers as Suppressors of Human Equality and Creativity

Still, beneath the Disneyesque world of happiness lays another world—A world of inequality, injustice, loneliness, and abuse. Computers foster conviviality and allow for participation in the public sphere, only for those who can afford them. The picture of the world as the global village may appear to be very appealing and interesting to dwell in, but this is only one side of the coin—the middle or upper-class western worldview side of the coin. Computers may have become cheaper; yet, a vast amount of people cannot afford them [17]. Eurostat reports [18] that broadband was used by 86% of the households in the EU-28 in 2018, 38 percentage points higher than the share recorded in 2008 (48%). Regardless of the high percentages of broadband access reported, our attention must be shifted to the remaining population in Europe alone (14%) who still do not have broadband connections. Lack of broadband connection becomes a form of social exclusion and marginalization when one considers the necessity for broadband access as a result of social distancing measures governments imposed amidst the COVID-19 crisis in 2020. Simply put, no broadband in-home quarantine means students without access to education.

This inequality becomes more intense taking into account not only the cost of buying a machine but all the other sideway costs that come with computer ownership (e.g., purchasing and updating software, Internet access, support). Thus, even when the traditional hierarchy in producing and consuming knowledge is challenged (like in the case of Zakgeorge21), the hierarchy in producing and consuming the actual product (the PC and the software and nowadays the smartphone) still endures. People still need to buy the product, they still need to be taught how to use it (in many cases formally and under fee), and companies still sell their products and expertise. The level of participation and the benefits that each individual may gain from ICT is analogous to the level of sophistication of different software and, of course, to their market price. As Illich [6] notes "the present organization of tools impels societies to grow both in population and in levels of affluence. This growth takes place at the opposite ends of the privilege spectrum. The underprivileged grow in number, while the already privileged (e.g. large computing enterprises) grow in affluence" (p. 28).

Even when PCs and smartphones (as basic machines) may be affordable by many people, affluence is constructed within the context of renewal. Illich [6] points out that the most effective way to open a market is to identify the use of what is new as an important privilege. Thus, the old model is devalued, and the self-interest of the consumer is wedded to the ideology of never-ending and progressive consumption. Consequently, individuals have been socially graded according to the number of years their bill of goods is out of date. Not all can get the latest iPhone model, not all can afford to buy the new version of MS Office, not all can attend a seminar on the latest edition of newly introduced software. Some people can afford to keep up, while others still use old machines and software. Subsequently, an elite rises from the herd, an elite distinguishable, yet, pseudo accessible to all. "The members of this minority within a minority recognize each other by the recent date at which the products they use came onto the market (…)" (ibid., p. 80). The fact that many new technological gadgets are not restrictive—in budgetary terms—for many people creates the need to constantly update and keep up with the pace of technological advancements, big or small, at the expense of many other essential things. Hence, a multilayered "digital divide" emerges that divides not only people by their capability to buy a computer. It also refers to the ability to keep up with technological advances.

One may argue that as long as one owns a computer and has access to the Internet, there is an infinite universe of available freeware and applications. However, being schooled through Microsoft products, it is more or less impossible to shift to Linux, and Open Office applications. Although open-source programs gain more and more acceptance, Microsoft, Apple, and Google will still keep the "lion's share" in the global computing market. One can argue that computer hardware and software usage can be restricted, thus becoming the monopoly of certain groups of people or certain professional trusts. Having the latest and more sophisticated computers and software purposely limits the capabilities of former models and editions rendering them insufficient to cope up with modern demands. As Illich notes, "tools can be purposely limited when simple pliers and screwdrivers are insufficient to repair modern cars" [6, p. 23].

Within this context, hackers may be considered as the Robin Hoods of the digital age [19, 20]. Considering hackers as members of a community with its own culture and ethics, Levy [21] argues that hackers are both soldiers and artists committed to the abolishment of inequalities. As he points out, access to computers and information should be unlimited and total. Since this basic principle is not conditioned, the communities of the hackers are a contemporary form of rebellion against all forms of authority that restrict freedom. Hacker communities not only challenge the control of access to a computer but the hierarchical organization of society as well. Thus, hackers should only be judged by their ability, in their very own form of art: hacking. Other criteria such as degrees, age, race, or position taking place in various systems (schools, universities, workplaces) have no place in the hacker community.

Hackers, in their ethicality, attempt to bridge some of the inequalities of cyberspace and transcend the barriers of the digital divide. However, their efforts are consumed within a group of people who can afford a computer but cannot buy all the software they need. Nevertheless, the digital divide is not only associated with economic factors. We should also consider the fact that many people not only cannot buy a computer (or software) but cannot also read or write. Moreover, many of these people do not have the chance to get a decent meal every day or even be certain that they will "live to fight another day". The digital divide is therefore not only an economic divide but also a usability divide. The latter form of the divide may be far worse than the former since many people couldn't use a computer even if they got one for free. Hackers' potential beneficiaries are in all cases computer literate people. However, very few people, in poor countries or lower economic layers within richer countries, own computers, simply because they are too poor, illiterate, or have other more vital concerns such as food, health care, and security. So, even if it were possible to magically deliver a computer to every household on earth, it would not achieve very much: a computer is not useful if you have no food or electricity and cannot read. Lower literacy may be the Web's biggest accessibility problem, but it seems that nobody cares about this colossal user group [22, 23].

Another kind of abuse is embedded in the infinite functions and countless capabilities that modern computers have. PCs, tablets, iPods, and smartphones are packed with limitless capacities. However, while addressing certain human needs, ICT is also manufacturing new ones. These needs are often aligned with tools and applications that ordinary people may never use. Moreover, most of these applications are "over-efficient": they immensely surpass human ability—the way an actual person would do things. Commenting on the notion of over-efficiency, Illich [6] points out that this upsets the relationship between what people need to do by themselves and what they need to obtain ready-made. "When over efficient tools are applied to facilitate man's relations with the physical environment, they can destroy the balance between man and nature" (ibid., p. 54). Hence, people may be deprived of the right to do hands-on work that they formerly enjoyed and consequently become alienated from the product of their labor. An architect using AutoCAD and a photographer using Photoshop are examples of the radical monopoly that contemporary ICT tools have on people. The photographer does not need to calculate all the angles, consider the light and speed of his/her camera. All these are done more efficiently through the machine. Similarly, the architect needs not to consume his/her precious time on a drawing board. He/she needs not to draw a building from the scratch. All these are done through sophisticated algorithms that minimize mistakes. Yet, the over-efficiency of tools impedes the artistry that used to be a fundamental condition of these professions.

The associated institutional monopoly and the selective ownership of tools are a form of abuse, as Illich [6] would probably argue since they impede equality in the digital world and alter human ecology. Still, there are many other ways of abusing ICT: They can be used for foul play such as child pornography, criminal impersonation, economic fraud, and many other illegal activities. They may lead to addiction and retrieval from social life or they may enhance temptations resulting in "broken homes". They may ignite long-forgotten passions and lusts such as gambling. However, abuse can also happen in the name of protection. Only in the USA, probably the most "fertile soil" for such undertakings, many laws have been proposed ranging from the protection of minors (i.e., COPA, COPPA, CIPA[3]) to the protection of trade and intellectual property (i.e., SOPA) and finally to the protection of the state (i.e., OFAC). Many of these bills have met significant public resistance since they were considered to collide with the First Amendment to the United States Constitution (that safeguards protections for freedom of speech and expression against federal, state, and local government censorship) and consequently, many governmental attempts to regulate content have been blocked, often after lengthy legal battles. Nonetheless, the debate about use vs. abuse and control vs. freedom is still at large.

In this context, one must consider issues of surveillance and regulation through an ever-watching eye, a "panopticon". The panopticon is a type of institutional building and a system of control designed by the English philosopher and social theorist Jeremy Bentham in the eighteenth century. The basic setup of Bentham's panopticon is that there is a central tower surrounded by cells. In the central tower is the watchman. In the cells are prisoners—or workers, or children, depending on the use of the building. The tower shines bright light so that the watchman can see everyone in the cells. The people in the cells, however, aren't able to see the watchman, and therefore have to assume that they are always under observation. Foucault [24] used

---

[3]The acronyms refer to laws, agencies or proposed legislations. The full names are:
  Child Online Protection Act (COPA), 1998.
  Children's Online Privacy Protection Act (COPPA), 2000.
  Children's Internet Protection Act (CIPA), 2000.
  Stop Online Piracy Act (SOPA), 2011.
  Office of Foreign Assets Control (OFAC) is an agency established under the Trading with the Enemy Act of 1917.

the panopticon to illustrate the inclination of disciplinary societies to subdue its citizens. As Foucault argues, the prisoner of a panopticon is seen, but he does not see; he is an object of information, never a subject in communication.

Nowadays, ICT has rendered Bentham's tower redundant [25]. The panoptic is realized via monitoring electronic communications from a central location. Even though the analogy between the panopticon and video surveillance (CCTV) is obvious, ICT provides limitless capabilities via digital surveillance and data capture. Despite believing that we learn about the world as we swipe on our smartphone screens, we are primarily objects of information. Modern-day types of visuality are far different from the central tower concept. In the panopticon, the occupants are constantly aware of being watched. Today surveillance on the Internet is invisible; there is no tower, no guard watching you; yet you are being monitored every time you enter a URL. As we live our lives carefree, surfing the World Wide Web, everything is under surveillance, not only by governments but also by corporations that invest and also make enormous profits capitalizing on the surveillance and monitoring.

3.3 ICT: Help or Hindrance

Despite the many benefits that the contemporary uses of ICT bear, there are still many unresolved issues concerning their capacity to deliver a more humane and democratic society. We need to consider the degree to which the contemporary uses of ICT meet the criteria of conviviality: Are PCs used "easily, by anybody, as often or as seldom as desired"? Are individuals in control of computers or is it the other way round? Revisiting Illich's [26] analysis of how the means of transportation (e.g., cars, buses, and planes) ultimately alternate the circumstances, obscure the hierarchy, and finally reduce people-transforming them into the means of industrial transportation—we need to be aware of the perils associated with the "homo programmandus" [27–29]. In an age when the computer becomes the "root metaphor" of existence, we need to question whether the tools are transformed from means to ends into the ends in themselves. Are computers serving people, or are people serving the uprising industry of manufacturing and consuming new technology? Do we choose which computer to buy, or are we chosen in advance by computer manufactures? Can I personalize my computer or my personalization options being set by default are dictating what kind of personalization I am allowed to have? Am I becoming someone else in my effort to keep up with technology?

Questions, therefore, need to be asked about who and what technology serves, who it excludes and why, and the strategies that should be pursued [30, 31]. We need to critically examine whether the promising proclaims of harmonious planetary communication in the digitized "one world" are in many ways a myth that cloaks inequalities [32, 33]. We need to reflect upon the notion of social justice within the context of infotainment and techno-capitalism in a globally networked economy driven by the forces of science and business.

Computers as most tools lend themselves to convivial use unless they are artificially restricted through some institutional arrangements [6]. Thus, while acknowledging that Information Communication Technologies contribute to and may cause, at times, many social problems, it is an inescapable fact that they have changed the world. ICT has fragmented, connected, converged, diversified, homogenized, flattened, broadened, and reshaped the world [34, 35]. The contemporary world is the world of ICT. In this context, not knowing how to use new technologies downgrades people, rendering them to illiterate and ignorant objects that are unable to function in modern societies and are vulnerable to manipulation. However, our relationship with technology is not simple. ICT skills and functions should not be regarded as "sanitized" and limited within a vacuum of utilization-focused applications. ICT needs to be examined in situ. As Ferguson [36] points out, contextualizing the understanding of ICT effects within its social and historical dynamics allows us to explore the interconnections between information and power. Not only do we need to learn how to use ICT but also to question them, identify power relations and underlying patterns and thereby embrace the potential for empowerment that critical pedagogy offers.

3.4 Critical Media Literacy

Contemporary societies, being globalized and interconnected, are heavily relying on technology [34]. Technology transformed the physical world into a digitized-one world. Cyberspace represents the agora of the ancient Hellenic city and becomes a forum of communication, discussion, and education that transcends former physical barriers. Still, as it also happened in the agora of ancient Hellas, Cyberspace turns out to be the main arena of politics. Within the ever-changing and deeply political contemporary digital world, "Politics that does not exist in the media … simply does not exist in today's democratic politics" [37, p. 61]. Thus, any apolitical approaches to media literacy (focusing strictly on how to use media effectively) resemble the tip of the iceberg, thereby failing to grasp the underlying intellectual, historical, and analytical factors of the information society [38].

Acknowledging the above, Critical Media Literacy (CLM) not only does it criticize mainstream approaches to literacy but also represents a politically oriented project aiming to democratic social change [39, 40]. Combining cultural studies with critical pedagogy, CLM expands the notion of literacy to include different forms of media culture and literacy (i.e., information literacy, technical literacy, multimodal literacy) and thereby enhances the potential of literacy education to critically analyze relationships between media and audiences, information and power [41]. Further, as an educational response, CLM engages students to a multilateral, yet, critical inquiry of popular culture and the cultural industries. It intrigues them to addresses flaming issues such as class, race, gender, sexuality, and power and aspires to empower students to challenge media texts and narratives and produce their own, alternative counter-hegemonic media [42, 43].

Critical Media Literacy does not come with rigid instructions nor is it associated with any specific pedagogical model. Nevertheless, it is firmly attached to the values of Freire's pedagogy. As discussed in his books [44, 45], Freire's philosophy rests on the belief that we are "unfinished" in our development as human beings. We are rather "conditioned" than "determined" [44, 45]. Thus, although in our era, a computer becomes the "root metaphor" of existence [46] reducing people into "homo programmandus" [27, 28] people can still fight back via ontological and epistemological curiosity, within an ethicality of respect, solidarity, and commitment to justice. People must therefore not reify knowledge, but critique it and develop critical consciousness [47].

Critical Literacy, the underlying framework of CML, was initially proposed by social critical theorists that were unsettled with social injustice and inequalities, due to unequal power relationships [48]. They believed that those predominant in society, commit the power to indicate the prevailing truths that are mediated through education, and formulate how things stand. Thus, knowledge is authenticated by specific groups of people where other groups are excluded. In the contemporary digitized, networked cyberspace, the so-called post-truth era,[4] inequalities in representation and participation are further fortified when texts and messages are naturalized and consequently masked in such a way that people seldom question them. Yet, critical literacy acknowledges that texts in all forms, ranging from traditional print documents to contemporary multimedia, are vehicles through which individuals communicate with one another using the codes and conventions of society [49]. While studying a text, individuals are reading the world [50]. Hence, texts must be investigated by asking questions on how their characteristics attempt to position us, and further, analyze how texts form our identity, construct cultural discourses, and support or disrupt the conventional [51].

Critical educators intend to make inequalities visible to their students. In this direction, Freire's [7] notion of generative themes becomes the starting point of any educational endeavor. Generative themes are codifications of complex experiences that are charged with political significance and, as such, are likely to provoke genuine and motivated discussion derived from a study of the specific history and circumstances of the learners. In this context, students could investigate how women, homosexuals, immigrants, handicapped people, or any other oppressed group is represented in the media. They can explore several websites, (i.e., corporate, governmental, NGOs) and comment if these are accessible for certain groups (e.g., people with limited eyesight) and discuss how and why these people are excluded or included. They can analyze the stereotypes and the hidden curriculum nested in websites, blogs, and forums—official and unofficial, corporate, governmental, or personal—and evaluate the messages and the intended receptors of the media designers.

CML should also help students examine media beyond the perspective of the "traditional" oppressed groups. They can examine other types of oppression that may apply to the "average Joes"—every day, "ordinary" people. Topics like addiction,

---

[4]Post-truth era signifies a world where "alternative facts" replace actual facts and feelings have more weight than evidence [49].

lack of physical social interaction, technophilia, technophobia, and many other ICT-associated problems could also constitute generative themes of investigation: Do you think that computers help or hinder genuine human interaction? How many hours a day do you use the Internet? Have you ever pretended to be someone else? Why?

Further, students can consider issues about consumerism and identity formation. Why do they need to buy the latest product by Apple? Why do they use MS Office and not Open Office? How did they become users of these particular products? How does being a Mac user make you feel and why? Do you think that being a Mac user constitutes a different identity than being a PC user?

Students can also discuss Illich's [6] notion of over-efficiency and the alienation of people from the "fruit of their labor". They can be challenged to consider the degree to which computers have helped them become more productive and the degree computers have deprived them of the joy of physical, manual activities. Which hands-on activities did you enjoy but now, due to ICT, stopped doing? Why? Thematic investigation circles can also be generated about control, censoring, banning, and freedom in using cyberspace. Students can critically reflect on the laws on Internet usage and the politics underneath abandoning or enforcing proposed legislation. They can further reflect on hackers and whether they are criminals or contemporary Robin Hoods.

Nevertheless, Critical Media Literacy is not only about interpreting the world. It is not only about revealing hidden agendas and challenging social inequalities. It is also about reconstructing more ethical and just media [52]. CLM aims to provide not just critical-reflective skills, but also the technical skills that students need to create their own alternative stories and communicate them to the world. Thus, students combine the analytical skills to deconstruct mainstream media with the artistic and technical skills to construct alternative counter-hegemonic media. In this context, deconstructing and reconstructing become natural processes. The deconstructive–reconstructive principles have been successfully applied in many projects such as the Educational Video Center (EVC) in New York City and REACHLA in Los Angeles [35]. Students learn video production, animation, digital arts, web site creation and maintenance, as well as the skills necessary to produce magazines. These technical skills incorporate their poetry, artwork, and short stories in public service campaigns for the larger goal of affecting change in their communities. Founder and Executive Director of EVC, Steven Goodman writes,

> This approach to critical literacy links media analysis to production; learning about the world is directly linked to the possibility of changing it. Command of literacy in this sense is not only a matter of performing well on standardized tests; it is a prerequisite for self-representation and autonomous citizenship. [35, pp. 7–8]

Yet, approaching generative themes or developing alternative media through the "banking method" of instruction [7] that considers students as empty vaults waiting for their teacher to deposit the riches of his/her wisdom is a priori doomed to failure. Generative themes become genuine tools for emancipation when they are approached in collegiality and methodized dialogically. For Freire, the "dialogical approach" to learning demands cooperation and the acceptance of mutuality and interchangeability in the roles of teacher and learner. It is founded upon mutual acceptance and trust. All teach and all learn. Students should be treated as equals and are expected to bring to the discussion their inputs and educational resources. However, many risks emerge when coupling the freedom of students to co-determine the learning agenda with the vast and uncensored material that is freely available online. In contrast to the approved knowledge that the banking method guarantees, the dialogical approach does not place any restrictions on what can or cannot be discussed.

Furthermore, since technological advancements allow synchronous and asynchronous communication, no one can limit where, when, and who will discuss what. Blogs, chat rooms, emails, tweets, and many other forms of messaging provide students infinite opportunities. In this context, transforming classrooms into learning circles that reside upon shared and equal participation, enhances politics. When discussing a provocative and ambiguous theme, a topic emotionally or politically charged, students may lobby against each other or their teacher. The "safety net" is removed. However, since societies are political and classrooms are the image of societies, classrooms inevitably will reflect these structures. Hopefully, the "consensual governance" [7] that is embedded in critical pedagogical approaches may protect from unethical decisions and foul play. Consensual governance requires the discussion of issues until all are in agreement. In contrast to decision-making by voting in which rule by the majority is imposed on those who dissent, consensual governance excludes no one by a decision. Nevertheless, the final consensus cannot be regulated. Should it be "right" or "wrong", nobody knows!

4 Conclusions

Digital technologies, immensely, changed our way of life, our way of thinking and feeling, our communication and social skills, and our social behavior. An increasing amount of research evidence [53, 54] suggests that the high-tech environment (computers, smartphones, video games, Internet search engines) is reshaping the human brain. In this landscape, the modern generation is inescapably participating in constant and intensive online interaction with information, people, and artifacts [55]. Not surprisingly, the modern generation is known as digital, socially digital, and generation Z. Contemporary education is inescapably interwoven with digital technologies. A new challenge consequently arises for education: to figure out how it can help students to master the technical skills needed to use contemporary ICT tools while at the same time inspire a critical disposition toward the new reality in the post-truth[5] era, where people increasingly believe their eyes, opinions, and "gut feelings" to a much greater extent than cogent argumentation backed with data. Media reportage, popular culture, and interpersonal communication, all now facilitated by

---

[5]Post-truth is a philosophical and political concept for "the disappearance of shared objective standards for truth" [56] and the "circuitous slippage between facts or alt-facts, knowledge, opinion, belief, and truth" [57].

ICT, can build up perceptions of reality that become more "real" than reality itself [57].

ICT not only has influenced the way we consume information. It has also changed how we interact with the world, ideologies, and politics. ICT has transformed activism [58, 59] developing new forms of exercising political pressure via digital tactics in human rights movements, including choices in messaging and discourses, selection of digital tools and techniques, and targeting of opponent movements. Activists exploit all the communicative capabilities to practice a politics of visibility, cultivate solidarity, diffuse a consciousness, enforce dominant governments' and corporations' trust and treaty responsibilities, constantly reminding humanity about the injustices that may appear. Baring these in mind, Critical Media Literacy is not an option but a necessity [43, 60]. Not only does it empower students to resist media manipulation, but it also enables them to learn from media and to use it in constructive ways, thereby crafting the citizens of the present and the future. Yet, Critical Media Literacy, like any other form of literacy, does not happen by chance or by accident! It is not an ability that people bring from birth nor is it something that can be developed effortlessly. It requires a process. Goals and objectives must be set, methods and strategies need to be developed, assessment tools need to be created. Education systems and teachers must search deeply into their armories and find the appropriate methods, techniques, and tools to facilitate learner-centered approaches to help students master the technical skills needed to use contemporary ICT tools while at the same time inspire a critical disposition toward post-truth reality.

The vigorous use of innovative instructional methods not only does it make the lesson more interesting, but more importantly, it motivates students, stimulates their cognitive abilities, enhances their capacity to solve nonstandard problems while steadily assimilating technological dexterities of practical significance [61]. A good teacher constantly improves his teaching skills and develops new methods and technologies of teaching. New requirements emerge for teachers who, themselves, need to master ICT to follow the ever-changing landscape, but more importantly keep up with their students, who may have already surpassed them! Teachers need to keep inspiring and motivating children. This cannot be achieved if teachers are illiterate in ICT.

Teacher training programs must be developed to provide practical training for the use of ICT, always in the context of critical pedagogy/critical media literacy: not just using ICT tools but using them as tools that empower, question, reflect, and purposively act. Act toward uncovering injustice, act to lobby against inequalities, influence policies, and decision-makers, applying pressure, raising money for noble purposes, etc. ICT can make education more political and politics more educational. Teachers, at all levels, are those who will organize and defend schools in the cyber age, as institutions essential to maintaining democracy, and portray themselves as transformative intellectuals who combine scholarly reflection and practice to train students to be responsible citizens [62, 63]. Further research should therefore be directed toward finding and testing appropriate methodologies of instruction of CML that would empower teachers to become transformative intellectuals [64] and to foster the technical and critical skills required for students not just to navigate in the post-truth-digital era but also be actively engaged as agents of change toward a society of justice.

References

1. Castells, M.: The information ag: economy, society and culture. Blackwell, Oxford (1996)
2. Bryman, A.: Social research methods. Oxford University Press, Oxford (2016)
3. Hennink, M., Hutter, I., Bailey, A.: Qualitative research methods. Sage Publications Limited (2020)
4. Rozas, L.W., Klein, W.C.: The value and purpose of the traditional qualitative literature review. J. Evid.-Based Soc. Work. **7**(5), 387–399 (2010)
5. Bengtsson, M.: How to plan and perform a qualitative study using content analysis. NursingPlus Open. **2**, 8–14 (2016)
6. Illich, I.: Tools for conviviality. Harper & Row, New York (1973)
7. Freire, P.: Pedagogy of the oppressed. Continuum, New York (1970)
8. Berg, B.L.: Qualitative research methods for the social sciences. Allynand Bacon, Boston (2001)
9. Patton, M.Q.: Qualitative research & evaluation methods. Sage, Thousand Oaks, CA (2002)
10. Gray, P.: Computer scientist: Alan Turing. Time Magazine U.S., March 29 (1999)
11. Felsenstein, L.: Convivial cybernetic devises: From Vacuum Tube Flip-Flops to the Singing Altair. An Interview with Lee Felsenstein (Part 1). The Analytical Engine. Newsletter of the Computer History Association of California. 3:1 (1995)
12. Hilbert, M.: The Maturing concept of e-democracy: From e-voting and online consultations to democratic value out of jumbled online chatter. J. Inf. Technol. Politics. **6**(2), 87–110 (2009)
13. Silverstone, R. (ed.): Media, technology and everyday life in Europe: From information to communication. Routledge (2017)
14. Habermas, J.: The structural transformation of the public sphere: An inquiry into a category of bourgeois society. MIT Press, Cambridge (1989)
15. Kellner, D., Kim, G.: YouTube, critical pedagogy, and media activism. Rev. Educ., Pedagog. & Cult. Studies. **32**(1), 3–36 (2010)
16. Benjamin, W.: Reflection. In Demetz, P. (ed.). New York: Hartcourt, Brace, Jovanovich. Cited in Kellner, D., Kim, G.: YouTube, Critical Pedagogy, and Media Activism. Review of Education, Pedagogy & Cultural Studies **32**(1), 3–36 (1934)
17. King, J., Reichelt, M., Huffman, M.L.: Computerization and wage inequality between and within German work establishments. Res. Soc. Strat. Mobility. **47**, 67–77 (2017)
18. Eurostat: Digital economy and society statistics—households and individuals (2019). Retrieved March 30, 2020 from https://ec.europa.eu/eurostat/statistics-explained/pdfscache/33472.pdf
19. Powell, A.: Hacking in the public interest: Authority, legitimacy, means, and ends. New Media & Soc. **18**(4), 600–616 (2016)
20. Richterich, A.: Tracing controversies in hacker communities: ethical considerations for internet research. Inf., Commun. & Soc. **23**(1), 76–93 (2020)
21. Levy, S.: Hackers: Heroes of the computer revolution. Nerraw Manijaime/Doubleday, New York (1984)
22. Abascal, J., Barbosa, S.D., Nicolle, C., Zaphiris, P.: Rethinking universal accessibility: a broader approach considering the digital gap. Univ. Access Inf. Soc. **15**(2), 179–182 (2016)
23. Nielsen, J.: Digital divide: The three stages. Jakob Nielsen's Alertbox, November 20 (2006). Retrieved February 26 2020 from http://www.useit.com/alertbox/digital-divide.html
24. Foucault, M.: Discipline and punish. A. Sheridan, Tr., Paris, FR, Gallimard (1975)
25. Galič, M., Timan, T., Koops, B.J.: Bentham, Deleuze and beyond: An overview of surveillance theories from the panopticon to participation. Philos. & Technol. **30**(1), 9–37 (2017)

26. Illich, I.: Deschooling society. Harper & Row, New York (1971)
27. Ellul, J., Illich, I.: Statements. Technol. Soc. **17**(2), 231–238 (1995)
28. Falbel, A.: The mess we're in. In: Hoinacki, L., Mitcham, C. (eds.) The challenges of Ivan Illich: a collective reflection. State University of New York Press, Albany (2002)
29. Finn, E.: What algorithms want: Imagination in the age of computing. MIT Press (2017)
30. Ellul, J.: The technological system. Wipf and Stock Publishers (2018)
31. Kahn, R.: Critical pedagogy, ecoliteracy, and planetary crisis: The ecopedagogy movement. Peter Lang Publishers, New York (2010)
32. George, É. (ed.): Digitalization of Society and Socio-political, Issues 1: Digital, Communication and Culture. Wiley (2020)
33. Kellner, D.: Media spectacle. Routledge, London and New York (2003)
34. Wellman, B.: Networks in the global village: Life in contemporary communities. Routledge, London and New York (2018)
35. Kellner, D., Share, J.: Critical media literacy is not an option. In Hunsinger, J.W., Nolan, J. (eds.), Learning inquiry. Springer (2007)
36. Ferguson, R.: Media education and the development of critical solidarity. Media Educ. J. **30**, 37–43 (2001)
37. Castells, M.: Flows, Networks, Identities: a critical theory of the information society. In: Castells, M., Flecha, R., Freire, P., Giroux, H.A., Macedo, D., Willis, P. (eds.) Critical education in the new information age. Rowman & Littlefield, Lanham (1999)
38. Ferguson, R.: Representing 'Race': Ideology, identity and the media. Oxford University Press, New York (1998)
39. Alvermann, D.E., Moon, J.S., Hagwood, M.C., Hagood, M.C.: Popular culture in the classroom: Teaching and researching critical media literacy. Routledge, London and New York (2018)
40. Kellner, D.: Technological transformation, multiple literacies, and the re-visioning of education. E-Learning **1**(1), 9–37 (2004)
41. Semali, L.: Intermediality: teachers' Handbook of critical media literacy. Routledge, London and New York (2018)
42. Funk, S., Kellner, D., Share, J.: Critical media literacy as transformative pedagogy. In Handbook of research on media literacy in the digital age, pp. 1–30. IGI Global (2016)
43. Kellner, D., Share, J.: Critical media literacy is not an option. In Hunsinger, J. W., Nolan, J. (eds.), Learning Inquiry. Springer (2007)
44. Freire, P.: Pedagogy of the city (D. Macedo trans.). Continuum, New York (1993)
45. Freire, P.: Pedagogy of Freedom. Rowman & Littlefield, New York (1998)
46. Illich, I.: In the Vineyard of the Text: a commentary to Hugh's didasacalicon. University of Chicago Press, Chicago (1992)
47. Weiner, E.J.: Secretary Paulo Freire and the democratization of power: Toward a theory of transformative leadership. Educ. Philos. Theory **35**(1), 89–106 (2003)
48. Hagood, M.: Critical literacy for whom? Read. Res. Instr. **41**, 247–264 (2002)
49. Robinson, E., Robinson, S.: What does it mean? Discourse, text, culture: An introduction. McGraw-Hill Book Company, Sydney (2003)
50. Freire, P., Macedo, D.: Literacy: reading the word and the world. Bergin and Garvey, Boston (1987)
51. Marsh, J.: Teletubby tales: Popular culture in the early years language and literacy curriculum. Contemp. Issues Early Child. **1**(2), 119–123 (2000)
52. Baker-Bell, A., Stanbrough, R.J., Everett, S.: The stories they tell: Mainstream media, pedagogies of healing, and critical media literacy. Engl. Educ. **49**(2), 130–152 (2017)
53. Myamesheva, G.: The virtue in the modern smart world. Bull. KazNU. Pedagog. Sci. Series. **44**(1), 152–156 (2015)
54. Soldatova, G., Zotova, E., Lebesheva, M., Shlyapnikov, V.: Digital literacy and internet safety. Methodological textbook for specialists of general education. Google, Moscow (2015)
55. Hietajärvi, L., Tuominen-Soini, H., Hakkarainen, K., Salmela-Aro, K., Lonka, K.: Is student motivation related to socio-digital participation? A person-oriented approach. Procedia-Soc. Behav. Sci. **171**, 1112–1156 (2015)

56. Biesecker, B.A.: Guest Editor's Introduction: Toward an Archaeogenealogy of Post-truth. Philos. & Rhetor. **51**(4), 329–341 (2018)
57. Neophytou, L., Hajisoteriou, C.: Intercultural emotional literacy in the post truth era: Challenges for education. Presentation at the 3rd International Conference: Literacy and Contemporary Society, Nicosia, 11–12 October (2019)
58. Duarte, M.E.: Connected activism: Indigenous uses of social media for shaping political change. Australas. J. Inf. Syst. 21(2017) https://doi.org/10.3127/ajis.v21i0.1525
59. Olabode, S.: Veterans of diaspora activism: An overview of ICT uses amongst Nigerian migrant networks. In The digital transformation of the public sphere, pp. 129–148. Palgrave Macmillan, London (2016)
60. Cruz, A., Dorsch, J.: Critical media literacy in global disquiet times. Int. J. Crit.Al Media Lit. **1**(2), 137–152 (2019)
61. Mynbayeva, A., Sadvakassova, Z., Akshalova, B.: Pedagogy of the twenty-first century: Innovative teaching methods, New pedagogical challenges in the 21st century—Contributions of research in education. In Bernad Cavero, O., Llevot-Calvet, N., IntechOpen (2017). https://doi.org/10.5772/intechopen.72341. Available from: https://www.intechopen.com/books/new-pedagogical-challenges-in-the-21st-century-contributions-of-research-in-education/pedagogy-of-the-twenty-first-century-innovative-teaching-methods
62. Neophytou, L.: The variations of the teacher profile as reflected in the curricula of teacher training in Cyprus. Educ. Res. ejournal **1**(1), 33–50 (2012). https://doi.org/10.5838/erej.2012.11.03
63. Neophytou, L., Valiandes, S.: Critical literacy needs teachers as transformative leaders. Reflections on teacher training for the introduction of the (new) Greek-language curriculum in Cyprus. Curriculum J. **24**(3), 412–426 (2013). https://doi.org/10.1080/09585176.2012.744331
64. Giroux, H.A.: Teachers as transformative intellectuals. Social Educ. **49**(5), 376–379 (1985)

Current Issues of Ethical Use of Information Technology from the Perspective of University Teachers

Liliana Mâță, Alexandra-Georgiana Poenaru, and Ioana Boghian

Abstract The purpose of the research is to investigate the perception of teachers regarding the ethical problems of the use of information technology (IT) in higher education teaching-learning-evaluation and research-development. A qualitative research methodology based on the use of the semi-structured interview was built. The research was attended by 31 teachers from the field of Informatics, but also the socio-human areas from five Romanian universities in the Northeastern part of Romania. The results of the research show that the ethical problems faced by teachers when operating with IT in academic activities are plagiarism, infringement of intellectual property rights, incorrect use of personal data, unethical use of computer programs, or multimedia resources. Preventing and reducing ethical issues related to the proper use of digital resources requires the development of programs for educating students and teachers in higher education.

Keywords Ethical issues · Information technology · Semi-structured interview university teachers

1 Introduction

Technology is an important factor of change in any society and as Bigum and Kenway [1] have argued, "it is generally associated with a change in many areas, which has quite a large impact on educational institutions" that have a special role in every society. The opportunities provided by information technologies lead to the use of computers in a variety of fields, including education; therefore, the use of computers for storing and processing the information as well as the use of the

L. Mâță (✉) · A.-G. Poenaru · I. Boghian
Vasile Alecsandri University of Bacău, Bacău, Romania
e-mail: liliana.mata@ub.ro

I. Boghian
e-mail: boghian.ioana@ub.ro

Internet for accessing information has become everyday practices in higher education. Computers and the Internet have become integrated into all areas of society because, as stated by İşman [2] and Yaman [3] they consolidate the "influential and unique position" of the respective fields. Resorting to technology for various academic activities must involve the retrieval and correct use of information as well as paying special attention to computer ethics. Otherwise, the incorrect use of information technologies, in a way that can harm data confidentiality and ownership, can lead to ethical dilemmas, which may lead to ethical problems regarding the use of technology. The use of technological resources determines, on the one hand, many benefits but generates, on the other hand, a series of difficulties that cannot be dismissed by teachers. From an ethical point of view, these problems are increasingly frequent in the academic space, but they are studied mainly at the level of students and very rarely among teachers.

The research objective aims to investigate the perception of teachers regarding the ethical problems of information technology (IT) use in higher education:

- the ethical obstacles involved in the teaching-learning-evaluation activities generated by the use of IT;
- the difficulties that arise in carrying out research and development activities from an ethical perspective as a result of IT integration;
- the problematic aspects of the use of social networks by teachers in the academic environment.

2   Background

In the literature, the education—IT binomial—is widely debated, with numerous references, both positive (ethical use of computers and IT) and negative (violation of principles of academic integrity by incorrect use of information technology and computers, namely plagiarism, cheating). Moreover, Baek et al. [4] consider that "one of the most interesting changes in education is related to the word technology" (p. 224) and unethical use of technology in education is a serious problem (Ki and Ahn) [5].

2.1   Computer Ethics

The concept of computer ethics is widely debated in The handbook of information and computer ethics coordinated by Kenneth Einar Himma and Herman T. Tavani [6]. In Chapter 2 entitled "Milestones in the History of Information and Computer Ethics" (authored by Terrell Ward Bynum) [7], it is stated that the origins of the concept of computer ethics would be in two of Wiener's writings (1948, 1950) as well as in the work of Walter Maner who coined the term "computer ethics" to refer to the new branch of applied ethics that Wiener had founded, the concept of computer ethics as it is typically understood today, is a subfield of Wiener's information ethics. Also, we can identify the fact that over time there have been numerous scientific contributions of researchers that have led to the development of the uniqueness of this concept (see Bynum [8]; Floridi and Sanders [9]; Himma [10]; Tavani, [11]).

According to Floridi [12], information ethics "must be able to address and solve the ethical challenges arising in the new environment based on the fundamental principles of respect for information (infosphere), its conservation and valorization" (p. 1). In other words, computer ethics has the role of addressing the confidentiality of the information within a certain infosphere, according to Tavani [13] Similarly, if computers and infosphere are to be used effectively and continuously, teachers must teach students about the potential dangers of unethical use of technology and the ethical challenges that arise in the educational environment regarding the use of information technology.

2.2 Unethical Use of Information Technology in Higher Education

Some researchers have argued that students and teachers are ethically linked as a "community" or with the world through technology (Prosser, Ward) [14] mainly through computers. If for Roh [15] IT development involves both positive and especially negative consequences such as "hacking, infringements of privacy or intellectual property" (p. 168), Baum [16] states that "the ethical problems that accompany educational technology have become more evident, as more and more teachers integrate technology into their courses" (p. 54). The concept of ethics is a key factor in higher education, and it is important to study the attitude of teachers toward ethical, especially unethical computer use because, as Brey [17] observed, "historically, universities have played a major role in transmitting social, cultural and academic values" such as ethics (p. 91).

Apart from the lack of policies and clear legislation strictly prohibiting the illegal/unethical use of computers such as confidentiality, privacy, data security, intellectual property/copyright, computer crime, in the higher education system, there are no courses on computer ethical use. The Impact of Policies for Plagiarism in Higher Education Across Europe (IPPHAE) is a European-level approach to plagiarism and academic integrity aimed at conducting an analysis that addresses this issue in the Member States of the European Union, based on the model proposed by Irene Glendinning [18]. According to [18], in the case of Romania, "51% of the students and 21% of the questioned teachers admit to having intentionally committed plagiarism" (p. 5). As it results from this study, the absence of a well-defined legislative framework leads to light or non-existent sanctions, which can lead to encouraging this phenomenon. As it also results from our research, the main ethical issues facing the academic environment are plagiarism, infringement of intellectual property rights, incorrect use of personal data, unethical use of computer programs, or multimedia resources.

2.3 Studies on the Attitude of Teachers Toward the Use of IT in the Educational Process

Recent studies have shown that the successful implementation of information technologies depends largely on the attitude of teachers, which ultimately determines how they are used in the classroom. For example, studies by Koohang [19] and Selwyn [20] have shown that teachers' attitudes toward computers involve major factors regarding both the initial acceptance of computer technology and future behavior regarding computer use. Bullock [21] has found that teachers' attitude is an important factor that either enables or disables the adoption of technology; similarly, Kersaint et al. [22] found that teachers who have positive attitudes toward technology feel more at ease with using it and usually integrate it into their activity. A similar opinion, that of Baylor and Ritchie [23] assumes that regardless of the level of development, technology will not be used unless faculty members have the skills, knowledge, and attitudes needed to implement it in the education process. Therefore, teachers' attitudes toward the use of computer technology in the teaching and learning process seem to be a determining factor for effective integration. Building teachers' positive attitudes toward IT is a key factor in improving computer integration and avoiding teachers' resistance to computer use, as Watson [24] noted. An essential element would be the teacher's competence to use a computer and, implicitly, the introduction of technology in the didactic activity. Therefore, in the study entitled Building attitudes: how a technology course affects preservice teachers attitudes about technology, on the correlation between teacher attitude and acceptance of technology, Francis-Pelton and Pelton [25] argued that many teachers consider computers an important component in the educational process, however, teachers' lack of knowledge and experience leads to low or absence of confidence in attempting to introduce them into their activities.

3 Methodology

To investigate the perception of university teachers regarding the ethical problems of using information technology, a qualitative research methodology based on the use of the semi-structured interview was constructed.

3.1 Participants

The research was attended by 31 teachers from five Romanian universities in the Northeastern part of Romania. Teachers were selected from the fields of Informatics and socio-human areas because the research topic concerns both informatics and ethics. The main selection criterion was the frequent use of IT by university teachers.

3.2 Research Method

The semi-structured interview was used because it is appropriate to deepen a topic and understand in detail the answers offered by Harrell and Bradley [26]. One of the characteristics of the semi-structured interview refers to the fact that many questions will be planned ahead of time, but during the interview, the research directions will be followed to track the interesting and unexpected paths that may emerge along the way (Blandford) [27]. The structure of the interview guide was elaborated according to the reference criteria (Arthur and Nazroo [28]: introduction, opening questions, basic questions, and conclusion). In the first part of the interview, introductory questions were asked, followed by open questions regarding the general context of the issue of IT ethical use in the academic environment and basic questions on the difficulties found by teachers regarding IT ethical use.

3.3 Research Procedure

The participants were informed about the purpose of the research and their right to withdraw at any time. Interviews were organized individually with each respondent for approximately one hour, as it is the optimal time to minimize fatigue for both interviewers and respondents, according to Adam [29]. Teachers' responses were recorded and then transcribed. Confidentiality regarding data collection, management, and reporting was ensured.

3.4 Data Analysis

The data were analyzed using the thematic content analysis method, which allows a statistical analysis of the coded form of the text, by Agabrian [30]. With the help of content analysis, the main categories of ethical problems of the use of information technology in the academic environment are established. Frequencies are recorded for each category of problems, as a result of coding the answers.

4 Results

The research results are analyzed and interpreted in close connection with the main objectives.

(a) *Ethical obstacles involved in teaching-learning-evaluation activities generated by IT use*

The analysis of the frequencies of the data obtained has led to the establishment of certain categories of ethical problems that can intervene in the use of information technology in teaching-learning-evaluation activities (Table 1).

One of the ethical issues frequently highlighted by teachers in the university environment is plagiarism. There are two types of plagiarism, as indicated by a university teacher: "hard plagiarism, in the sense of taking large passages from other works, without citation and without any adaptation and soft plagiarism, in which the paraphrases are more or less faithful to the original text, which are also lacking an honest and necessary quotation". Therefore, the ethical problems that arise regarding the incorrect use of sources in the elaboration of teaching materials are the incorrect quotation of the references taken from the technological resources, the insertion of multimedia elements in the materials elaborated for didactic purpose without specifying the source, inaccurate notes on the source.

There is the possibility that some teachers "may take significant or even integral parts of a power-point presentation for a particular learning unit from the Internet". Sometimes these materials "can be taken from another language of international circulation and can be translated without specifying the source". As a university teacher specified, "the materials taken are distributed from one author to another, without knowledge of the source of the material". To avoid this problem, it is advisable to use anti-plagiarism software, such as Plagiarism Detector, to check both the graduation papers of undergraduates and masters' dissertations, including portfolios for the teacher training department.

As a university teacher stated, "the bachelor's graduation papers are checked with an anti-plagiarism program that is officially provided, purchased by the university". Another participant in the interview highlighted the importance of using the anti-plagiarism scanning software along with other qualitative checks. The evaluation of the materials elaborated by the students is carried out, as mentioned by a teacher, to "establish their contribution to the achievement of the graduation projects". According to the regulations that exist at the level of universities, "80% must be originality, 7–8% is the percentage of allowed plagiarism, the remaining proportion being references, links". One of the problems is also the lack of access to a licensed anti-plagiarism program at the university level. Another academic teacher stated that there has emerged an "overestimation of the accuracy of the evaluations of students' works through plagiarism programs". There are "certain shortcomings of such software or programs", as one interviewee noted, in the sense that they can lead to "increasing

Table 1 Ethical issues of IT use in teaching-learning-evaluation activities

No.	Ethical problems at didactic level	Frequency
1	Plagiarism issues	28
2	Infringement of intellectual property rights	20
3	Problems regarding the use of software, equipment, audio-video media, platforms during teaching	13
4	Incorrect use of personal data	5

the percentage of similarities or plagiarism, just because very common phrases and some notions which can be found in many other reports are used". An interviewed teacher found that "most of the time there are identified cases of plagiarism, copy-pasting materials found on various sites, although the plagiarism programs, which are used under license, do not identify these texts as a result of a plagiarism process". Therefore, there is a need to "improve these technologies because there are simple techniques that can pose problems in identifying a text that was retrieved and not created".

The role of the university teacher, as one participant emphasized, is "to verify the entire content of the students' works, by referring to the sources on the Internet and the databases with existing bachelor and dissertation papers at the university level". A solution proposed by a university teacher consists of "giving access to both teachers and students to periodically check their papers, essays, not just the graduation paper". The issue of plagiarism is serious, as one participant in the interview noted because in other countries "a line of five words identical with other works can be considered plagiarism". Another university teacher proposed, as a means of counteracting plagiarism, asking students to go to the library and perform their documentation work based on written sources. A university teacher stated that "greater attention should be paid to the careful citation of the sources, specifying the authors, the works used, the materials used in teaching". It would also be necessary, in the opinion of one interviewee, to create "technologies that provide greater accuracy in terms of identifying online materials".

In the elaboration of the course and seminar materials, "problems related to mentioning the sources, as well as the use of some images" may appear, as observed by an academic teacher. Therefore, it is necessary to indicate the source for a text, as well as for images, graphs, tables, because there is the practice of inserting these multimedia elements in the materials that a university teacher elaborates. As a university teacher stated, "the source from which the material was taken, whether an electronic volume, a particular site, a public institution or any website or platform that broadcasts information" must always be specified. As there are many sources of documentation for the elaboration of teaching materials, teachers must select approved sources", as indicated by an interview participant.

The correct use of the sources should also be respected in the case of distributing the study materials on the platforms used in teaching in partial attendance study programs, according to a university teacher. Following the analysis of the responses of the interviewed teachers, there were reported several causes that lead to plagiarism issues in the preparation of teaching materials in the academic environment. One of the causes of plagiarism may be "overcrowding of the job description, the responsibility that the teacher has for preparation of the teaching act, corroborated with the other dimensions, which concern the research activity, the administrative activity, the tutoring activities, counseling, coordination and supervision of elaboration of the graduation paper for bachelor's or master's studies", as one participant in the interview mentioned. Another cause is the lack of financial resources to access IT use. A university teacher emphasized the fact that the use of information technology is expensive and costly, negatively impacting access to information. For example, some teachers can afford to pay subscriptions to different platforms, but others do not. Software purchase is very expensive, which causes differentiated access to the use of IT. The teacher also mentioned the problem of the lack of basic technological tools essential to carrying out teaching-learning activities in higher education. Under these circumstances, it would be necessary to have "agreements signed between the university and various institutions or associations, which provide certain databases."

As regards the occurrence of plagiarism in projects developed by students, one of the main causes may be, according to a university teacher, "the formulation of very complex, long assignments, disproportionate to the students' time, energy and cognitive resources". For example, if very long assignments are assigned for a short time interval, students will be tempted to retrieve information uncritically from sources on the Internet, websites such as referate.ro and hence their unethical behavior is triggered by teachers. As one interviewee noted, "we are at the beginning regarding the safe use of the content, which, at times, is being perceived as a common good, given that it is circulating on the Internet."

Regarding the violation of intellectual property rights, the main ethical issues refer to the distribution of materials for the course and seminar activities without the author's permission, the lack of protection of the course materials posted in the online environment before being published. A university teacher mentioned that "the use of technological applications implies respect of copyright or if they are open-source they can be used in compliance with the conditions imposed by those who developed it". One consequence may be the loss of financial gain for legal authors, as the same teacher stated. If university teachers do not use open source, then copyright issues arise because "there should be a permission to use the materials given by the person who owns those rights." Lack of protection of the course materials posted in the online environment before being published is an ethical issue, as teachers share with students new study materials at risk of being further forwarded. Under such circumstances, it is important to respect "the intellectual property right of the person who developed the course", as mentioned by a university teacher.

To respect the copyright, it should be noted that on each material used by the teachers in the academic environment "a warning message should be written to say that the respective content cannot be distributed without the author's permission". Also, to prevent students from sharing the course and seminar media offered by the teachers, an interview participant offered the solution to mention the author's name, the header, and the name of the faculty and university. Therefore, the same university teacher mentioned that "students should be warned that if they further share, multiply, print the respective material, or distribute it by any other form, they will fall under the law and are subject to the corresponding penalties." There are situations where "the materials taken by someone else can be found under a different name on different sites and the material belongs to another person", as stated by a university teacher.

Concerning the problems regarding the use of software, online equipment, audio-video media, and platforms, there are different ethical issues involved, such as downloading movies, demonstrations from the Internet, without specifying the source from where they were taken, the use of unlicensed platforms in teaching-learning activities, preparation of a CD for students with study materials, without indicating the sources, providing students with online sources that do not meet the specific standards of ethical higher education, not informing students on the rules for the use of platforms, equipment, sharing of inadequate information on platforms intended for teaching-learning activities. As one university teacher noted, these applications must "be open-source or purchased by the university." It is advisable to use those platforms for which "licenses are allocated to all students and teachers, including laboratories". As a solution, teachers "can provide students with links or other sources to download informative materials."

By indicating these links, ethical issues regarding the use of IT in the academic environment will be eliminated. In this regard, a university teacher drew attention to "providing students with sources such as referate.ro, which do not correspond qualitatively, ethically, deontologically to standards in higher education." If the university teacher "prepares for students a CD with a series of useful articles to provide a bibliography for certain papers or studies, it is recommended to identify those articles that are open-source". As one interviewee noted, there should be a "faculty platform" to make study materials available to students. One interviewee mentioned that "at some point, the students were signing an agreement form that they were legitimately using computer networks." Therefore, informing students about the rules for using platforms, equipment, and requesting signatures could prevent ethical issues from occurring.

Another problem mentioned by a university teacher refers to "uploading on the platforms of higher education some materials for which there is no copyright". Therefore, it is needed a "more rigorous selection of audio-video media for teaching, taken from the Internet", as another university teacher mentioned. There should be compliance with the "conditions of use of video materials that can be used for educational purposes". An appropriate solution proposed by a university teacher would be "collaboration with a person specialized in the IT field and team elaboration of teaching materials at the university level, to be included in the archive and used by all". From another perspective, "the use of platforms during teaching activities is discriminatory", as pointed out by a university teacher. Specifically, "learners who are more assertive and experienced in using these learning tools may unfairly demand resources and time from us as trainers, there being left no time and attention to support others in learning". There may also be problems related to the topics uploaded on the platform by students or regarding the assessment of knowledge with the help of digital tools, which raises the problem of visual contact with distance learning students. Also, in terms of evaluating in this context, one participant in the interview considered that "the main ethical problem that may arise would be access to a series of information that would be unnecessary for the evaluation of the students".

The main ethical problems that arise concerning the incorrect use of personal data concern the violation of the General Data Protection Regulation or the lack of agreement of the filmed persons to make a teaching-learning material. Infringement of the General Data Protection Regulation (GDPR) is one of the ethical issues that arise at the university level, as mentioned by one of the participants, as a result of collecting personal data as a private data operator, such as name, surname, the students' school situation, financial situation, etc. Therefore, it is not advisable to

Table 2 Ethical issues of IT use in research-development activities

No.	Ethical issues at scientific level	Frequency
1	Plagiarism problems	27
2	Ethical issues concerning the processing of research data	15
3	Infringement of intellectual property rights	6
4	Incorrect use of personal data	2
5	Unethical use of computer programs or multimedia resources	2

publish student names, marks, and other confidential information. Ethical problems can also arise if there is a lack of agreement of the persons filmed for the elaboration of the teaching-learning material. A university teacher stated that the video recorded material cannot be used or disseminated for educational purposes unless there is an agreement of the persons concerned. Also, security issues arise when using the platforms for learning activities in the academic environment, because, as a university teacher noted, there is the possibility that some users may "log in under another identity and post a material that is non-compliant or plagiarized".

All these ethical problems "could have negative consequences on the cognitive, affective-motivational and attitudinal paths used by students to receive and process data, information transmitted by the teacher", as found by a university teacher. Table 2 presents the frequencies regarding the ethical problems of IT use in the research-development activity.

(b) *Difficulties that arise in carrying out research-development activities from an ethical perspective as a result of IT integration*

Plagiarism is the main ethical problem in the use of IT in research activities, such as the search for documentation materials, the elaboration, and editing of articles in their journals. This problem arises when "either citation or paraphrasing is omitted when searching for reference materials", as specified by a university teacher. It is very important that "a scientific article contains some amount of original, authentic contribution", as mentioned by another university teacher. Another problem related to plagiarism is copying materials translated from other languages, without specifying the bibliographic reference. A university teacher formulated such an example: "the material is translated from Spanish into Romanian, then reformulated into Romanian, put into text, as if it were original, and then translated back into Spanish and thus it no longer appears in its original form."

One problem of plagiarism may also be "citing a secondary source instead of the authentic source," as one interviewee observed. A relevant and useful solution proposed by a university teacher for the prevention of plagiarism would be to create a national platform, where all assignments, articles, would be uploaded to observe the degree of novelty and originality. One interviewee pointed out that "teachers are more aware of the rules that must be followed to prevent plagiarism", as opposed to students. Problems related to the use of IT documentation involve the observance of the right to use in one's work documents existing in other bibliographic sources, on the Internet or in other fields, specifying that this information can be processed but not used. As one teacher also stated, "information should be retrieved, critically interpreted by authors, and quotation marks should be used when various information is inserted in one's work". Other problems related to the processing of information obtained with the help of IT could be avoiding the presentation of unfavorable results already published or problems related to the inclusion or exclusion of authors. These problems arise because "the resources for searching for documentary materials are usually limited to the libraries to which we have access." Another university teacher drew attention to the fact that "there may be situations when you do not have access to a particular article and you cite it second hand, so it will be specified that a certain author says that someone did that, but you do not know exactly what that author did, and then it becomes a problem because you should know exactly what somebody else did, otherwise you might do the same thing again."

Self-plagiarism is another ethical issue of using information technology, as a result of using similar information in several articles, without being aware of it. There occurs the problematic situation of "republishing articles or books as new editions, with very small changes", as observed by a university teacher. Also, there are situations in which some articles appear in a certain form, after which they will be republished in other volumes or scientific journals following only slight modifications. It is recommended to use the specific software to check articles with the plagiarism detector program. There are situations in which publications with a high percentage of plagiarism are identified by the reviewers of a journal, which causes the material to be rejected. Another problem mentioned by a university teacher is that of not checking the articles with anti-plagiarism programs, which enables the repeated publication of a similar article by the same author in different journals. A university teacher found that "anti-plagiarism programs are outdated, as a result of discovering that some misused sources were not cited."

From the analysis of the answers regarding the use of IT in research activities, one of the causes underlying the plagiarism problem was identified. This cause is related to the lack of financial resources to access information. As a university teacher observed, there emerge problems that refer to "downloading materials that cannot be accessed because of very high prices". There is, therefore, a lack of equity, as one participant in the interview noted, regarding access to the database of quality scientific materials. Therefore, property rights should be better regulated, according to the interviewed teacher, and the possibility of accessing certain materials should be ensured, provided that the author contributes to the creation of a database." In recent years, "special platforms at the national level have been created that provide academic teachers with access to international bases, based on an account".

The ethical problems that result from processing the research data are those that concern the possibility of presenting distorted or non-existent information. The use of statistical data tools can lead to several ethical issues, such as "data fabrication, data forgery or misreporting of data that do not match the research hypotheses" as one university teacher found. Other problems highlighted by an academic teacher refers to the complete reproduction in their study of a methodological approach copied from digital resources, reporting research results different from those obtained, on different platforms. In the opinion of another participant, "it is extremely serious to present a research that did not take place or a research in which you have somehow manipulated the parameters of the application or various results or have removed some of the unfavorable results so that on average or after various statistical parameters to achieve a better result than the real one."

The infringement of intellectual property rights is an ethical and scientific issue. One university teacher mentioned that one of the frequently encountered ethical problems is "fraudulent downloading of programs by breaking their access codes". Under these conditions, it is necessary to "obtain the license to use data analysis and processing software, such as SPSS, STATA programs". The use of statistical programs for processing the research data, therefore, requires their use with a license, as specified by a university teacher.

Another category of problems concerns the unethical use of personal data, such as accessing the personal data of other users. There are situations in which passwords of other teachers, researchers are used to accessing certain platforms, thus avoiding paying a membership fee, as mentioned by a university teacher. In this unethical manner, files can be accessed from certain professional institutions or organizations such as, for example, the European Sociologists Association or the International Sociologists Association. The same university teacher stated that "the membership data are transmitted from one researcher to another to avoid paying the respective annual fee", which leads to the emergence of ethical problems. One consequence of these problems may be obtaining false data from respondents on online platforms. Thus, a university teacher noted that applying questionnaires using the Google Drive tool entails "the risk that the respondent may not respond correctly or provide the actual data."

There are also problems regarding the unethical use of computer programs or multimedia resources. Among them, the problem of verifying participation in virtual conferences, as some teachers mention in their CV that they have delivered papers online, without them participating.

Following the analysis of the aspects specific to the didactic and scientific dimension, it was emphasized that "a teacher must be supported, in the teaching-learning-evaluation and research activities, by a specialist in the IT field". As the university teacher stated, "many of the problems that arise in the use of information technology are due to ignorance, insufficient updating of information in a world of fantastic dynamics."

(c)   *Problematic aspects of the use of social networks by teachers in the academic environment*

Three basic categories have been delimited regarding the problematic aspects of the ethical use of social networks (Table 3).

Problems related to online communication in the academic environment refer to the use of inappropriate, trivial language on social networks, excessive communication on the same topic, violation of privacy, trespassing the limits imposed by formal communication between teacher and student, creating ideological conflicts

Table 3 Ethical problems related to the use of social networks

No.	Ethical issues at the relational level	Frequency
1	Issues regarding online communication	19
2	The unethical use of personal data	16
3	The low level of safety of closed groups	7

manifested as very subtle forms of xenophobia, anti-Semitism, neo-Nazism, denigrating the image of students or colleagues, posting criticisms of students. For this reason, "we must be very careful what we communicate, how we communicate, so as not to disturb others, to be polite even if we are not face-to-face". Also, the same university teacher stated that it is important to set the "limit between professional and personal communication" so that communication is maintained at an optimal level. Ethical problems arise when "the language used exceeds the academic framework of politeness and mutual respect between those who use such channels, respectively teacher or student, and when the content of the communication exceeds the academic institutional framework", as emphasized by a university teacher. The same participant recommended communication with the students through the faculty platform and the use of professional email addresses on the respective platform, through the secretariat".

One way to communicate professionally, in the opinion of an interviewed teacher, is the e-mail because it "imposes limits on the elaboration of the text and is asynchronous", providing the option to read messages and reply whenever, as opposed to Facebook. It is very important to "clearly communicate the purposes of communication in the online environment", as emphasized by a university teacher and, at the same time, "to require the students' signature to use the e-mail address for communication on a didactic basis". The purpose of requesting personal e-mail addresses must be strictly academic, for the dissemination of course or seminar materials or other educational activities. Some teachers consider the Facebook social network as "a trap that determines the use of a more informal language". Therefore, the use of this language could also affect communication between teachers and students. The same teacher mentioned that he does not agree with accepting friend requests on Facebook from students, because there is personal information to which they should not have access.

Violation of the right to personal life and privacy or "the tendency of some persons to violate the electronic privacy of another person" is an ethical problem determined by the use of social networks in the academic environment. Violation of teacher privacy occurs when students want to communicate with teachers or request study materials outside of the working schedule. Therefore, the mandatory break of two days per week according to the law is not respected, which can lead to physical and mental exhaustion of the teacher, as stated by an interview participant. Communication with students on social networks should only be done within closed groups created for academic purposes. It is necessary to carry out, as one interviewed teacher stated, "education, self-education of users using online communication tools". Another university teacher has made the distinction between online teacher–student communication for teaching and personal communication. Thus, he stated that these groups "are intended for the didactic activity that was carried out with the students", and such communication is useful for "sharing various information concerning the didactic activity and not aspects that concern personal life". Another suggestion of a university teacher is to indicate to the students very clearly what address they can use for and only for purposes related to the respective academic course. In the opinion of a participant in the interview, in the academic field, communication should be done only through computer structures, so that there is no mixing in one's personal life".

Regarding the use of e-mail, a university teacher pointed out as an ethical problem the "sharing, by some colleagues, messages in which internal issues of faculties or even personal issues with the entire university group network". As another participant in the interview has specified, an ethical problem may also result from "sending e-mail messages to third parties by using the CC and BCC e-mail options". Another university teacher drew attention to the impolite communication between teacher and student, as some students do not know the rules of addressing and formulating an e-mail. Several teachers (7) stated that they do not use the Facebook social network to communicate with students, and if they are contacted on these networks, they direct them to e-mail. Among the communication problems, there is also the one related to the "erroneous acquisition by students of the information transmitted by teachers". In this situation, "problems of misunderstanding appear in online communication", which causes some teachers to avoid using technological tools. Also, in this category of problems, there is the one regarding the "use of social networks as a means of manipulation in the academic environment".

The unethical use of personal data or other people's documents includes various issues aimed at breaching the confidentiality of certain information, identity theft, cyber-bullying, borrowing the image of others in the academic environment, lawfully pursuing the activity of a particular user, trying to obtain information and even money from other people, threats of having one's account broken, the interpretation of personal information posted by others. Security issues arise, as one university teacher noted, because "there is a very high likelihood that our messages will reach other directions as well as receive many messages that are not for us or sent in the Spam folder." A university teacher mentioned that "the most popular attacks included in social engineering are spam and phishing messages". The phishing messages consist, as one interviewee stated, of "the intention to find out some personal information about someone to send an announcement with intent".

As stated by a university teacher, one can talk about "SPAM in the academic area", meaning that e-mails are sent aggressively and irritatingly about various false announcements related to publication opportunities in certain ghost magazines. Under these conditions, the same participant draws attention to the fact that "teachers and researchers need to be very careful because the lack of information in the field of IT ethics can cause serious financial damage". In the same context, the university teacher highlighted the problem of displaying an image different from the real one by some colleagues in the academic space. The data posted on different social networks demonstrates the lack of agreement between the information displayed and the actual data. Other serious security issues mentioned were identity theft or personal account theft.

Another risk of communication on social networks is that "the person or several of the persons involved in the communication have fake profiles", as stated by a university teacher. The main problems that may arise in this case are identity theft or the creation of fake accounts, as another university teacher has stated. As one interviewee mentioned, it is recognized that "social networks can facilitate the construction, distortion of academic identity". Among these ethical issues, there was also mentioned: "the distribution of non-personal materials, which are elaborated by others, by groups or individuals we collaborate with, be they students or other teachers with whom we work in research teams". In the opinion of a university teacher, a current ethical problem is "the use of personal information for commercial purposes". For example, a simple search for information on the site of a conference leads to a search for a series of incoming spam which provides information about other conferences, showing that the intention toward a particular domain is also exploited by other sources".

The last category of problems refers to the low level of safety of closed groups created on social networks for educational purposes. These ethical problems are related to the risk of sending incorrect documents to the group, uncertainty about understanding, the deciphering of the message transmitted in a text posted on a communication platform, the posting of materials by teachers, which can be transmitted further by the users, without requesting consent, breaking into other people's accounts (hacking). A university teacher pointed out that some students are dissatisfied with the information posted on online groups, even if it is not confidential. Therefore, there is the risk to share documents, without the consent of those who had originally submitted it. Also, on the workgroups created on social networks, "materials can be circulated by teachers and then reposted on other networks, although the teacher explicitly forbade forwarding of the lecture notes", according to one participant in the interview.

5 Conclusions

The purpose of this qualitative study was to investigate the perception of teachers in higher education regarding the ethical problems of using information technology. The ethical problems frequently mentioned by the teachers, both in the preparation of materials for lectures and seminars, as well as in the research activity, are related to plagiarism, concerning issues of incorrect use of the sources in the elaboration of teaching materials taken from digital resources, the insertion of multimedia elements in the materials elaborated for didactic purpose without specifying the source, the incorrect and/or incorrect mentioning of the source. From the perspective of the relational dimension, which concerns the use of social networks in the academic environment, problems have arisen regarding online communication, as well as difficulties related to the use of personal data or documents of other people, or regarding the security level of the closed groups created for a didactic purpose.

Acknowledgements "This work was supported by a grant of the Ministry of Research and Innovation, CNCS—UEFISCDI, project number PN-III-P1-1.1-TE-2016-0773, within PNCDI III".

References

1. Bigum, C., Kenway, J.: New information technologies and the ambiguous future of schooling—some possible scenarios. In Hargreaves, A. (ed.), Extending educational change, pp. 95–115. Springer, Dordrecht (2005)
2. İşman, A., Çağlar, M., Dabaj, F., Altinay, Z., Altinay, F.: Attitudes of students towards computer. Turk. Online J. Educ. Technol. **3**(1), 11–21 (2004)
3. Yaman, M.: The competence of physical education teachers in computer use. Turk. Online J. Educ. Technol. **6**(4), 79–87 (2007)
4. Baek, Y., Junk, J., Kim, B.: What makes teachers use technology in the classroom? Exploring the factors affecting facilitation of technology with a Korean sample. Comput. Educ. **50**(1), 224–234 (2008)
5. Ki, H., Ahn, S.: A study on the methodology of information ethics education in youth. Int. J. Comput. Sci. Netw. Secur. **6**(6), 91–100 (2006)
6. Himma, K., Tavani, H. (eds.).: The handbook of information and computer ethics. Wiley (2008)
7. Bynum, T.W.: Milestones in the History of Information and Computer Ethics" In: Himma, K., Tavani, H. (ed): The handbook of information and computer ethics, pp. 25–48. Wiley, Canada (2008)
8. Bynum, T.W.: Flourishing ethics. Ethics Inf. Technol. **8**(4), 157–173 (2006)
9. Floridi, L., Sanders, J.W.: The foundationalist debate in computer ethics. In: Francis-Pelton, L., Pelton, T. (ed.), Building attitudes: how a technology course affects pre-service teachers attitudes about technology, Waynesville, NC USA (1996)
10. Himma, K.E.: The relationship between the uniqueness of computer ethics and its independence as a discipline in applied ethics. Ethics Inf. Technol. **5**(4), 225–237 (2003)
11. Tavani, H.T: The uniqueness debate in computer ethics: What exactly is at issue and why does it matter? Ethics Inf. Technol. **4**(1), 37–54 (2002)
12. Floridi, L.: Informational ethics: An environmental approach to the digital divide. Philos. Contemp. World **9**(1), 1–7 (2001)
13. Tavani, H.T.: Floridi's ontological theory of informational privacy: Some implications and challenges. Ethics Inf. Technol. **10**, 155–166 (2008)
14. Prosser, B.T., Ward, A.: Kierkegaard and the internet: Existential reflections on education and community. Ethics Inf. Technol. **2**(3), 167–180 (2000)
15. Roh, Y.R.: Democratic citizenship education in the information age: A comparative study of South Korea and Australia. Asia Pac. Educ. Rev. **5**(2), 167–177 (2004)
16. Baum, J.J.: CyberEthics: The new frontier. TechTrends **49**(6), 54–55 (2005)
17. Brey, B.: Social and ethical dimensions of computer-mediated education. Inf. Commun. & Ethics Soc. **4**(2), 91–101 (2006)
18. Glendinning, I.: Impact of Policies for Plagiarism in Higher Education Across Europe. Plagiarism Policies in Romania. Acta Universitatis Agriculturae et Silviculturae Mendelianae Brunensis. **6**(1), 207–216 (2014)
19. Koohang, A.A.: A study of the attitudes toward computers: anxiety, confidence, liking, and perception of usefulness. J. Res. Comput. Educ. **22**(2), 137–150 (1989)
20. Selwyn, N.: Students attitudes toward computers: validation of a computer attitude scale for 16–19 education. Comput. Educ. **28**(1), 35–41 (1997)

21. Bullock, D.: Moving from theory to practice: an examination of the factors that preservice teachers encounter as they attempt to gain experience teaching with technology during field placement experiences. J. Technol. Teach. Educ. **12**(2), 211–237 (2004)
22. Kersaint, G., Horton, B., Stohl, H., Garofalo, J.: Technology beliefs and practices of mathematics education faculty. J. Technol. Teach. Educ. **11**(4), 549–577 (2003)
23. Baylor, A., Ritchie, D.: What factors facilitate teacher skill, teacher morale, and perceived student learning in technology-using classrooms? Comput. Educ. **39**(1), 395–414 (2002)
24. Watson, D.M.: Pedagogy before technology: Re-thinking the relationship between ICT and teaching. Educ. Inf. Technol. **6**(4), 251–266 (2001)
25. Francis-Pelton, L., Pelton, T.: Building attitudes: how a technology course affects pre-service teachers attitudes about technology (1996)
26. Harrell, M.C., Bradley, M.A.: Data Collection Methods Semi-Structured Interviews and Focus Groups. RAND National Defense Research Institute, USA (2009)
27. Blandford, A.: Semi-structured qualitative studies. In Soegaard, M. Dam, F. (eds.), The Encyclopedia of human-computer interaction, 2nd Edition, The Interaction Design Foundation, Denmark (2013)
28. Arthur, S., Nazroo, J.: Designing fieldwork strategies and materials. In: Ritchie, J., Lewis, J. (eds.) Qualitative research practice: a guide for social science students and researchers, pp. 109–137. Sage, London (2003)
29. Adam, W.C.: Conducting semi-structured interviews. In Newcomer, K.E., Hatry, H.P., Wholey, J.S. (eds.), Handbook of practical program evaluation. Jossey-Bass (2015)
30. Agabrian, M.: Analiza de conținut [Content Analysis]. Polirom, Iași (2006)

Ethical Responsibility of the University Teacher in Online Teaching and Evaluation

Alexandra-Georgiana Poenaru

Abstract Humanity goes through one of the most dynamic stages, characterized by profound structural changes in all areas of life. It was computer science, the age of robots, the digital age, etc., all forming a new environment of life and a new consciousness about them. In a relatively short time, the role of the teacher has undergone a dramatic change. In the context of the current pandemic, higher education teachers have had to refocus on new practices that ensure continuity of teaching and evaluation. This chapter examines the ethical competencies of the university professor from the perspective of online teaching and evaluation. Since the teaching activity has "moved" in the online environment, it is necessary to respect ethical and legal rules in the digital space. In the first part of the chapter, the author gives a presentation on the current meanings of the concept of ethical competence and will analyze in the second part the main digital and ethical competencies that university teachers must possess, with the European Parliament's Recommendation on Key Competences (2006) as a benchmark. EU Regulation 679/2016 on the protection of personal data has to be respected in the context of transitioning from classical to online education.

Keywords Competency · Digital era · Data protection · Ethics · Ethic competency · Higher education

1 Introduction

Information technology plays an important role in the twenty-first century causing profound changes in all areas of life, which signals that we have reached a new era, *the digital age*. Education is one of the fundamental areas in any society that must adapt to change to function effectively in this new era. The real transformation lies not in the increased and diversified pathways of access to information, but in

A.-G. Poenaru (✉)
Vasile Alecsandri University of Bacău, Bacău, Romania

© The Author(s), under exclusive license to Springer Nature Singapore Pte Ltd. 2022   181
L. Mâță (ed.), *Ethical Use of Information Technology in Higher Education*,
EAI/Springer Innovations in Communication and Computing,
https://doi.org/10.1007/978-981-16-1951-9_12

the increased opportunities for individuals to contribute to content production and knowledge creation.

We live in a digital age that facilitates free access to a panoply of information resources. New technologies have caused major changes in the way people access information. The current global situation has put humanity in the face of unpredictable, disruptive situations. The global pandemic has changed the daily lives of social actors, both individually and collectively. Major changes have taken place in each area of activity. The educational field has not been bypassed by these changes either. The transition from classical, face-to-face education, to online education, has been a major step. Important changes have been made to teaching programs, online admissions, and online support for various exams. All of this sparked a discussion of what a post-coronavirus university landscape might look like.

As of the March 11, 2020, following the decision of the Romanian Ministry of Education and Research to suspend face-to-face courses, the Romanian education system had to refocus on new communication and cooperation practices to ensure continuity of learning and organizational functioning. Since April, through a ministerial order, the online school has become mandatory for all actors involved in the educational process, and the online attendance of students and teachers in courses has been monitored. The online movement of the educational instructional activity, a transition that has taken the educational environment in Romania by surprise, involves various problems. In the context of compliance with European legislation on the security of students' data, the teacher must have certain ethical competencies concerning the conduct of teaching in the online environment.

In other news, as assessed in the Evaluative Research Report entitled Online School, conducted by P. Botnariuc et al. [1], the main element that led to major pressure on the education system and society as a whole was the exclusive use of remote media to educate. It is important to note that the Romanian education system is only partially prepared, some teachers do not currently possess sufficient information and skills specific to computer-assisted training and the curriculum allows to a variable/sequential/revised extent the transposition into remote activities. Thus, in addition to several obvious advantages of online learning, some disadvantages can be listed, including limits in teacher–student relations, lack of real feedback, genuine communication, etc.

In this study, the author aims to answer a few questions: How is the concept of ethical competence defined and what are the ethical implications in the online environment, what is the role of the online teacher, what ethical competencies one should have from the perspective of the use of information technology.

2 The Concept of Competence: Ethical Competencies of Teachers

Nowadays, the concept of competence is increasingly used in various organizations. In particular, educational institutions are keen to use the term competence to refer to tools for the development of human resources or to new educational methods. The literature invokes various definitions and ways of operating the concept of competence. The concept of competence was defined as follows: "competency is knowledge, skill, ability, or characteristic associated with high performance on a job, such as problem solving, analytical thinking, or leadership. Some definitions of competency include motives, beliefs, and values" [2]; "a competency is: a cluster of related knowledge, skills and attitudes that affects a major part of one's job (a role or responsibility), that correlates with performance on the job, that can be measured against well-accepted standards, and that can be improved via training and development" [3]; "human competence ... is displayed behavior within a specialized domain in the form of consistently demonstrated actions of an individual that are both minimally efficient in their execution and effective in their results" [4].

Tarrant [5] assesses that the definition of competence is not easy to achieve as it involves epistemological and ethical elements. One will find it very common that competence is described as an ensemble of skills, knowledge, attitudes, and values that enable the efficient carrying out of an activity. Regarding the concept of ethical competence, there are several ways of defining and operationalization [6–9].

De Schrijver et al. [6] summarizes three types of definitions specific to ethical competencies: general definitions, definitions based on James Rest's theory (1986) and definitions based on the KSAs structure (knowledge, skills, and attitudes). The first category of definitions attempts to illustrate a general view of ethical behavior. For [8], for example, an ethical relationship is of this type: Person-Role. By assuming an ethical position, the individual considers himself as a member of a profession and wondering how he or she must behave to successfully fulfill this role. To highlight the second type of definition, the model of [9] Rest can be invoked, according to which moral action is the result of four psychological sub-processes: moral awareness, judgment or moral reasoning, moral motivation, and moral character. Finally, the third type of definition can be analyzed based on [7], which considers that an ethical competence includes high ethical awareness, individual skills to handle ethical issues, functional organizational structure and routines, communication and argumentation skills, trust, and emotional strength.

As Ghiațău has appreciated [10], ethical competence can be understood as the psychological skill that supports teachers to find morally adequate solutions to daily professional problems. Ethical competence is not limited to the relational aspects of the teacher's work but is also connected to the whole set of a teacher's professional responsibilities: curricular design, lesson achievement, selection of teaching, and evaluation methods. In its core, according to OECD [11], competency is defined as "more than just knowledge and skills. It involves the ability to meet complex demands, by drawing on and moving psychosocial resources (including skills and attitudes) in a certain context".

2.1 Ethics in the Digital Era

Ethics, in general, is defined as a code of behavior, usually that of a particular group, profession, or individual. We can discuss the concept of ethics from at least two perspectives. On one hand, ethics understood as a way of behaving, relating to several rules of conduct, and on the other hand, ethics understood from the perspective of the use of information technology in the educational process.

In the field of education, ethics has its roots in the concern regarding equal access to education by anyone no matter the gender, nationality, ideological differences, and physical or mental disabilities, according to Toprak et al. [12]. At the same time, ethics highlights the code of behavior that guides the conduct of members of an educational institution. Mutual respect, justice, tolerance, and goodwill lay the foundations for this code of conduct. Specifically, it implies that, in any situation in the classroom, as well as in the virtual classroom, both pupils and teachers must know and follow acceptable ethical norms, thus creating an educational atmosphere that leads to optimal teaching and learning; everyone knows their role and should exercise it.

Anderson and Simpson [13] explored the ethical issue in an online environment and have highlighted the complexity of dealing with it due to online discourses that could go across physical and cultural borders. In that directive, Gearhart [14] considers that "when we interact with others face-to-face, we immediately see the results of inappropriate and unethical behaviors. When we use information technology in a way that harms others, the act feels less personal because we can't see or hear the other person in exchange". But in this study, we want to emphasize particularly the concept of ethics understood from the perspective of the use of information technology in the educational process, as well as the role that the teacher has in supporting online activities. The transition from face-to-face to online education, in the context of the current pandemic, requires some debate about the ethical and/or moral use of computers. This issue, widely analyzed by the literature, includes elements referring to several indicators such as confidentiality, online safety, fairness, data security, equal access, software reliability, as evidenced by the research of specialists such as Frohmann [15], Burnam and Kafai [16], Croy [17], Lin [18], Van Den Hoven and Lokhorst [19], Weckert [20].

For university education, Barcalow et al. [21] propose an ethical code for the use of information technology by teachers, concerning seven areas of interest. The seven indicators, as shown by The Rules for the use of information technology in the code of ethics in higher education, developed by Mâță and Poenaru [22] are the application of technology, access, student guidance, intellectual property, confidentiality, security, and equipment maintenance which implies the existence of rules (Table 1).

Carril et al. [23] report that the need to use information and communication technology in online teaching changes both the nature of teaching and learning processes and the need to develop ICT and other pedagogical skills. As the online environment changes and new technologies become available, the nature of the role of the online

Table 1 Rules of the ethical use of technology for teachers in higher education

Ethical issues	Norms/rules
Application of technology	– Teachers use information technology to improve the overall quality of education – Teachers must follow the guidelines on introducing technology into the syllabus
Access	– Teachers should provide equal access to technology to all students – Teachers will provide equitable technological resources to all students – Teachers need to use Internet filters and blocking software when students can access certain dangerous information
Guidance of students	– Teachers will inform the students about the conditions of use of the technology
Intellectual property	– Teachers must respect the intellectual property of their peers – Teachers have the responsibility to teach students about intellectual property
Confidentiality	– The teachers monitor the use of the computer by the students to ensure the security and confidentiality rights of the students – Teachers provide a general notification about accessing and/or deleting user files – Teachers must monitor the safety of the users and the integrity of the network – The teachers protect the personal information of the students and keep the data confidential
Security	– Teachers will only use those protected accounts based on passwords that have been assigned to them – Teachers respect the confidentiality of files and resources on the networks – Teachers have the responsibility to check all technological resources – Teachers must report any breach of security
Maintenance of equipment	– Teachers are responsible for maintaining the technological equipment they use

teacher will change. There are several references in the literature on the changing nature of the teacher's role in the online environment [24–27].

For example, the view of academics regarding the change in their roles was investigated by Coppola, Hiltz, and Rotter [28] who identified three roles that require change: cognitive, affective, and managerial. The cognitive role could involve a deeper level of understanding in online teaching, the affective role is necessary to maintain relationships with students online, and the managerial role involves changes in class management that could be different from now on.

The role of the teacher is key in this context. To be capable of developing pupils' basic skills and specialized knowledge, teachers must develop their professional digital competence during their initial teacher education and later, through continuing professional education and development, during their teaching career. Badia et al.

Table 2 Online teachers roles

Role	Definition
Designer	Includes teachers' behavior about course planning, organizing, leading, and controlling (Alvarez et al. [30])
Life skills promoter role	Can be defined as personal management and social skills that are a must-have for adequate functioning on an independent basis (Gómez-Rey et al. [31])
Facilitator	(Baran et al. [32]) gave no definition
Learning support role	Corresponds to different teaching tasks, such as monitoring, guidance, and evaluation of student participation in social interaction activities, explanation of the methodology and the organization of study time, and the presentation and sequencing of learning activities (Badia et al. [29])
Content expert	Chang et al. [33] appreciate that the teacher needs to prepare his materials for the presentation, upload resources for the participants, constantly improve their online skills
Personal	Complies with ethical and legal standards, adopts a positive attitude and commitment to e-learning, shows sensitivity during the communication process, and in online contacts [23]

[29] examined the roles of online teachers concerning different approaches regarding the teaching process in a survey. They identified a new role, the learning support role. When acting in learning support or the social role, online educators often use a collaborative learning approach. The main roles identified since 2010 in the literature are defined in Table 2.

As one can see in Table 1, the roles of teachers online are quite varied. For example, Abdous [34] invokes three central roles, namely organizational, social, and intellectual, and Berge [35] defined four roles (managerial, social, pedagogical, and technical). Several studies also examined the roles of the central and peripheral point of view. Carril et al. [23] considered the pedagogical role as the main, central role, and all seven others as peripheral. According to Metz & Bezuidenhout [36], the content facilitator, metacognition facilitator, technologist, process facilitator, assessor, advisor, and resource provider are all central roles and manager/administrator, designer, co-learner, and researcher are peripheral.

2.2 New European Recommendation for the Protection of Personal Data

Another important issue to be taken into account in the conduct of online activities concerns the protection of student data in the context of the new European regulations. In the present case, we are talking about the two normative acts that make up the data protection legislative package at the European Union level and which on the May

4, 2016, were published in the Official Journal of the European Union. This is the Regulation (EU) 2016/679 on the protection of individuals about the processing of personal data and the free movement of such data [37] and Directive (EU) 2016/680 on the protection of private information in the context of specific activities carried out by law enforcement authorities [38].

As is apparent from the EU Regulation 679/2016, rapid technological developments and globalization have created new challenges for the protection of personal data. The extent of the collection and exchange of personal data has increased significantly. Technology allows both private companies and public authorities to use personal data at an unprecedented level in their activities. Increasingly, individuals are making personal information public worldwide. Technology has transformed both the economy and social life and should further facilitate the free movement of personal data within the Union and the transfer to third countries and international organizations while ensuring a high level of protection of personal data.

In the context of the pandemic, moving learning and evaluation activities online requires certain directives on the protection of student and teacher data. Moreover, students must be in complete consent to the processing of personal data by which they agree to the storage, use, and processing of personal data by the university for contractual purposes, to carry out university studies, i.e., for the exercise by the controller of legitimate interests, provided for by law. At the same time, several rights must be respected in the event of online examinations. In the case of video surveillance, it is important not to infringe the right to privacy of the persons being filmed, in particular by respecting the right to the image of others in the room.

Last but not least, several principles relating to the processing of personal data are set out in Article 5 of [37]. These are as follows: (1) processed lawfully, fairly and transparently with the data subject ("legality, fairness, and transparency"); (2) collected for specific, explicit, and legitimate purposes and not subsequently processed in a manner incompatible with those purposes; further processing for archiving purposes in the public interest, for scientific or historical research purposes or for statistical purposes shall not be considered incompatible with the original purposes in accordance with Article 89(1) ("purpose limitations"); (3) adequate, relevant, and limited to what is necessary in relation to the purposes for which they are processed ("data minimization"); (4) accurate and, if necessary, up-to-date; all necessary measures must be taken to ensure that personal data which are inaccurate, having regard to the purposes for which they are processed, are deleted or rectified without delay ("accuracy"); (5) kept in a form which allows the identification of data subjects for a period not exceeding the period necessary to fulfill the purposes for which the data are processed; personal data may be stored for longer periods in so far as they are processed exclusively for archiving purposes in the public interest, for scientific or historical research purposes or for statistical purposes, in accordance with Article 89 (1), subject to the implementation of the appropriate technical and organizational measures provided for in this Regulation with a view to guaranteeing the rights and freedoms of the data subject ("storage limitations"); (6) processed in a way that ensures the proper security of personal data, including protection against unauthorized or unlawful processing and accidental loss, destruction or damage, by taking appropriate technical or organizational measures ("integrity and confidentiality").

Therefore, student information can only be processed, recorded, and used for a precise, legal, and legitimate purpose, and a fixed period of data retention should be established, depending on the type of information and the reason for processing, for example, until the expiry of the period during which the examination is carried out. The information processed must be relevant and of strict necessity to the purpose of the processing (principle of minimization of the data processed), and personal data must be processed only if the same purpose that cannot be achieved by less invasive means.

3   The Teacher's Digital Skills in the Ethical Use of Online Technology

More and more specialists are bringing to the public's attention theoretical and empirical information on the skills that a teacher must possess when using information technology to carry out their activities, and in this case, the educational activities carried out online. In this respect, several scientific contributions are representative. For example, Shakeel Ahmad Khan, Bhatti, &Aqeel Ahmad Khan [39] appreciate that "the purpose of ICT in education is generally to familiarize students with the use and workings of computers and related social and ethical issues." Thus, teachers must have the necessary competencies for them to appropriately and efficiently guide the students. J. Kerkula [40] concludes that teachers need to be "technologically knowledgeable and competent" but may not be "technology savvy". Moore & Ellsworth [41] argued that there is a low level of ethical integration of educational technology. Lin [42] gathered nine important ethical issues in technological development in teaching and learning that focus more on the understanding of the identified skills. Next, Table 3 mentions several ethical problems relating to information technology, as shown by D. Marcial [43].

The use of IT in the educational domain includes competencies related to social, ethical, legal, and human issues and community linkages. In this sense, the teacher must detain a series of competencies among which: understanding the legal implications of Software Licenses & Fair Use; understanding and explaining the basic concepts of intellectual property rights; identifying and differentiating the copyright; detecting plagiarism in the work of students; advocating the responsible use of various technologies; monitoring how students use the computer specifically for software, hardware, computer games, and Internet activities; to help minimize the effects of the digital divide by providing access to digital materials for all students.

As it results from the Recommendation of The European Parliament and of the Council of December 18, 2006, on key competences for lifelong learning (2006/962/EC) [44], "digital competence involves the confident and critical use of

Table 3 Ethical problems with information technology

Issues	Description
Copyright	Is protection for any published work that helps to prevent that work from being used without prior authorization
Digital divide	Is a term which refers to inequality between one or more groups in terms of access to, use of, or knowledge about information and communication technologies
Etiquette	Refers to a code, manners, or set of rules that allow you to behave and interact correctly with other users in a social environment
Information rights	Are access details given by users or network administrators that define access rights to files on a network
Privacy	Refers to information shared with visiting sites, how that information is used, who that information is shared with, or if that information is used to track users
Software license	Is an agreement between a user and a software company that allows that individual to use the program
Software piracy	A term used to describe the act of illegally using, copying, or distributing software without ownership or legal rights

Information Society Technology (IST) for work, leisure and communication. It is underpinned by basic skills in ICT: the use of computers to retrieve, assess, store, produce, present and exchange information, and to communicate and participate in collaborative networks via the Internet". In general, digital competence can also be defined as the creative, critical, and confident use of information and communication technologies to achieve the objectives related to work, employability, learning, leisure, inclusion, and participation in society. The main domains of the common area of the digital competences are shown in Fig. 1.

Each of the five areas is operationalized by several specific indicators, as shown in Table 4.

A clear evolution of digital competence is seen in the definition proposed in the European Digital Competence Framework DigComp [45], updated and published in 2013, describing the areas that define the individual "digitally competent": the processing of information (identification, location, recovery, storage, organization and analysis of digital information, taking into account its relevance and purpose); communication (communication in digital media, the exchange of digital resources through online tools, communication and collaboration through digital tools, interaction with others through communities and social networks); creating content (creating and editing educational content); safety (protection of personal data, protection of digital identity, taking security measures); problem solving (identification of digital needs and resources, decision-making by choosing the most appropriate digital tools according to purpose, solving conceptual problems by digital means, using creative technologies, and solving technical problems).

Compliance with ethical and legal norms in the digital space is an area specific to the standards of digital competence for teachers (squirrel) [46] and contains several

Fig. 1 Areas of the common digital competence framework for teachers

Problem solving

Information and data literacy

Communication and collaboration

Safety

Digital content creation

Table 4 Operationalization of teachers' digital skills

Domain	Indicators
Information and data literacy	– Browsing, searching, and filtering data, information, and digital content – Evaluation of data, information, and digital content – Managing and retrieval of data, information, and digital content
Communication and collaboration	– Interacting through digital technologies – Sharing information and digital content – Online participation for citizens – Collaborating through digital technologies – Netiquette – Managing digital identity
Digital content creation	– Developing digital content – Integrating and re-elaborating digital content – Copyright and licenses – Programming
Safety	– Protecting devices – Protecting personal data and privacy – Protecting health – Protecting the environment
Problem solving	– Solving technical problem – Identifying technological needs and responses – Innovation and creative use of digital technologies – Identifying gaps in digital competence

indicators. To comply with ethical and legal norms in the digital space, the teacher must use electronic resources, respecting environmental protection rules; identify the positive and negative effects of IT on the environment and human health; know and use pre-established cybersecurity tools for data and equipment protection in the personal digital environment; identify and take protective measures in the event of security threats; configure security applications in line with problem-solving requirements; explain to students and colleagues the risks to individuals when distributing personal information over the Internet; use tools that ensure the confidentiality of personal information and make decisions about applications that collect personal data; use and promote tools for detecting plagiarism; know, comply with, and promote the provisions of the legislation in the field of child protection in the digital environment, digital education, cybercrime, and data protection.

4 Discussions

The purpose of this study was to carry out an analysis of the concept of competence, in the general sense, and of ethical and digital competence, in the specific sense, for teachers who use information technology in the educational instructional process as a result of the current context. The recommendation of the European Parliament and the Council of the European Union considers "competence" as a proven capacity to use personal, social, and/or methodological knowledge, skills, and abilities in work or study situations and for professional and personal development. For [47], digital competence can be broadly defined as the confident, critical, and creative use of ICT to achieve goals related to work, employability, learning, leisure, inclusion, and/or participation in society. Digital competence is a transversal key competence that enables the acquisition of other key competencies. It is related to many of the so-called twenty-first Century skill, which should be acquired by all citizens, to ensure their active participation in society and the economy. For university education, the literature considers that teachers should consider an ethical code for the use of information technology, which includes the application of technology, access, student guidance, intellectual property, confidentiality, security, and equipment maintenance. This framework requires that European regulations on the protection of personal data are taken into account. Another aspect analyzed in this study concerns the role of the teacher in the online space. Several roles performed by teachers have been brought to the attention as evidenced by the studies of the specialists who have addressed this issue. Among the roles mentioned are designer, life skills promoter role, facilitator, learning support role, content expert, managerial, social, etc. Information processing, communication, content creation, safety, and problem solving are examples of key digital skills that a teacher must possess to streamline online activities.

5   Conclusions and Recommendations

In this theoretical study, the author presented a series of scientific information on the concept of ethical competence in the digital era. Another issue analyzed referred to the protection of personal data among students regarding the activity carried out in the online environment. The suspension of face-to-face courses has forced them to be conducted online, which implies compliance with European and national rules. In the second part of the study, the author presented and analyzed the main digital and ethical competencies that a university professor must possess, with the European Parliament's Recommendation on Key Competences (2006) as a benchmark and some ethical problems about information technology. The main teachers' digital skills are correlated with the following areas: information and data literacy, communication and collaboration, digital content creation, safety, and problem solving, and for each of these areas, the main reference indicators were mentioned.

6   Limitations and Future Work

The main limitation of this study would be the lack of empirical research on the issue under discussion. As mentioned, this study brings together several theoretical concepts and relates to studies already conducted by other researchers. However, a future direction of research could be to conduct an empirical study on the ethical competencies of public and private university teachers and the difficulties that may arise in complying with data protection rules in online activity.

Acknowledgements "This work was supported by a grant of the Ministry of Research and Innovation, CNCS—UEFISCDI, project number PN-III-P1-1.1-TE-2016-0773, within PNCDI III."

References

1. Botnariuc, P., Cucoș, C., Glava, C., Iancu, D., Ilie, M., Istrate, O., Labăr, A., Pânișoară, I., Ștefănescu, D., Velea, S.: Școala online. Elemente pentru inovarea educației [Online school. Elements for educational innovation]. University of Bucharest Publishing House, Bucharest (2020)
2. Mirabile, R.J.: Everything you wanted to know about competency modeling. Training & Develop. **51**(8), 73–77 (1997)
3. Parry, S.B.: The quest for competences: Competency studies can help you make HR decision, but the results are only as good as the study. Training **33**, 48–56 (1996)
4. Herling, R.W.: Operational definitions of expertise and competence. Adv. in Develop. Human Res. **5**, 8–21 (2000)
5. Tarrant, J.: What is Wrong with Competence? J. Further High. Educ. **24**(1), 77–83 (2000)
6. De Schrijver A., Maesschalck, J.: A new definition and conceptualization of ethical competence. In Menzel, D., Cooper, T. (eds.) Achieving ethical competence for public service leadership,pp. 29–51. Routledge (2013)

7. Kavathatzopoulos, I.: Making ethical decisions in professional life. In: Montgomery, H., Lipshitz, R., Brehmer, B. (eds.) How Professionals Make Decisions, pp. 277–288. L. Erlbaum, Mahwah, NJ (2005)
8. Gardner, H.: Mintea umană: cinci ipostaze pentru viitor [The human mind: five hypostases for the future]. Sigma, Bucharest (2007)
9. Rest, J.: Moral development: Advances in research and theory. Praeger, New York (1986)
10. Ghiațău, R.: Ethical competence for teachers: A possible model. Symposion **2**(3), 387–403 (2015)
11. OECD: The definition and selection of key competencies. Executive Summary. [Online]. Retrieved from http://www.oecd.org/pisa/35070367.pdf
12. Toprak, E., Özkanal, B., Aydin, S., Kaya, S.: Ethics in E-Learning. The Turkish Online J. Educ. Tech. **9**(2), 78–86 (2010)
13. Anderson, B., Simpson, M.: Ethical issues in open and distance learning. J. Open, Distance and e-Learning **22**(2), 129–139 (2007)
14. Gearhart, D.: Ethics in distance education: developing ethical policies. Online J. Distance Learning Admin. **4**(1), 1–4 (2001)
15. Frohmann, B.: Subjectivity and information ethics. J. Am. Soc. Inform. Sci. Technol. **59**(2), 267–277 (2008)
16. Burnam, B., Kafai, Y.B.: Ethics and the computer: Children's development of moral reasoning about computer and Internet use. J. Educ. Comp. Res. **25**(2), 111–127 (2001)
17. Croy, M.J.: Ethical concerns in computer-assisted instruction. Metaphilosophy **16**(4), 338–349 (1985)
18. Lin, H.: The ethics of instructional technology: Issues and coping strategies by professional technologists in design and training situations in higher education. Education Tech. Res. Dev. **55**(5), 411–437 (2007)
19. Van Den Hoven, J., Lokhorst, G.J.: Deontic logic and computer-supported computer ethics. Metaphilosophy. **33**(3), 376–386 (2003)
20. Weckert, J.: Computer ethics: Future directions. Ethics Inf. Technol. **3**(2), 93–96 (2001)
21. Barcalow, T., Creech, M., Gerrietts, G., Marassa, M., Sallas, P., Sierra-Perry, M., Weinert, B.: Code of Technology Ethics for Educators. University of Illinois, Champaign/ Urbana (2001)
22. Mâță, L., Poenaru, A.: Rules for the use of information technology in the code of ethics in higher education. The 16th International Scientific Conference eLearning and Software for Education. Bucharest, 537–544 (2020). https://doi.org/10.12753/2066-026x-20-070
23. Carril, P.C.M., Gonzalez Sanmamed, M., Hernandez Selles, N.: Pedagogical Roles and Competencies of University Teachers Practicing in the E-Learning Environment. The International Review of Research in Open and Distributed Learning **14**(3), 462–487 (2013)
24. Muge, A., Kalelioglu, F., Gulbahar, Y.: Assessment of a multinational online faculty development program on online teach: Reflections of candidate e-tutors. Turkish Online Journal of Distance Education. **18**(1), 22 (2017)
25. Baran, E., Correia, A.P., Thompson, A.: Transforming online teaching practice: Critical analysis of the literature on the roles and competencies of online teachers. Distance Educ. **32**(3), 421–439 (2011)
26. Bezuidenhout, A.: Analysing the Importance-Competence Gap of Distance Educators With the Increased Utilisation of Online Learning Strategies in a Developing World Context. The International Review of Research in Open and Distributed Learning **19**(3) (2018). https://doi.org/10.19173/irrodl.v19i3.3585
27. Vaill, A.L., Testori, P.A.: Orientation, Mentoring and Ongoing Support: A Three Tiered Approach to Online Faculty Development. Online Learning **16**(2), 111–119 (2012)
28. Coppola, N.W., Hiltz, S.R., Rotter, N.G.: Becoming a Virtual Professor: Pedagogical Roles and Asynchronous Learning Networks. J. Manag. Info. Syst. **18**(4), 169–189 (2002)
29. Badia, A., Garcia, C., Meneses, J.: Approaches to teaching online: Exploring factors influencing teachers in a fully online university: Factors influencing approaches to teaching online. Br. J. Edu. Technol. **48**(6), 1193–1207 (2017)

30. Alvarez, I., Guasch, T., Espasa, A.: University teacher roles and competencies in online learning environments: A theoretical analysis of teaching and learning practices. European J. Teacher Educ. **32**(3), 321–336 (2009)
31. Gómez-Rey, P., Barbera, E., Fernández-Navarro, F.: Students' perceptions about online teaching effectiveness: A bottom-up approach for identifying online instructors' roles. Australasian J. Educ. Tec. **34**(1), 116–130 (2018)
32. Baran, E., Correia, A.P., Thompson, A.: Transforming online teaching practice: Critical analysis of the literature on the roles and competencies of online teachers. Dist. Educ. **32**(3), 421–439 (2011)
33. Chang, C., Shen, H.Y., Liu, Z.F.: University faculty's perspectives on the roles of e-instructors and their online instruction practice. The International Review of Research in Open and Distributed Learning **15**(3), 73–92 (2014)
34. Abdous, M.: A process-oriented framework for acquiring online teaching competencies. J. Comp. High. Educ. **23**(1), 60–77 (2011)
35. Berge, Z.: Facilitating Computer Conferencing: Recommendations From the Field Educational Technology 15 (1995)
36. De Metz, N., Bezuidenhout, A.: An importance–competence analysis of the roles and competencies of e-tutors at an open distance learning institution. Australian J. Educ. Tech. **34**(5) (2018). https://doi.org/10.14742/ajet.3364
37. Regulation (Eu) 2016/679 of the European Parliament and of the Council of 27 April 2016 on the protection of natural persons with regard to the processing of personal data and on the free movement of such data, and repealing Directive 95/46/EC (General Data Protection Regulation)
38. Directive (EU) 2016/680 on the protection of personal data in the context of specific activities carried out by law enforcement authorities
39. Shakeel A. K., Bhatti, R., Aqeel A. K.: Use of ICT by Students: A Survey of Faculty of Education at IUB. Library Philosophy and Practice (e-journal) **677** (2011)
40. Kerkula Foeday, J.: Social Work in the ICT Age. How to Ensure Ethical and Competent Practice in the 21st Century and Beyond (2011). Retrieved from https://www.academia.edu/1172248/Social_Work_in_the_ICT_Age_How_to_Ensure_Ethical_and_Competent_Practice_in_the_21st_Century_and_Beyond
41. Moore, S.L., Ellsworth, J.B.: Ethics of Educational Technology. In Spector, J., Merrill, M., Elen, J., Bishop, M. J. (eds.), Handbook of Research on Educational Communications and Technology. Springer, New York (2014)
42. Lin, K.Y.: Ethical Issues in Technology Education in Taiwan. J. Tech. Stud. **33**(1), 17–24 (2007)
43. Marcial, D.E.: ICT social and ethical competency among teacher educators in the Philippines. Info. Techn. Learning Tools **57**(1), 96–103 (2017). https://doi.org/10.33407/itlt.v57i1.1533
44. Recommendation of the European Parliament and of the Council of 18 December 2006
45. Ferrari, A.: A framework for developing and understanding digital competence in Europe. Publications Office of the European Union, Luxembourg, 50 (2013)
46. Veveriță, T.: Metodologia dezvoltării competenței digitale în procesul formării inițiale a cadrelor didactice filologi [Methodology for developing digital competence in the process of initial training of philological teachers], Doctoral thesis, Tiraspol State University, Chisinau (2019)
47. Ferrari, A.: Digital competence in practice: European commission joint research centre. Institute for Prospective Technological Studies. Spain, Seville (2012)

Responsible Online Ethical Teaching in Higher Education During the COVID-19 Pandemic

Ioana Boghian, Carmen-Violeta Popescu, and Roxana Ardeleanu

Abstract In the context of the COVID-19 pandemic, when a relevant amount of education at all levels has shifted online, there has occurred a series of unprecedented issues related to ethical technology use by teachers and students. Behind the anxiety generated by the online teaching–learning environment and the joy of discovering the benefits of online education of both teachers and students, there have been reports of serious unethical technology use issues manifested as, for example, violations of the General Data Protection Regulation, of intellectual and authorship rights, software piracy. Such issues call for immediate response aimed at diminishing and controlling unethical technology use in online teaching. To this effect, this paper aims to outline the problems connected to online (un)ethical teaching and provide a series of guidelines to be included in the teacher training curriculum as soon as possible. Our proposal provides possible solutions to such issues as the recording of online teaching sessions without the consent of the participants and use of the recording by third parties for various purposes; attendance of third parties to online teaching sessions without the participants—teacher and/or students—being aware of a third party's presence in the online meeting; decreased motivation of both teachers and students to participate and give their best to the online teaching–learning process.

Keywords COVID-19 · Ethics · Higher education · Online teaching · Solutions

I. Boghian (✉) · C.-V. Popescu · R. Ardeleanu
Vasile Alecsandri University of Bacău, Bacău, Romania
e-mail: boghian.ioana@ub.ro

C.-V. Popescu
e-mail: cmuraru@ub.ro

R. Ardeleanu
e-mail: rardeleanu@ub.ro

© The Author(s), under exclusive license to Springer Nature Singapore Pte Ltd. 2022   195
L. Mâță (ed.), *Ethical Use of Information Technology in Higher Education*,
EAI/Springer Innovations in Communication and Computing,
https://doi.org/10.1007/978-981-16-1951-9_13

1 Introduction

The World Health Organization (WHO) declared COVID-19 as a global public health emergency of international concern on January 30, 2020, as well as a pandemic on March 11, 2020 [1]. There have been other cases of viruses negatively impacting human life in several countries in recent years (the SARS-CoV, the H1N1 Flu), but the COVID-19 pandemic has affected the entire world, globally impacting a wide variety of human activities domains with serious economic, social, and health-related consequences: health care (body care, mental care), education, traveling (whether for business or tourism), and the leisure industry (sports, hotels and restaurants, arts and entertainment, etc.). Short-term closure of academic institutions under emergencies is not recent; however, the global scale of today's educational instability is unparalleled and, if sustained, may inflict psychological distress and misery at various levels [2].

The COVID-19 pandemic has had a serious impact on students, instructors, and educational organizations around the globe [3], causing schools, colleges, and universities to close their campuses so that students could follow social distancing measures [4]. Shifting from the conventional, on-site educational environment to the online, virtual one has generated challenges, obstacles, and increased effort to tackle newly emerged issues in areas ranging from limited to total absence of social interaction to technological devices breakdown. As nobody knows when the COVID-19 pandemic will be overcome, educational institutions around the world have undertaken the use of already available technical resources to create online educational materials for students of all academic fields, as well as develop, together with companies in the domain of technological research and development, innovative digital applications to enhance the virtual educational experience [5]; also, academic organizations need to constantly improve their curriculum by adding new instructional methods and strategies [4].

As early as the 2000s, UNESCO researched the challenges implied by implementing the use of the Internet in schools from the perspective of computer coordinators; the research concluded by highlighting ethical issues as one of the critical obstacles in online education, revealing, at the time of the study (1998–2001) a 10% increase in concerns about ethical issues, meaning that ethical and cultural worries have been continuously soaring [6]. The need for responsible online ethical teaching has also become equally imperative. Should young people be educated/taught how to learn, promoting flexibility in thinking, adaptability, cooperation, and dialogue and perhaps most importantly the ability to anticipate change in the context of the future (challenges)? The digital generation, those born between 1996 and 2010, spends more and more time in the virtual world, playing, writing, or reading blogs, visiting and creating, using one or several virtual identities. In this context, what is online ethical teaching and what should the aims of online ethical teaching be?

The permanent contact with the virtual world brings not only benefits but also specific dangers that education should diminish. The inappropriate use of modern technologies in educational activities not only has become a major problem at the international level, as more and more specialists in the field are trying to find solutions to mitigate the negative effects that derive from this aspect.

Based on the term of computer ethics as defined by Moor and Bynum in 2002 [7], various authors try to answer the following question: what is wrong and right from the ethical point of view in the educational process carried out in the virtual environment. According to Beycioglu [8], the term *computer ethics* could be a subfield of information ethics which was defined by Reitz in "Information Ethics" as "the branch of ethics that focuses on the relationship between the creation, organization, dissemination, and use of information, and the ethical standards and moral codes governing human conduct in society" [8, p. 202].

When we choose to use a certain computer application in carrying out teaching activities for students, we should also be concerned with issues related to the safety and security of the identity of all those involved in the teaching act. It is important that the computer applications or educational platforms used in the educational act gain the trust of those whose data are collected.

Within the virtual team comprising the teacher and the students, the ethical aspects must be maintained as it happens in the case of a face-to-face experience. Blockages in communication due to depersonalization in the online environment can lead to actions of violation of ethical principles and the temptation to cheat or copy.

In general, unethical behavior is related to individual actions that a person performs in the idea of selfishly gaining advantages over others. Ethical issues regarding online learning are focused primarily on copyright, fair-use and plagiarism, and cheating. Even if studies show that students who cheat in face-to-face learning systems will do the same in online learning, there is a perception that the virtual environment could encourage cheating and unethical practice by using a different identity, a virtual one. The students are more and more receptive to creating several virtual identities through which they can become whatever they want. Data privacy is a very important aspect of security and safety in the online environment which has implications for ethical issues.

This chapter aims to define responsible online ethical teaching and provide answers to a series of related issues: challenges and problems connected to online education from the perspective of ethical technology use by *teachers* and solutions; challenges and problems connected to online education from the perspective of ethical technology use by *students* and solutions; a series of guidelines on ethical online education to be officially included in the teacher training curriculum at national and international level.

2 Method

This paper is based on a literature review type of research. This type of approach supports researchers to identify, evaluate, and systematize the literature on the undertaken research topic as well as extract and formulate solutions to the research objectives. The literature search was begun in March 2020, following worldwide news of the outbreak of the SARS-Cov-2 pandemic, and was conducted in the databases EBSCO, Google Scholar, ProQuest, ResearchGate, and others, using the following keywords: "online education, COVID-19", "online ethical/ unethical teaching", "ethical/unethical technology use by teachers", "ethical/ unethical technology use by students", "online teaching, teacher training", and "online teaching, teacher training curriculum". The selection of relevant studies consisted of covering by hand all the articles on one or several of our study's research objectives:

O1: to define online ethical teaching in higher education during the COVID-19 pandemic;

O2: to highlight the challenges and problems connected to online education from the perspective of ethical technology use by *teachers*;

O3: to highlight the challenges and problems connected to online education from the perspective of ethical technology use by *students*;

O4: to provide solutions to the challenges and problems connected to online education from the perspective of ethical technology use by teachers and students and guidelines on ethical online education to be officially included in the teacher training curriculum at the national and international level as soon as possible.

3   Results

The literature research generated a relevant number of articles published in 2020, or under publication, which illustrates the acuteness of education in the COVID-19 pandemic context. Numerous articles contain the words "COVID-19" and education in their titles, and the topics of such articles draw on such themes as problems related to online learning and teaching in various domains of education and for different educational cycles or learner ages; advantages and disadvantages of online education; positive and harmful effects of online education at the physical, mental, and emotional level of both teachers and learners; proposals and suggestions of best practices for conducting online education at various disciplines; ethical aspects connected to the use of information technology in education; personal data protection in the virtual environment and risks associated with online teaching–learning for teachers and students from this perspective; online education as generator of even more inequality in terms of the right to education for children and students from vulnerable groups, the social, economic, cultural, physical, mental, moral, emotional effects of online education on the short and long terms, etc.

We shall further present our findings for each of the research objectives.

Regarding O1, to define online ethical teaching in higher education during the COVID pandemic, online ethical teaching may be defined as a set of rules both for e-Learners and e-Teachers that guides their conduct in the online environment in the direction of mutual respect, justice, tolerance, and avoidance of all acts and discourses that are harmful to others [9].

Online teaching implies the use of information technology. A series of studies have been elaborated on the unethical use of IT in education, resulting in the identification of unethical online practices: plagiarism, inappropriate use of programs, pirated software, or, in other words, all activities involving the violation of copyright [10, 11]. Mâță et al. [12] have identified a series of models and theories of unethical use of information technologies in higher education: general theories (the theory of planned behavior, the theory of reasoned action, the theories of Jean Piaget and Lawrence Kohlberg on the stages of moral development, etc.); decision-making models (e.g., Hunt and Vitell's comprehensive model for ethical decision making, detailing the factors that determine attitude); information technology models (Mason's PAPA model, the ethical behavioral model of information technology use elaborated by Banerjee et al. [13], Chatterjee's model of unethical use of information technology [14], Leonard and Cronan's model of ethical computer use attitudes [15], etc.). Of the latter, the most relevant for our definition of online ethical teaching in higher education is Mason's 1986 PAPA model that comprises four ethical aspects that are essential for the digital era: privacy, accuracy, property, and access. Privacy or confidentiality concerns people's thoughts, feelings, beliefs, fears, and fantasies as well as the ability to hide from others; the information system should not invade the private space of a person. Accuracy is related to the accuracy of information. Property refers to the fact that information systems should protect intellectual property and the flow of information. Accessibility is represented by the idea that information systems should be available to all [16].

Regarding the importance of ethics in online educational environments, to take moral decisions regarding online education, the educational institutes should promote and build a culture of trust, define the ethical and unethical application of electronic contents, and support accurate understanding of privacy and intellectual rights. This implies a common perception of universal privacy and copyright laws and of what an ethical educational environment should be [17].

Online teaching implies teachers working in electronic environments and encountering challenges in terms of providing electronic content, learning facilities, the use of a reliable network, and effective software programs, with network security and ethical issues coming into the foreground now more than ever before. Feng Chen Miao [6] argues that online ethical teaching is ensured when teachers make fair and appropriate use of technology, exploit technological resources effectively, and conduct good activities [6].

At the level of each higher education institution in correlation with university autonomy, there should be a code of ethics as an extension of the already existing code of ethics for face-to-face learning because a series of ethical rules regarding on-site education also remain valid in the virtual environment.

The need for an ethical code may be imposed by the fact that an online community within a higher education institution may include persons of various ages, with different cultural and religious backgrounds, or even diverging opinions and attitudes regarding online education. A common denominator should be found for all these aspects to ensure the best educational process based on a shared agreement concerning ethical norms.

Concerning O2: to highlight the challenges and problems connected to online education from the perspective of ethical technology use by *teachers*, there have been identified two major problems connected to online learning.

Firstly, as full-time online education has only been a recent practice, there are no studies yet to establish the effects and efficacy of online learning [18].

Secondly, the capacity to teach digitally differs according to a wide range of factors: learning goals, educational priorities, availability of technological devices and data connection, the age of learners, etc. [19]. Online education can be effective in digitally advanced countries, whereas, in the communities where an Internet connection and/or technological devices are almost nonexistent or completely absent and families struggle with poverty, online education has come across as a factor generating even more inequalities on the short and long term; also, students accessing the Internet through smartphones do not take full advantage of online education because a relevant amount of online content is not accessible via smartphones. Other problems associated with online education include lack of proper interaction with teachers and classmates; further questions and clarifications on the learning content are usually discussed over the e-mail, which implies even more time effort from both teacher and students; online education does not comply with the tactile learning style of some learners; there is limited to no classroom socialization, students communicate with their fellows digitally, and the real-time sharing of ideas, knowledge, and information among them is not possible in online learning; such aspects define online education as crisis education [20, 21].

Dhawan [22] proposes a SWOT analysis for e-learning modes in times of crisis. The ethical issues connected to online learning are included in the challenges section of the SWOT analysis and mainly refer to the violation of the universal right to equal education: unequal distribution of ICT infrastructure; the doubtful/poor quality of online education as a result of some factors (teachers with poor digital skills, poor Internet connection, obsolete learning content, etc.); the digital divide (the gap between those able to benefit from the Internet and those who are not); technology cost and obsolescence [22, p. 10]. There is a lack of standards on how to make the transition from offline to online learning efficiently, with good time management and proper motivation of students to actively take part in online education, as well as no general rules on e-resources quality, quality control, development, and delivery.

Besides the problems mentioned above, as the use of educational technologies and software tools in the education system has become unavoidable in the current pandemic context, there have also emerged concerns about the ethical use of technology for educational purposes. Thus, the need for the school to teach young people, to develop those modern skills on which an educational action should be based in the twenty-first century, has become imperative.

Another important challenge is to ensure correct and efficient evaluation. If in face-to-face learning the teacher can ensure that the works submitted after tests during the classes are the students', in online education, this aspect can be difficult to control. In online evaluation, the teacher should find solutions for the positive validation of the fact that the paper truly belongs to the student and not somebody else and whether the respective paper is the result of partial or full plagiarism.

About O3: to highlight the challenges and problems connected to online education from the perspective of ethical technology use by *students*, students' voices need to be taken into consideration when it comes to online learning if we want to examine the challenges faced by students [3, 23] and find solutions to issues such as enhancing the quality and efficiency of online learning and diminishing unethical information technology use by students, as well as its consequences.

There is a series of studies on students' perception of online learning in terms of efficiency, but fewer on students' perception of the issue of the ethical use of information technology in education [24, 25]. For example, the study by Anwar and Adnan [25] on a sample of 126 higher education students attending online education in Pakistan found that, among other things, 71.4% of students feel that they are well qualified to use computer/laptop for online learning, 61.1% of students reported that they are comfortable communicating digitally, while 11.1% feel that they face problems in digital communication; 67.5% reported that online learning is way different from conventional learning mode, while 18.3% feel that there is little difference between online and conventional learning; only 10.3% of students feel that online learning is more motivating than conventional learning, while the majority of the students (71.4%) voted against the notion that online learning is more motivating than conventional learning; 50.8% students reported that it is not possible to effectively complete entire university courses through online means, while 18.3% reported that it is possible to complete an entire course through distance learning; 42.9% of students reported that they feel difficulties while doing group projects or assignments through distance education, while 34.1% of students feel that group projects and assignments can be completed digitally; 78.6% of students feel that face-to-face contact with an instructor is necessary for learning and distance learning [25].

We have identified several studies on students' challenges and problems connected to online education from the perspective of ethical technology use [26, 27]. Hamity, Reka, and Baloghová's study, conducted on a sample of 225 students from the State University of Tetova, in Macedonia, revealed that the difference between students who claim to have enough knowledge about online ethics and those who have little or no knowledge about Internet ethics is relatively small, 53% vs. 47%, indicating that nearly half of the students that had declared themselves to be massive users of the Internet did not have enough knowledge about the ethical use of the Internet [26].

Another study also found that undergraduates at higher educational institutions are using information communication technologies in their daily lives but are not taught how to do so ethically, the most common ethical violations in this respect being, as of the pre-COVID-19 pandemic world, software piracy, plagiarism, and cheating [27], with expectations in recent research for such acts to increase in number and relevance in today's full-time online education.

The reasons behind such expectations regarding increased unethical information technology use by students include

- demotivation and diminished interest in online learning as a result of poor to no social interaction and connectivity issues;
- lack of access to physical libraries;

– long hours spent in front of the computer for educational purposes which generate a desire to solve assignments quickly and thus reduce the time spent online for learning purposes as much as possible;
– lack of proper training on the ethical use of information technology for educational purposes (intellectual property rights concerning digital content).

The study by Cilliers [27] found that first-year students understood what software piracy was but did not think it was wrong to copy software from the Internet; eventually, they did understand that cheating, while making use of technology, was wrong and should be avoided.

An example of good practice connected to online education from the perspective of ethical technology use by students can be provided by Wawasan Open University.

At the level of this institution, created in 2006 and providing distance education in the online environment, these measures are stipulated under the "Rules and Regulations for Information Technology and Facilities" section of the University's Student Handbook. This guide can be accessed from the student portal and Wawasan-Learn. The guide sets out rules and measures that students will follow in an informed manner. Some of the rules regarding the example in a discussion forum concern both the "tone" of the language in which these messages are written and examples of messages that are forbidden, advertisements, or messages with a religious or political connotation. Other forbidden messages are those that can invade privacy (e.g., posting another person's phone number without their permission) [9].

Concerning O4, providing solutions to the challenges and problems connected to online education from the perspective of ethical technology use by teachers and students and guidelines on ethical online education to be officially included in the teacher training curriculum at the national and international level as soon as possible, based on the literature analysis, there should be reconsidered and reformulated the ethical codes for academic education to include the approaches to the specificities of online education in the COVID-19 context.

The study of Basilaia and Kvavadze [23] reveals that the lesson learned from the COVID-19 pandemic will force a generation of new laws, regulations, platforms, and solutions for future cases, so that the countries around the world may be more prepared than they are today [23].

Information security in a higher education institution is an extremely important element for any device connected to the Internet or connected to an intra/extranet network [28]. Thus, it must be taken into account that the organization minimizes the risks regarding the security of the information and data it manages [29]. This can be done in several ways such as adopting a strict policy on personal data protection and information security, reporting information security incidents, training all stakeholders on the importance of managed information and the consequences, dissemination, alienation of important data, but also the use of materials without copyright.

Educational institutions, as well as all organizations that have their networks, must restrict access to certain devices that store vital information. These computers will only be accessed by designated personnel who will be logged in with a username and password. Regardless of the work platform, users will be differentiated in terms of access to an application or other information, depending on their responsibilities and duties. Only the zero-level administrator can install or change the settings of a used system or application, and the rest of the users have restricted rights. For example, students participating in a course should not be able to give participation to any other person inside or outside the institution.

Backups of applications, information, and system data should be performed at all times to avoid the risks caused by external factors with or without intention. We mention here power outages, system failure, and hackers.

The information in the system must also be encrypted to be invulnerable. They become illegible and inaccessible to people who do not know about digital information management.

Both antivirus programs and firewall applications will be used to block data communications over a network and/or malicious programs.

Strict measures will be initiated when information is transmitted by e-mail. Thus, antivirus programs must have the option to scan both sent and received messages, including attached documents.

Regarding the activity of direct participants in the online educational act, teachers, and students, but also indirect (parents), the keyword should be *responsibility*. We are the only responsible people in our lives. Improving the quality of online education is closely related to the desire for the personal development of teachers. In general, young teachers are most willing to use digital resources in the teaching–learning assessment process, while older teachers use these methods to a lesser extent and under the influence of external factors [30]. In the new context created by the COVID-19 pandemic, all teachers are forced to use digital resources and adapt to the use of platforms from the simplest, such as e-mail, to the most complicated such as Google Classroom, Google meets, and Microsoft Teams. Teachers work under the paradigm of lifelong learning and adapt to the new context also that involves personal effort.

For Feng Chen Miao [6], to ensure online ethical teaching, teachers should do the following: use technology fairly; effectively exploiting technological resources; appropriate uses of technological resources; demonstrating good activities [6].

The transition to online education involves a fundamental change in the teaching strategies used. Now, the emphasis must be placed on interactive strategies, on the use of didactic methods with a pronounced formative character. Interactive methods are based on action; they are those that require the maximum mechanisms of thought, imagination, intelligence, and creativity. Thus, the teacher must give up the actor–spectator teaching style and encourage cooperation between students, collaboration, expressing their own opinions. The teacher is no longer the transmitter of information, the one who makes the decisions during the lecture, but the one who stimulates the student to discover, to investigate, to develop new skills and behaviors. The student becomes an active participant in his/ her own training and development. The emphasis is no longer on the volume of information transmitted, but on the way of thinking, intrinsic motivation, and cognitive autonomy of the student.

Regarding the evaluations, they can no longer be only summative, but of a continuous type, therefore formative. The problem encountered by teachers is that of cheating/copying by students. In this regard, on the one hand, students must be informed about plagiarism, what it is and how it can be avoided, and on the other hand, assessments must be designed in such a way as to avoid copying. The themes/evaluations must stimulate creativity, originality but also the spirit of competition [31, 32].

The contents of the online lessons must be presented in an attractive but at the same time flexible and engaging form. It is advisable to use experiential learning, learning that stimulates the ability of analysis and creativity of students. The lack of direct contact must be replaced by arousing interest in new knowledge, stimulating imagination, memory, and the power of anticipation, but also the ability to communicate. Given the social distance to which students are subjected, they should be stimulated to solve the assigned tasks individually or in small groups.

In supporting online lessons, teachers may also encounter difficulties in involving students. This is because: there may be members of the group who do not want to expose themselves, due to shyness or lack of self-confidence; some students may be used to waiting for the team's results and then expressing themselves; the lack of interest/experience in the subject of the lesson; monopolizing the discussion by a student who can be seen as an authoritarian leader; due to verbal conflicts between group members; due to the large number of students who are part of the team.

Teachers and students should be made aware of the many advantages and benefits that the human society has from the use of information technology, but also of the possibility that the information technology can be abused by various users to the detriment of other people and, sometimes, of society.

The recommendation of a study by Cilliers [27] is that information ethics must be included in the undergraduate curriculum to prepare students to deal with these ethical problems. To carry out the teaching activity effectively, an ethical guide to online activities should be created. It will be addressed to all parties involved: pupils, students, but also teachers and researchers, and support staff from the institution. An ethical guideline will be useful not only for an educational institution but for an entire education system. Thus, students and teachers will once again be guided to adopt and respect values such as integrity, honesty, and appreciation of truth. Intellectual property and copyright are a central element in teaching and research.

Academic integrity requires that each of the parties involved in the education system act in the interest of the institution and support its strategies and objectives to achieve the mission of education and training. The parties involved also have the obligation to defend the image and prestige of the educational institution, not to harm the image or its interests, to be loyal to the institution, and fulfill their professional duties.

The online ethical conduct guide will be based on universal ethical principles. Among these, we mention

1. the principle of autonomy;
2. the principle of dignity;

3. the principle of fair play;
4. the precautionary principle;
5. the principle of justice.

From these general principles, we can make up a set of rules of moral (ethical) conduct in the form of obligations or prohibitions that indicate what to do/not to do from an ethical point of view.

1. Respect for academic and personal autonomy and freedom, respect for research consent;
2. Respect for dignity in the sense of prohibiting online misinformation, ensuring the transparency of both scientific and administrative information, ensuring intellectual correctness (plagiarism, intellectual fraud are prohibited);
3. Respect for professional integrity, prohibiting mental injury of the persons involved; respect for confidentiality;
4. Fair and non-discriminatory treatment for all pupils/students, reward on merit, elimination of conflicts of interest, rejection of corruption, and abuse.

To implement an ethical guide, it must be disseminated, known, and applied by all students and all teaching and support staff. This can be done with the help of online training sessions with teachers and/or students, parents to study, analyze, understand the rules of conduct online, or with the help of movies, games, and case debates.

4 Discussions

We have systematized our findings for each research objective in Table 1.

As shown in Table 1, there is a stringent need for standardizing laws, rules, and regulations that concern all aspects of online education:

- ensuring curriculum coverage in parallel with a motivational, engaging virtual environment for learners;
- developing high-quality teaching materials, contents, and tools for online education;
- ensuring personal data protection and information security in the virtual environment for both teachers and students;
- ensuring backup applications that may activate automatically in case of security breaches;
- ensuring redundant systems that may be used in "emergency" mode, when the main platform/connection has failed;
- instruct both teachers and students on the ethical use of information technology regularly;
- elaboration and dissemination among teachers and students of a national ethical code of conduct in the online teaching–learning-evaluation process;
- elaboration and dissemination among students of an easy-to-read netiquette poster on communication rules in the online environment; for example, avoid off-topic,

Table 1 Systematization of findings for each research objective

Research objective	Findings	References
O1: definition of online ethical teaching in higher education during the COVID-19 pandemic	– Online ethical teaching as equal access to education – Online ethical teaching as the code of behavior based on mutual respect, justice, tolerance, and goodwill that guides the conduct of the members of an educational institution (teachers and learners) – Online ethical teaching as compliance with the four ethical aspects that are essential for the digital era: Privacy, Accuracy, Property, and Access (the PAPA model)	[9, 16, 33]
O2: challenges and problems connected to online education from the perspective of ethical technology use by *teachers*	– Increased student academic dishonesty in exams and assignments – Concerns about having one's intellectual copyright violated through plagiarism, sharing of one's work without permission, etc.	[9, 33]
O3: challenges and problems connected to online education from the perspective of ethical technology use by *students*	– The challenges faced by students: software piracy, plagiarism, and cheating – Students' perception of the issue of the ethical use of information technology in education is biased or truncated – Challenges and problems connected to online education from the perspective of ethical technology use: poor quality of education and learning content; low level of interaction during online classes; inefficient study time management; exposure to a vast amount of spam, hate, and hoax messages	[3, 23] [24, 25] [9, 26, 27]
O4: solutions to the challenges and problems connected to online education from the perspective of ethical technology use by teachers and students and guidelines on ethical online education to be officially included in the teacher training curriculum at national and international level as soon as possible.	– New laws, regulations, platforms, and solutions for online learning – Information security – Restrict access to devices that store vital information – The differentiated possibility of access – Backups of applications – Encrypted information – Using antivirus programs and firewall application – Personal development of teachers – Use technology fairly; effectively exploiting of technological resources; appropriate uses of technological resources; demonstrating good activities – A fundamental change in the teaching strategies used – Evaluations must stimulate creativity, originality but also the spirit of competition	[23] [28] [29] [6, 30] [31, 32] [27]

insulting, hate or personal-attack messages; do not post advertisements, political and/or religious messages, spam or hoaxes on the educational platforms used by your educational institution; do not share another person's data without their permission (telephone number, photo, address, e-mail) or any other offensive, abusive, racist, and discriminative messages.

Within higher education institutions, postgraduate courses can be held to focus on issues related to the security of activities in the online environment together with the ethical issues involved, to train specialists at the level of each institution. In our country, there are already concerns in this area, and specialists in the field are trying to find solutions to these current challenges. Thus, the Romanian Intelligence Service through the National Cyberint Center, together with the Ministry of National Education and companies in the IT&C field, initiated the steps for the development, adaptation, and implementation of curricula in the field of cybersecurity, at the level of technical universities and in some high schools in Romania. Also, twenty higher education institutions have introduced or are about to introduce in the university program post-university studies (short-term) and master studies dedicated to security in the online environment. The first series of students specialized in this field graduated in 2019 (source https://intelligence.sri.ro/educatia-investitie-securitatea-cibernetica/). The Cyberint Center continues the initiatives dedicated to professional training in the field of security in the online environment, coming to meet the possible legislative changes in the field of cybersecurity at the national and international level—implementation of the Network and Information Systems Security (NIS) Directive and the EU General Data Protection Regulation (GDPR).

Given the special importance that security and ethics in the online environment will have in the educational activities, at the level of decision-making forums there should be considered the possibility of introducing a study discipline through which students are informed about the dangers to which they may be exposed in the online environment but especially how to proceed in such situations.

There is a wide range of the aspects impacted by (un)ethical online education that all the actors engaged in education should be aware of decision-makers in education such as government officials, management staff of educational institutions, members of the academic teaching staff, and representatives of students' unions and students.

5 Conclusions

Although it is too early to generate large scale and long-term results of online education in terms of teaching and learning efficiency, its impact on the physical, mental, and emotional dimensions of human development, we may conclude that online learning is a solution in times of crisis given its potential to send vast amounts of information/learning content to a large number of people in the remotest corners of the world. It has already been hypothesized that online education is not as effective as on-site education and this is true where the right to quality education is violated due to monetary issues.

In technologically advanced countries, one of the most undesired effects of using information technology in education is its unethical use associated with harmful consequences such as violation of data privacy and intellectual rights, as well as offensive online discourse directed at others. This paper highlights a series of solutions to the above-mentioned problems that should be implemented and disseminated at the level of higher education institutions nationally and internationally; as human rights to property and privacy are universal, so should the standards for the ethical, unharmful use of information technology in education, and not only, be.

Acknowledgements "This work was supported by a grant of the Ministry of Research and Innovation, CNCS—UEFISCDI, project number PN-III-P1-1.1-TE-2016-0773, within PNCDI III".

References

1. Cucinotta, D., Vanelli, M.: WHO Declares COVID-19 a Pandemic. Acta Bio. Med. [Internet] **91**(1), 157–160 (2020)
2. McCarthy, K.: The global impact of coronavirus on education (2020). Retrieved November 13, 2020, from https://abcnews.go.com/International/global-impact-coronaviruseducation/story
3. Mailizar, Almanthari, A., Maulina, S., Bruce, S.: Secondary school mathematics teachers' views on e-learning implementation barriers during the Covid-19 pandemic: The case of Indonesia. Eurasia J. Math., Sci. Tech. Educ. **16**(7), em1860 (2020)
4. Toquero, C.M.: Challenges and opportunities for higher education amid the COVID-19 pandemic: The Philippine context. Pedagogical Res. **5**(4), em0063 (2020)
5. Kaur, G.: Digital Life: Boon or bane in teaching sector on COVID-19. CLIO an Annual Interdisciplinary J. His. **6**(6), 416–427 (2020)
6. Miao, F.C.: ICT in Teacher education: Case studies from Asia-Pacific region. UNESCO (2020)
7. Moor, J.H., Bynum, T.W.: Introduction to cyberphilosophy. Metaphilosophy. **33**(1–2), 4–10 (2002)
8. Beycioglu, K.: A cyberphilosophical issue in education: Unethical computer using behavior—The case of prospective teachers. Comput. Educ. **53**, 201–208 (2009)
9. Vighnarajah, S., Chuah, K.M.: Ethical Conduct of E-Learners and E-Teachers in Online Learning Community. Pakistan J. Dist. & Online Learn. **3**(2), 1–12 (2017)
10. Phukan, S., Dhillon, G.: Ethical and intellectual property concerns in a multicultural global economy. Elec. J. Info. Syst. Develop. Count. **7**(3), 1–8 (2001)
11. Ghiațău, R.M., Mâță, L.: Factors influencing higher education teachers' attitudes towards unethical use of information technology: A review. Revista Romaneasca pentru Educatie Multidimensionala. **11**(1), 287–300 (2019)
12. Mâță, L., Boghian, I., Poenaru, A.G., Ghiațău, R.M.: Models and Theories of Unethical Use of Information Technology in Higher Education. Proceedings of the International Scientific Conference eLearning and Software for Education. Bucharest, 138–144 (2019)
13. Banerjee, D., Cronan, T.P., Jones, T.W.: Modelling IT ethics: A study in situational ethics. MIS Q. **22**(1), 31–60 (1998)
14. Chatterjee, S.: A Model of Unethical Usage of Information Technology. AMCIS 2005 Proceedings 51, 2891–2896 (2005)
15. Leonard, L.N.K., Cronan, T.P.: Attitude toward ethical behavior in computer use: a shifting model. Indus. Manag. & Data Syst. **105**(9), 1150–1171 (2005)

16. Mason, R.O.: Four ethical issues of the information age. Manag. Info. Syst. Quart. **10**(1), 5–12 (1986)
17. Mitchell, R., Garza, L.: Ethics in an online environment. New Directions for Community Colleges **148**, 63–70 (2009)
18. McPherson, M.S., Bacow, L.S.: Online higher education: Beyond the hype cycle. J. Econ. Perspec. **29**(4), 135–153 (2015)
19. Liguori, E., Winkler, C.: From offline to online: Challenges and opportunities for entrepreneurship education following the COVID-19 pandemic. Entrepreneurship Educ. Pedagogy **3**(4), 346–351 (2020)
20. Britt, R.: Online education: A survey of faculty and students. Radiol. Technol. **77**(3), 183–190 (2006)
21. Pace, C., Pettit, S.K., Barker, K.S.: Best practices in middle level quaranteaching: Strategies, tips and resources amidst COVID-19. Becoming: J. Georgia Association for Middle Level Educ. **31**(1), 2 (2020)
22. Dhawan, S.: Online learning: A Panacea in the time of COVID-19 crisis. J. Educ. Tech. Syst. **49**(1), 5–22 (2020)
23. Basilaia, G., Kvavadze, D.: Transition to online education in schools during a SARS-CoV-2 coronavirus (Covid-19) pandemic in Georgia. Pedagogical Res. **5**(4), 1–9 (2020)
24. Mishra, L., Gupta, T., Shree, A.: Online Teaching-Learning in Higher Education during Lockdown Period of COVID-19 Pandemic. International Journal of Educational Research Open. Journal pre-proof. Retrieved November 13, 2020, from https://reader.elsevier.com/reader/sd/pii/S2666374020300121?token=D14ABEE41B77608690FE8D14DF2DA96CDD6E8CFD245C2870363CE58A5FF51E7489179BA6B179A24066BE839507E2BD16
25. Anwar, K., Adnan, M.: Online learning amid the COVID-19 pandemic: Students perspectives. J. Pedagogical Res. **1**(2), 45–51 (2020)
26. Hamiti, M., Reka, B., Baloghová, A.: Ethical use of information technology in high education. Procedia—Social and Behav. Sci. **116**, 4411–4415 (2014)
27. Cilliers, L.: Evaluation of information ethical issues among undergraduate students: An exploratory study. SA J. Info. Manag. **19**(1), a767 (2017). https://doi.org/10.4102/sajim.v19i1.767
28. Nechita, E., Timofti, I.C.: Instruire asistată de calculator [Computer aided training]. Alma Mater, Bacău (2011)
29. Oprea, D.: Protecția și securitatea informațiilor [Information protection and security]. Polirom, Iași (2007)
30. Baek, Y., Junk, J., Kim, B.: What makes teachers use technology in the classroom? Exploring the factors affecting facilitation of technology with a Korean sample. Comput. Educ. **50**(1), 224–234 (2008)
31. Prohaska, V.: Encouraging students' ethical behaviour (2013). Retrieved November 13, 2020, from https://www.apa.org/ed/precollege/ptn/2013/05/ethical-behavior
32. Prohaska, V.: Teachers can have an effect: Strategies for encouraging ethical student behavior. In: Landrum, R.E., McCarthy, M. (eds.) Teaching ethically: Challenges and opportunities. American Psychological Association, Washington, DC (2012)
33. Toprak, E., Özkanal, B., Aydin, S., Kaya, S.: Ethics in elearning. The Turkish Online J. Educ. Tech. **9**(2), 78–86 (2010)

Glossary

Academic dishonesty It takes into account a range of unethical behaviors including cheating plagiarism, the misuse of technology, as well as additional practices to gain an unfair advantage, such as using outside help

Academic integrity It is a set of specific practices revolving around independent work production of original scholarship, accurately and transparently tracing of sources and others' contributions, and following stated and unstated norms of academic conduct for academic rewards

Accessibility of data It refers to students' capacity to access and correct their own data as well as it can refer to the establishment of who can have access to raw and analyzed data

Attitude towards the unethical information technology use It aims at the appreciation by the individual of what is right or wrong in the case of digital instruments. The ethical attitude toward the unethical use of information technology is dynamic because it depends on the evaluated situation and changes as society changes

Computer ethics This domain includes consideration of personal and social policies for the ethical use of computer technology

Cyberplagiarism The text is copied with the Ctrl + C function and pasted with Ctrl + V directly into the text from the materials available online on the Internet and not from books or articles

Ethical behavior Ways of acting that are consistent with what society and individuals typically think are good values. It tends to be good for business and involves demonstrating respect for key moral principles that include honesty fairness, equality, dignity, diversity, and individual rights

Ethics It is a morale code comprising rules for the good of the individual and society and can have different connotations across time and cultures

Information ethics It is as a set of rules or principles used for moral decision making regarding computer technology and computer use. The aim is to develop

L. Mâță (ed.), *Ethical Use of Information Technology in Higher Education*, EAI/Springer Innovations in Communication and Computing, https://doi.org/10.1007/978-981-16-1951-9

the moral behavior of information users from the perspective of forming their responsibility

Information technology It represents the use of computers in managing data, i.e., to store, retrieve, transmit, and manipulate data or information. IT is typically used within the context of business operations as opposed to personal or entertainment technologies

Learning analytics Learning analytics entails the measurement collection, and reporting data regarding the learners and their contexts. The purpose of learning analytics is understanding and optimizing learning

Plagiarism It constitutes the act of using someone else's work without proper recognition or unauthorized unacceptable use of someone else's ideas as if they were original or common knowledge

Privacy It is a basic right of every human, and the legal systems in developed countries include this human right

Software piracy It refers at a situation where an individual uses software illegally; thus, the person does not pay for the usage of the software

Transparency in learning analytics Universities should offer students information regarding the purpose of data usage and data controllers/processors

Unethical information technology use The concept is defined as the violation of privacy property, accuracy and access of any individual, group, or organization by any other individual, group, or organization

Bibliography of Selected Titles

1. Abolarinwa, O.L., Tiamiyu, M.A., Eluwa, S.E.: Computer ethics and security awareness behaviour of tertiary institution students in South-Western, Nigeria. ESTIJ **5**(3), 260–265 (2015)
2. Acilar, A.: Demographic factors affecting freshman students' attitudes towards software piracy: An empirical Study. Issues Informing Sci. Inf. Technol. **7**, 321–328 (2010)
3. Adam, A.: Computer ethics in a different voice. Inf. Organ. **1**(4), 235–261 (2001)
4. Akbulut, Y., Uysal, Ö., Odabasi, H.F., Kuzu, A.: Influence of gender, program of study and PC experience on unethical computer using behaviors of Turkish undergraduate students. Comput. & Educ. **51**(2), 485–492 (2008)
5. Akbulut, Y., Şendağ, S., Birinci, G., Kılıçer, K., Şahin, M.C., Odabaşı, H.F.: Exploring the types and reasons of Internet-triggered academic dishonesty among Turkish undergraduate students: Development of Internet-Triggered Academic Dishonesty Scale (ITADS). Comput. & Educ. **51**(1), 463–473 (2008)
6. Akdemir, O., Vural, O.F., Çolakoğlu, O.M.: Prospective teachers' likelihood of performing unethical behaviors in the real and virtual environments. Turk. Online J. Educ. Technol. **14**(2), 130–137 (2015)
7. Alakurt, T., Bardakçi, S.: ICT student teachers' judgments and justifications about ethical issues. Turk. Online J. Educ. Technol. **3**(4), 48–63 (2012)
8. Al-Dheleai, Y.M., Tasir, Z.: Facebook and education: students' privacy concerns. Int. Educ. Stud. **8**(13), 22–26 (2015)
9. Almseidein, T.A.: Attitudes of undergraduate management information systems Students towards computer ethics at Al-Balqa' applied university. Asian J. Inf. Technol. **13**, 438–441 (2014)
10. Ashman, H., Brailsford, T., Cristea, A.I., Sheng, Q.Z., Stewart, C., Toms, E.G., Wade, V.: The ethical and social implications of personalization technologies for E-learning. Inf. Manag. **51**, 6 (2014). https://doi.org/10.1016/j.im.2014.04.003
11. Barcalow, T., Creech, M., Gerrietts, G., Marassa, M., Sallas, P., Sierra-Perry, M., Weinert, B.: Code of technology ethics for educators. University of Illinois, Champaign, Urbana (2001)
12. Baum, J.J.: CyberEthics: The new frontier. TechTrends **49**(6), 54–55 (2005)
13. Bennett, J.B.: Do colleges and universities need ethics officers? Acad. Lead. Ship: Online J. **1**(2), Article 4 (2003)
14. Beycioglu, K.: A cyberphilosophical issue in education: Unethical computer using behavior—The case of prospective teachers. Comput. & Educ. **53**, 201–208 (2009)
15. Blum, S.D.: Academic integrity and student plagiarism: A question of education, not ethics. Chron. High. Educ. **55**(24), A35 (2009)

L. Mâță (ed.), *Ethical Use of Information Technology in Higher Education*,
EAI/Springer Innovations in Communication and Computing,
https://doi.org/10.1007/978-981-16-1951-9

16. Brey, B.: Social and ethical dimensions of computer-mediated education. Inf. Commun. & Ethics Soc. **4**(2), 91–101 (2006)
17. Bush, P., Bilgin, A.: Student and staff understanding and reaction: Academic integrity in an Australian university. J. Acad. Ethics **12**(3), 227–243 (2014). https://doi.org/10.1007/s10805-014-9214-2
18. Calluzzo, V.J., Cante, ChJ: Ethics in information technology and software use. J. Bus. Ethics **51**, 301–312 (2004)
19. Capurro, R., Pingel, C.: Ethical issues of online communication research. Ethics Inf. Technol. **4**, 189–194 (2002)
20. Chankova, M.: Teaching academic integrity: The missing link. J. Acad. Ethics **18**, 155–173 (2020). https://doi.org/10.1007/s10805-019-09356-y
21. Chatterjee, S.: A model of unethical usage of information technology. AMCIS Proceedings **51**, 2891–2896 (2005)
22. Cilliers, L.: Evaluation of information ethical issues among undergraduate students: An exploratory study. S. Afr. J. Inf. Manag. **19**(1), (2017). https://doi.org/10.4102/sajim.v19i1.767
23. Cvejic, R., Kostic, D., Crvenković, B.: Emerging ethical concerns in information systems. Ann. Univ. Oradea, Fascicle Manag. Technol. Eng. **1**, 9–14 (2016)
24. Davis, L.: Arresting student plagiarism: Are we investigators of educators? Bus. Commun. Q. **74**(2), 160–163 (2011)
25. Deveci, A., Kolburan, A.: Unethical behaviours preservice teachers encounter on social networks. Educ. Res. Rev. **10**(14), 1901–1910 (2015)
26. Dika, A., Hamiti, M.: Challenges of implementing the ethics through the use of information technologies in the university. Procedia Soc. Behav. Sci. **15**, 1110–1114 (2011)
27. Engler, J.N., Landau, J.D., Epstein, M.: Keeping up with the Joneses: Students' perceptions of academically dishonest behavior. Teach. Psychol. **35**, 99–102 (2008)
28. Ess, C.: Universal information ethics? Ethical pluralism and social justice. In: Rooksby, E., Weckert, J. (eds.) Information technology and social justice, pp. 69–92. Information Science Publishing, London (2007)
29. Fishman, T.: Academic integrity as an educational concept, concern and movement in US institutions of higher learning. In: Bretag, T. (eds.), Handbook of academic integrity. Springer Science+Business Media Singapore, pp. 1–2 (2015). https://doi.org/10.1007/978-981-287-079-7_1-2
30. Floridi, L.: Informational ethics: An environmental approach to the digital divide. Philos. Contemp. World **9**(1), 1–7 (2001)
31. Gasser, U., Ienca, M., Scheibner, J., Sleigh, J., Vayena, E.: Digital tools against COVID-19: taxonomy, ethical challenges, and navigation aid. Health Policy **2**(8), E425–E434 (2020). https://doi.org/10.1016/S2589-7500(20)30137-0
32. Ghiațău, R.M., Mâță, L.: Factors influencing higher education teachers' attitudes towards unethical use of information technology: A review. Rev. Rom.Easca Pentru Educ. Multidimens. **11**(1), 287–300 (2019)
33. Glendinning, I.: Impact of policies for plagiarism in higher education across Europe. Plagiarism Policies in Romania. Acta Universitatis Agriculturae et Silviculturae Mendelianae Brunensis **6**(1), 207–216 (2014)
34. Halawi, L.: Evaluation of ethical issues in the knowledge age: An exploratory study. Issues Inf. Syst. **14**(1), 106–112 (2013)
35. Hamiti, M., Reka, B., Baloghová, A.: Ethical use of information technology in high education. Procedia—Soc. Behav. Sci. **116**, 4411–4415 (2014)
36. Himma, K.E.: The relationship between the uniqueness of computer ethics and its independence as a discipline in applied ethics. Ethics Inf. Technol. **5**(4), 225–237 (2003)
37. Hosny, M., Fatima, S.: Attitude of students towards cheating and plagiarism: University case study. J. Appl. Sci. **14**, 748–757 (2014)
38. Hyytinen, H., Löfström, E.: Reactively, proactively, implicitly, explicitly? Academics' pedagogical conceptions of how to promote research ethics and integrity. J. Acad. Ethics **15**, 23–41 (2017). https://doi.org/10.1007/s10805-016-9271-9

39. Ives, B., Alama, M., Mosora, L.C., Mosora, M., Grosu-Radulescu, L., Clinciu, A.I., Cazan, A.-M., Badescu, G., Tufis, C., Diaconu, M., Dutu, A.: Patterns and predictors of academic dishonesty in Romanian university students. Higher Educ. **74**(5), 815–831 (2017)
40. Jamil, M., Tariq, R-u-H., Shah, J. H.: Ethical attitudes towards the use of computer and information technology. Int. Res. J. Arts Soc. Sci. **2**(4) 72–78, (2013)
41. Karim, N.S.A., Zamzuri, N.H.A., Nor, Y.M.: Exploring the relationship between Internet ethics in university students and the big five model of personality. Comput. & Educ. **53**(1), 86–93 (2009)
42. Kaya, S., Durmus, A.: Investigation of relationship between preservice teachers' unethical computer using behavior and attitudes towards the using of internet. Procedia—Social Behav. Sci. **28**, 667–672 (2011)
43. Ki, H., Ahn, S.: A study on the methodology of information ethics education in youth. Int. J. Comput. Sci. Netw. Secur. **6**(6), 91–100 (2006)
44. Kuo, F., Hsu, M.: Development and validation of ethical computer self-efficacy measure: The case of softlifting. J. Bus. Ethics **32**(4), 299–315 (2001)
45. Kuzu, A.: Problems related to computer ethics: origins of the problems and suggested solutions. Turk. Online J. Educ. Technol.Turk. Online J. Educ. Technol. **8**(2), 91–110 (2009)
46. Landau, J.D., Druen, P.B., Arcuri, J.A.: Methods for helping students avoid plagiarism. Teach. Psychol. **29**, 112–115 (2002)
47. Leonard, L.N.K., Cronan, T.P.: Attitude toward ethical behavior in computer use: a shifting model. Ind. Manag. & Data Syst. **105**(9), 1150–1171 (2005)
48. Lin, H.: The ethics of instructional technology: Issues and coping strategies by professional technologists in design and training situations in higher education. Educ. Technol. Res. Dev. **55**(5), 411–437 (2007)
49. Lin, K.Y.: Ethical issues in technology education in Taiwan. J. Technol. Stud. **33**(1), 17–24 (2007)
50. Liu, X., Chen, Y.: A cross-cultural comparison between Americans and Chinese in their attitudes towards information ethics. Issues Inf. Syst. **13**(1), 59–67 (2012)
51. Löfström, E., Trotman, T., Furnari, M., Shephard, K.: Who teaches academic integrity and how do they do it? Higher Educ. **69**(3), 435–448 (2015). https://doi.org/10.1007/s10734-014-9784-3
52. Macdonald, R., Carroll, J.: Plagiarism—A complex issue requiring a holistic institutional approach. Assess. & Eval. High. Educ. **31**, 233–245 (2006)
53. Macer, D.: Computing ethics: Intercultural comparisons. Ethical pluralism and social justice. In: Rooksby, E., Weckert, J. (eds.) Information technology and social justice, pp. 1899–2204. Information Science Publishing, London (2007)
54. Macfarlane, B., Zhang, J., Pun, A.: Academic integrity: A review of the literature. Stud. High. Educ. **39**(2), 339–358 (2014). https://doi.org/10.1080/03075079.2012.709495
55. Mahabeer, P., Pirtheepal T.: Assessment, plagiarism and its effect on academic integrity: Experiences of academics at a university in South Africa. S. Afr. J. Sci. **115**(11/12), 1–8 (2019). https://www.sajs.co.za/article/view/6323
56. Manly, T.S., Leonard, L.N.K., Riemenschneider, C.K.: Academic integrity in the information age: Virtues of respect and responsibility. J. Bus. Ethics **127**, 579–590 (2015). https://doi.org/10.1007/s10551-014-2060-8
57. Marcial, D.E.: ICT social and ethical competency among teacher educators in the Philippines. Inf. Technol. Learn. Tools **57**(1), 96–103 (2017). https://doi.org/10.33407/itlt.v57i1.1533
58. Martin, K., Shilton, K., Smith, J.: Business and the ethical implications of technology: Introduction to the symposium. J. Bus. Ethics **160**, 307–317 (2019). https://doi.org/10.1007/s10551-019-04213-9
59. Mason, R.O.: Four ethical issues of the information age. Manag. Inf. Syst. Q. **10**(1), 5–12 (1986)
60. Mâță, L., Boghian, I., Poenaru, A. G., Ghiațău, R. M.: Models and theories of unethical use of information technology in higher education. Proceedings of the International Scientific Conference eLearning and Software for Education. Bucharest,138–144 (2019)

61. Mâță, L., Poenaru, A.: Rules for the use of information technology in the code of ethics in higher education. The 16th International Scientific Conference eLearning and Software for Education. Bucharest, 537–544 (2020). https://doi.org/10.12753/2066-026X-20-070
62. Mâță, L., Clipa, O., Tzafilkou, K.: The development and validation of a scale to measure university teachers' attitude towards ethical use of information technology for a sustainable education. Sustainability 12(15), 6268 (2020). https://doi.org/10.3390/su12156268
63. McCabe, D.L., Butterfield, K.D., Treviño, L.K.: Academic dishonesty in graduate business programs: Prevalence, causes, and proposed action. Acad. Manag., Learn. Educ. 5, 294–305 (2006)
64. Mitchell, R., Garza, L.: Ethics in an online environment. New Dir. Community Coll.Es 148, 63–70 (2009)
65. Mohamed, N., Karim, N.S.A., Hussein, R.: Computer use ethics among university students and staffs: The influence of gender, religious work value and organizational level. Campus-Wide Inf. Syst. 29(5), 328–334 (2012)
66. Moore, S.L., Ellsworth, J.B.: Ethics of Educational Technology. In Spector, J., Elen, M.J., Bishop, M.J. (eds.), Handbook of research on educational communications and technology. Springer, New York (2014)
67. Moores, T.T., Chang, J.C.-J.: Ethical decision making in software piracy: Initial development and test of a four-component model. Manag. Inf. Syst. Res. 30(1), 167–180 (2006)
68. Murdock, T.B., Anderman, E.M.: Motivational perspectives on student cheating: Toward an integrated model of academic dishonesty. Educ. Psychol. 41(3), 129–145 (2006)
69. Namlu, A.G., Odabasi, F.H.: Unethical computer using behavior scale: A study of reliability and validity on Turkish university students. Comput. & Educ. 48(2), 205–215 (2007)
70. Nordkvelle, Y.T., Olson, J.: Visions for ICT, ethics and the practice of teachers. Educ. Inf. Technol. 10(1–2), 19–30 (2005)
71. O'Connell, J.: Networked participatory online learning design and challenges for academic integrity in higher education. Int. J. Educ. Integr. 12(4), 1–15 (2016). https://doi.org/10.1007/s40979-016-0009-7
72. Olcott Jr. D., Carrera Farran, X., Gallardo Echenique, E.E., González Martínez, J.: Ethics and education in the digital age: Global perspectives and strategies for local transformation in Catalonia. RUSC. Univ. Knowl. Soc. J. 12(2), 59–72 (2015). http://dx.doi.org/10.7238/rusc.v12i2.2455
73. Owunwanne, D., Rustagi, N., Dada, R.: Students perceptions of cheating and plagiarism in higher institutions. J. Coll.E Sci. Teach. 7(11), 59–68 (2010)
74. Özer, N., Uğurlu, C.T., Beycioglu, K.: Computer teachers' attitudes toward Ethical use of computers in elementary schools. Int. J. Cyber Ethics Educ. 1(2), 15–24 (2011)
75. Prohaska, V.: Teachers can have an effect: Strategies for encouraging ethical student behavior. In: Landrum, R.E., McCarthy, M. (eds.) Teaching ethically: Challenges and opportunities. American Psychological Association, Washington, DC (2012)
76. Ramdani, Z.: Construction of academic integrity scale. Int. J. Res. Stud. Psychol. 7(1), 87–97 (2018). https://doi.org/10.5861/ijrsp.2018.3003
77. Roig, M.: Plagiarism and paraphrasing criteria of college and university professors. Ethics & Behavior. 11, 307–323 (2001)
78. Roig, M., Marks, A.: Attitudes toward cheating before and after the implementation of a modified honor code: A case study. Ethics & Behavior. 16, 163–171 (2006)
79. Scanlon, P.M.: Student online plagiarism: how do we respond? College Teach. 51(4), 161–165 (2003)
80. Seif, M.H.: Presenting a casual model for ethical behavioral intention of information technology among students of Shiraz University of Medical Sciences. Medical Ethics J. 10(35), 177–198 (2016)
81. Stahl, B.C., Timmermans, J., Flick, C.: Ethics of emerging information and communication technologies: On the implementation of responsible research and innovation. Sci. Public Policy 44(3), 369–381 (2017)

82. Starovoytova, D., Namango, S.S.: Viewpoint of undergraduate engineering students on plagiarism. J. Educ. Pract. **7**(31), 48–65 (2016)

83. Taebi, B., van den Hoven, J., Bird, S.J.: The importance of ethics in modern universities of technology. Sci. Eng. Ethics **25**, 1625–1632 (2019). https://doi.org/10.1007/s11948-019-001 64-6

84. Tavani, H.T: The uniqueness debate in computer ethics: What exactly is at issue and why does it matter? Ethics and Info. Tech. **4**(1), 37–54 (2002)

85. Toprak, E., Özkanal, B., Aydin, S., Kaya, S.: Ethics in eLearning. Turk. Online J. Educ. Technol. **9**(2), 78–86 (2010)

86. Vighnarajah, S., Chuah, K.M.: Ethical conduct of e-Learners and e-Teachers in online learning community. Pak. J. Distance & Online Learn. **3**(2), 1–12 (2017)

87. Weckert, J.: Computer ethics: Future directions. Ethics Inf. Technol. **3**(2), 93–96 (2001)

88. Whitley Jr., B.E., Keith-Spiegel, P.: Academic integrity as an institutional issue. Ethics & Behav. **11**, 325–342 (2001)

89. Woodward, B., Davis, D.C., Hodis, F.A.: The relationship between ethical decision making and ethical reasoning in information technology students. J. Inf. Syst. Educ. **18**(2), 193–202 (2001)

90. Yeaman, A.R.J.: The origins of educational technology's professional ethics: Part two—establishing professional ethics in education. TechTrends **49**(2), 14–17 (2005)

Lightning Source UK Ltd.
Milton Keynes UK
UKHW050836210722
406114UK00007B/12